The Bartered Bride
Prodaná nevěsta

Praise for *The Bartered Bride—Prodaná nevěsta*:

"No more excuses! Whether your questions about Smetana's opera *Prodaná nevěsta* pertain to translation and pronunciation of the Czech language, the opera's history, its traditions or performance practices, Timothy Cheek has answered them all in his marvelous new book. This is a stunning achievement; one that I hope will place this masterful work where it belongs, in the repertoire of every professional opera company and every university opera workshop … and in its original language. Bravo, Dr. Cheek, and thank you!"—*Benton Hess, Distinguished Professor of Voice, Eastman School of Music; Musical Director, Eastman Opera Theatre*

"Wow! This book is a treasure! It's put together so expertly, so thoroughly, and so lovingly. Thank you, Professor Cheek, for demystifying *The Bartered Bride* and giving us both the resources and the confidence to produce this wonderful opera *in Czech.*"—*Stephen Dubberly, Opera Music Director, University of North Texas*

"Professor Timothy Cheek's new performance guide of *The Bartered Bride*, including literal and practical translations in English as well as an IPA transcription, is a masterful work. The first part of the work is dedicated to the *The Bartered Bride* in its various versions along with a fascinating detailed performance history—productions, singers, conductors, choreographers—as well as a crystal clear guide to the pronunciation of the Czech language. The second part is a pristine layout of the original Czech, the IPA guide, a literal translation as well as a practical one. It couldn't be easier to use. I can't imagine a finer work on *The Bartered Bride* in the English language appearing any time soon. For anyone interested in studying or performing this glorious piece, Professor Cheek's new work is without competition and utterly invaluable. Bravo, Tim!"—*Craig Rutenberg, international collaborative pianist and vocal coach; Head of Music Administration, Metropolitan Opera*

"With this book Timothy Cheek not only contributes greatly toward the feasibility of presenting Smetana's *Prodaná nevěsta* in its native tongue beyond the Czech Republic, he also presents perspectives on the opera's history and music that indeed every opera buff will savour."—*Sonya Szabo-Reynolds,* Dvořák Society Newsletter, *UK*

Praise for *Singing in Czech: A Guide to Czech Lyric Diction and Vocal Repertoire*, with a foreword by Sir Charles Mackerras:

"For singers, coaches, and conductors, this book is a godsend. When I think of the repertoire I could have programmed if such a reference had existed all these years! But never mind—it exists now, and we are all the luckier for it. Here is everything you need to dare to sing (and play) in this beautiful language, and clearly presented by an experienced, caring teacher. No one involved in vocal music can afford to be without it."—*Martin Katz, international collaborative pianist and vocal coach; Professor of Collaborative Piano, University of Michigan*

The Bartered Bride
Prodaná nevěsta

Performance Guide with Translations and Pronunciation

Timothy Cheek

The Scarecrow Press, Inc.
Lanham, Maryland • Toronto • Plymouth, UK
2010

SCARECROW PRESS, INC.

Published in the United States of America
by Scarecrow Press, Inc.
A wholly owned subsidiary of
The Rowman & Littlefield Publishing Group, Inc.
4501 Forbes Boulevard, Suite 200, Lanham, Maryland 20706
www.scarecrowpress.com

Estover Road
Plymouth PL6 7PY
United Kingdom

British Library Cataloguing in Publication Information Available

Library of Congress Cataloging-in-Publication Data
Cheek, Timothy, 1957–
  The bartered bride = Prodaná nevesta : performance guide with translations
and pronunciation / Timothy Cheek.
      p. cm.
  Includes a transcription in the International Phonetic Alphabet, and a word-for-
word English translation, of Karel Sabina's lbretto.
  Includes bibliographical references, discography, videography, filmography,
and index.
  ISBN 978-0-8108-7260-8 (pbk. : alk. paper) — ISBN 978-0-8108-7261-5
(ebook)
  1. Smetana, Bedrich, 1824–1884. Prodaná nevesta. 2. Singing–Interpretation
(Phrasing, dynamics, etc.) 3. Opera–Interpretation (Phrasing, dynamics, etc.)
4. Operas–Librettos. I. Sabina, Karel, 1813–1877. II. Smetana, Bedrich, 1824–
1884. Prodaná nevesta. Libretto. English. I II. Title. IV. Title: Bartered bride.
  ML410.S63C5 2010
  782.1–dc22   2009032277

To my son, Timothy Joseph Cheek—
may you have many enjoyable moments with this opera!

Contents

Illustrations

Cover
Chodská svatba [Chodsko wedding], oil on canvas, 104 x 168 cm., by Jaroslav Špillar (1869–1917). (Chodsko is in the Plzeň region of Bohemia.)

Following page 93
Composer Bedřich Smetana; librettist Karel Sabina

Ema Destinnová as Mařenka, Adolf Krössing as Vašek
    Prague National Theatre, 1909

Choreographer Otakar Bartík and dancer Gina Torriani
    New York Metropolitan Opera, 1909

Jarmila Novotná as Mařenka
    New York Metropolitan Opera, 1941

Marilyn Horne professional debut as Háta
    Los Angeles Guild Opera, 1954

Teresa Stratas as Mařenka, Nicolai Gedda as Jeník
    New York Metropolitan Opera, 1978

Ara Berberian as Kecal in his Met debut
    New York Metropolitan Opera on tour at the Detroit Opera House, 1979

Dancer Bohuslava Jelínková, Act III; with husband, author Timothy Cheek
    Prague National Theatre, 1992; 1999

Chorus, Act I; Amita Prakash as Mařenka, Bernard D. Holcomb as Jeník
    University of Michigan, 2007

Simone Osborne as Mařenka, Eric Olsen as Jeník
    Opera Nuova summer program, Edmonton, Alberta, 2007

Preface

This book has its origins in a production of *Prodaná nevěsta, The Bartered Bride*, March 15–18, 2007, that I helped coach in Czech at the University of Michigan, for a cast of all students. Throughout preceding years at the university, I and my colleague Joshua Major, stage director for the production, had always assumed we would perform the opera in English. When the decision was made to produce the opera, I thought of all the singers involved in the double-cast production (over forty, with chorus). With the full support of my colleagues, we then decided not to lose this wonderful opportunity to give so many students the valuable experience of singing in the original language, opening the door for them to perform more great Czech repertoire in their careers.

The opera was cast in October, I taught two group sessions on Czech lyric diction in November, the singers received copies of the main part of this book, as well as access to my book *Singing in Czech*, and they arrived in January after Christmas break completely prepared for private music and diction coachings by our staff. Recitatives proved to be just the right length for all the individual roles, so that while they were certainly challenging (like any recitatives!) they were not overwhelming. In the end, one could not have asked for better results —the Czech was clear and communicative (attested to by native Czechs in the audience) so that it became a natural means of expression bound to the lyric fabric of the opera. I supplied English surtitles, and the audience's experience was enhanced by hearing the work with all the rich, earthy colors of the original Czech. Several of the cast have already gone on to perform in significant Czech performances, especially Seth Mease Carico, Jody Doktor, Elizabeth Gray, Bernard Holcomb, Amita Prakash, Steven Tompkins, and David Wilson.

The main part of this book was further tried and tested with a production by the summer Canadian program Opera Nuova in Edmonton, Alberta, where I was invited by Kim Wannat to coach the music in Czech for performances in late June–July 2007. Again, the young singers, double-cast, rose to the challenge with outstanding results, singing beautifully, expressively, and naturally. One Mařenka, Simone Osborne, went on to win the Ninth International Czech and Slovak Voice Competition in Montreal that November. Using Mařenka's arias in every round, she then became one of the winners of the Metropolitan Opera 2008 National Council Auditions, at only twenty-one years old.

My first experience with the opera, besides the overture and dances, began on Tuesday, November 21, 1978, when I happened upon the Metropolitan

Opera's first simulcast of the season, showing in one of the dormitories at Oberlin College where I was a student. Besides the stellar cast (Stratas and Gedda conducted by Levine), the choreography of Czech guest Pavel Šmok proved a revelation for opera lovers. My next experience had to wait until Tuesday, February 21, 1995, when I caught a performance at the National Theatre in Prague. It was the eighty-second performance of the twenty-sixth production (which ran seven years), and it was conducted by Bohumil Gregor, who would soon become my mentor. This time Šmok not only choreographed, but was the stage director for the entire production. In that performance I first saw dancer Bohuslava Jelínková, who would become my wife three years later. It was around her one-hundreth performance in this work, and she would dance in three productions at the National Theatre. I saw quite a few more performances of that sparkling production over the next few years and even went on to collaborate with one of the main Mařenkas, Dana Burešová, on a Supraphon CD of the songs of Vítězslava Kaprálová. Both Burešová and Miloslav Podskalský (one of the Míchas) also demonstrated Czech sounds for the CD in my book *Singing in Czech*. Finally, I had the great privilege to observe *all* the stagings, triple-cast, of the next Prague production—their twenty-seventh—with conductor Bohumil Kulínský and stage director Josef Průdek, while sitting next to the diction coach, Věra Herečková, and asking her countless questions. The live Czech television broadcast of the premiere on Saturday, June 5, 1999, was a joy to hear and to watch.

I do advocate performing *Prodaná nevěsta* in the original language, as I think many singers now have the means, ability, opportunity, and knowledge of IPA to carry this out as much as any other foreign language. That the opera is a comedy really makes no difference—audiences get most of the jokes in *Le nozze di Figaro* and *L'elisir d'amore* with English supertitles. (It is only with extensive spoken dialogue that the argument for a translation into English becomes stronger, as in *Die Fledermaus* or *Die Zauberflöte*.) Still, performing operas in the language of the audience certainly has its valid arguments. For those who choose to perform *The Bartered Bride* in English, I believe this book is also very useful, as it provides word-for-word English translations of the Czech, vital for those creating their own singing translations.

This book centers on Czech and English-language performances, with an occasional bow to German and other translations. The performance history in chapter two reveals that the most successful performances were those that approached the work as a folk opera, not treating the characters as caricatures, but as real people. The section on debuts, I hope, will be enjoyable reading for opera buffs, and serve as an inspiration for young singers who may be debuting themselves with one of these roles.

I use the designation "Czech lands" to refer to the area that became Czechoslovakia, and later the Czech Republic. "Bohemia" refers to the western part of the country, with "Moravia" in the eastern part. In the early part of the twentieth century, Czechs were usually referred to as "Bohemians." I also use the Czech city name "Plzeň" instead of the English "Pilsen." The opera takes place in a

Bohemian village, usually set in the Plzeň region.

Instead of the title *The Bartered Bride*, I usually use the Czech title *Prodaná nevěsta*. (Czechs often refer to their beloved opera with the affectionate name *Prodanka*.) I also use the Czech names of characters, such as "Mařenka," even when referring to an English or German production where the character is called "Marie." I use the name "National Theatre" instead of the Czech name "Národní divadlo," and the spelling "theater" unless "theatre" is the specific spelling for a proper noun. I have used the English title *Jenůfa* for Janáček's opera, instead of the original *Její pastorkyňa*.

In the process of writing my previous books on Janáček's *Příhody lišky Bystroušky, The Cunning Little Vixen*, and *Kát'a Kabanová*, they became more than translations and IPA, and were received by reviewers as performance guides. Therefore, I have decided to approach this book as a basic performance guide—not daring to presume to give definitive stylistic niceties (we luckily have recordings of great artists to get a feel for the Czech spirit and style of this work)—but rather to give information, my own observations, practical suggestions, and possibilities. Language, of course, is the main focus.

Either way, in Czech or English, I hope that this book can serve as one tool to help bring this truly great comic folk opera to life.

Acknowledgments

Research for this book was supported in part by a grant from the International Research and Exchanges Board (IREX) with funds provided by the National Endowment for the Humanities, and the United States Department of State, which administers the Title VIII Program. None of these organizations is responsible for the views expressed. First of all, I wish to thank the students at the University of Michigan who, after some slight trepidation, dove in to their work enthusiastically and sang beautifully in Czech in the school's wonderful 2007 production of *Prodaná nevěsta*. Many thanks go to my colleagues at the university—especially Joshua Major, for his full support and his wonderful, funny, and above all human portrayal of the characters in the opera; and to Martin Katz, for rallying behind me to perform the opera in Czech. Thanks certainly go to the computer team at the school, as well—Greg Laman, Elizabeth Burr, Cathy Behrendt, and Jeremy Edwards. As usual, my wife Bohuslava Jelínková was of great help and amazing support, and I loved hearing her stories of personalities and incidents behind the scenes in her many performances of the opera! Thanks, too, to Marie Jelínková and Bohuslav Jelínek for their help, as well as to my son Timothy Joseph Cheek, who at six years old happened to notice a missing accent mark in one of the musical examples. Thanks also to Zdenka Brodská, Kerianne Tupac, Marc Shepherd, Tomáš Vrbka of the Státní opera, Ivana Nováková of the Gallery of West Bohemia Plzeň, Rita Richter of Lübeck Opera, John Pennino of the Metropolitan Opera Archives, Andrea Kunešová and Václav Krejčí of the Prague National Theatre Archives, soprano Jadwiga Wysoczanská, Jaroslav Hostinský, Diane M. Glass of the Buffalo Bill Historical Center McCracken Research Library, Thomas Bandy of the University of Oklahoma, Peter Smith of Smith Photography, Ed Ellis of Ellis Brothers Photography, Art Joslin, Ginny Berberian, and to the wonderful staff at Scarecrow Press.

Part One

Kdo, Kdy, Kde a Jak—
Who, When, Where, and How

1

Opera Essentials

Imagine a land where an opera house stands as a symbol of a proud people and their fight for national identity. The opera house is the Prague Národní divadlo, the National Theatre, funded almost completely by private donations collected across the Czech lands. It took thirty years to raise the necessary funds for this magnificent edifice, which though unfinished, opened in 1881 with the premiere of the epic nationalistic opera *Libuše* by Bedřich Smetana (1824–84). *Libuše* had been written almost ten years earlier and reserved for the occasion. Within months, fire destroyed much of the new theater before it could even be completed. Having come so close to their treasured dream, citizens responded immediately with more contributions, and the reconstructed and fully complete National Theatre that stands today quickly reopened in 1883, again with *Libuše*.

Before the opening of the National Theatre, the Austrian government had provided state funds to the Czechs to build a theater for them alone, mostly as a means of appeasing their nationalist aspirations. With these limited funds, the Czechs chose to build a temporary building, the Prozatímní divadlo, Provisional Theatre, which opened in 1862. It was a tiny theater and stood at the back of the present National Theatre. In fact, it became incorporated into the rear of the new building. Meant to serve as a temporary structure until the Czechs could build their permanent theater, the cramped quarters became a place to lay the artistic groundwork for the great theater to come. It was in the Provisional Theatre that *Prodaná nevěsta* first saw light—from its promising, though tenuous beginning, through Smetana's masterful revisions, and even beyond. Since its premiere, the opera has been performed every year in Prague.[1]

Birth of the Opera

In his later years, Smetana pointed to one evening as being decisive for his whole life, stating:

> ". . . I swore there and then that no other than I should beget a native Czech music."

The evening occurred in 1857 in Weimar at a gathering of musicians and artists to celebrate the birth of Grand Duke Karl August (1757–1828), organized largely by composer Peter Cornelius (1824–74). Cornelius was at work on his German comic opera *Der Barbier von Bagdad* [The barber of Baghdad]. This through-composed opera, Cornelius felt, would serve both as a modern alternative to Wagner and as a response to comic operas of the time, which usually had spoken dialogue. At the gathering was the influential Viennese conductor and composer Johann Ritter von Herbeck (1831–77). He was of the opinion that, although the Czechs were excellent musicians, they were incapable of creating any music of their own. Resolved to lay a solid foundation for Czech opera, Smetana then returned from Weimar to his post in Sweden, where he worked in Göteborg as a conductor and piano teacher from 1856 to 1859. It was during this same year, 1857, that Czech writer Karel Sabina (1813–77) began writing his novel *Věčný ženich* [Eternal bridegroom], featuring some characters who were analogous to those that would be featured six years later in *Prodaná nevěsta*.[2]

In 1861, anticipating the opening of the Provisional Theatre, Czech patriot Count Jan Harrach (1828–1909) announced a competition for an opera on a Czech libretto. There would be one prize for a historical opera and one for a comic opera, and both operas were to be in two acts. There would be separate prizes for the best composer and the best librettist. Smetana finished his first opera, *Braniboři v Čechách* [The Brandenburgers in Bohemia], to a Czech libretto by Karel Sabina (1813–77) in 1863. Before putting the finishing touches on this historical opera, he commissioned a comic opera libretto from Sabina the same year, and began sketching themes for it even before receiving any text. In fact, in 1862 Smetana had already entered the words "chorus in comedy" in his "sketchbook of motives" next to the theme that would become the opening chorus from *Prodaná nevěsta*, "Proč bychom se netěšili." Also in the sketchbook are eight measures marked "In comic opera. Duetto!," that would become "Věrné milování," sung by Mařenka and Jeník in Act I, sc. ii. The earliest preexisting music for the opera dates from 1849, when Smetana had composed a set of three piano pieces called *Svatební sceny* [Wedding scenes]. These had been written as a wedding present for one of his piano pupils, Countess Marie von Thun-Hohenstein. The third piece, titled "Svatební veselí: Tanec" [Wedding revelry: dance], in ABA form, consists of a fast waltz-like section in its outer parts and a middle section marked "Tempo di polka." It is this middle section that is quoted in the opening scene of the opera, note for note, mm. 10–75 and 443–460. The obvious inspiration of a Czech wedding, with a festive Czech polka, served Smetana well to introduce the chorus of revelers that opens the opera. While all these connections have been pointed out by previous authors, the present author also notes that music from the second piano piece, titled "Ženich a nevěsta" [Bridegroom and bride], makes its way into the Act I, sc. iv quartet, in which Kecal and Mařenka's parents try to persuade Mařenka to marry their chosen groom.[3]

Just as Smetana had had a confident and successful approach to forging a new nationalistic serious opera with *Braniboři v Čechách*, so was he clear in his ideas for a new Czech comic opera. This can be seen in an argument the composer had with the intendant of the Provisional Theatre, František Ladislav Rieger (1818–1903). Rieger, one of the most prominent Czech politicians and intellectuals of the second half of the nineteenth century, stated that a Czech comic opera would be more difficult to write than a serious one. He asserted that it would need to be based on Czech folksongs. Smetana vehemently argued that this was totally wrong, and such an approach would not allow for dramatic truth or artistic depth. Smetana claimed that Rieger did not understand the matter, and as a composer, he would have to show him. Rieger represented the principles of the Old Czech (*staročech*) conservative party, which was especially leery of any music that alluded to the German strains of Wagner. Smetana's tendencies found resonance in the Young Czech (*mladočech*) liberal party. Each of these strong political factions believed they knew what was best for determining the future of the Czech nation and its art. Smetana's confrontation with Rieger is probably what lost him his initial bid for the musical directorship of the Provisional Theatre.[4]

On July 5, 1863, Smetana received and paid for Sabina's still untitled libretto. Actually not quite yet a libretto, it was only a short sketch written in one act, and only in German. Smetana insisted on two acts and much more detail. Because Sabina could not come up with a title, the composer himself eventually named the opera *Prodaná nevěsta*, which literally means "the sold bride." "The bartered bride" is more euphonious, however, so this English title has always been used.

Why Smetana chose Karel Sabina for his librettist was very simple—at this time in history there seemed to be no one else who could fashion a Czech opera libretto, and do it quickly. Sabina's work was quite mercenary, so that Harrach's competition jury condemned the libretto of *Braniboři v Čechách* as "hastily written patchwork."[5] In 1849 Sabina had been arrested by the Austrian police for being a member of a revolutionary committee. He was held prisoner in Vyšehrad for over a year, and then a military tribunal condemned him to death by hanging. The young Emperor Franz Joseph I (1830–1916) commuted his sentence to eighteen years in prison, and Sabina was sent to the fortress in Olomouc. Under a general amnesty for political prisoners, he was freed after serving eight years of his sentence. Sabina was a very active novelist and journalist, but his writings were constantly censored by the police. As a result, he had little work, he was in and out of jail, and he often lived on the edge of poverty. So, while Sabina's artistic abilities were limited, his Czech nationalistic fervor was seemingly boundless. However, in 1872, after the final version of *Prodaná nevěsta* had been hailed as a model for Czech opera, Sabina was exposed as a traitor to the Czechs.[6]

Rather than sit idly waiting for Sabina's revisions, Smetana wrote into his notebook two months later nineteen bars for the Principál/Esmeralda duet in Act III, "Milostné zvířátko." He then abandoned his usual procedure of writing his opera overtures last, and spent the fall working on the famous overture. In December 1863, the musical paper *Slavoj* reported that a "comic overture" by Smetana had been performed on the piano on November 18 at a celebration given by Umělecká beseda (an important Czech cultural society founded that year, with Smetana as its musical head). This was probably Smetana's four-hand arrangement. It is interesting that the popular overture, with its infectious exuberance that so perfectly captures the vitality of the opera, was composed months before the bulk of the work was written.[7]

Sabina's revisions finally arrived, although piecemeal. Some of them seem to have been dictated to Smetana's wife, Betty, as they resemble her handwriting. Other lines were added by Smetana himself. The two-act expanded libretto was in Czech verse, but included a condensed German prose translation as an aid. (Smetana's Czech was not yet at the level of his German. See chapter 5.) Words would still be revised in the course of composition and early rehearsals.

In October 1865, Smetana completed a pencil sketch of the entire opera. According to his lifelong friend, Josef Srb-Debrnov (1836–1904), music critic, promoter, and writer on music:

> "Most of the beautiful melodies in *Prodaná nevěsta* originated in late evening on the bank [of the Vltava river] within sight of the castle and Malá strana [Lesser Town, in Prague]. There the master strolled almost every day toward evening, and while he was walking he read over the text, which Sabina sent him in fragments. Melodies flowed into his head. Arriving at his apartment in the Lažanský Palace, he would sit at the table and immediately make a sketch of the part he had thought out."[8]

This description is exactly in line with Smetana's own description of his method of opera composing:

> "Walking up and down the room, I read it aloud until the words changed into music."[9]

Over the next five months, Smetana refined his sketches and completed the orchestration of the opera on March 15, 1866. This year was one of Smetana's happiest. His first opera, *Braniboři v Čechách*, had its premiere conducted by the composer at the Provisional Theatre on January 5, and was an immediate success. When the new Provisional Theatre had opened, on November 18, 1862, Smetana had applied for the musical directorship, but was rejected. The post was instead granted to his bitter rival, Jan Nepomuk Maýr (1818–88). Count Jan Harrach, too, suffered disappointment, for he had hoped to award his prize for the best Czech opera in time for the opening of the theater. Smetana was the first entrant when he submitted the score to *Braniboři v Čechách* on the very day he completed it, April 23, 1863. The jury had been deliberating this whole time, and was reluctant to award Smetana the prize because of the work's modern German traits and lack of Czech folk elements. However, the wonderful music, the patriotic sentiments of the opera, surpassing any previous Czech opera, along with the rousing approval of critics and the public, swayed Harrach's jury to award Smetana the prize on March 27, 1866, less than two weeks after completing the score of *Prodaná nevěsta*. On May 30, 1866, Smetana's new comic opera had its premiere with the composer at the podium, and in September Smetana replaced Maýr as head conductor of opera at the Provisional Theatre.[10]

First Version

The first production of *Prodaná nevěsta* was performed twice. Unlike Smetana's first opera, it was not a success. There is a list of reasons for this. First, the opera was not as it is today. Much like a Singspiel, *Prodaná nevěsta* consisted of dialogue between its musical numbers, with almost no recitative, and there were two acts instead of three. Both acts took place in the village green. Mařenka's second aria had not been written yet, although the recitative before it had. The three dances were not yet written, nor was the men's beer chorus. Missing was the "pochod komediantů" [march of the comedians], with its onstage band. One duet was eventually dropped in a later revision—a nonessential couplet for Esmeralda and the Principál, called "Ten staví se svatouškem" [He acts like a goody two-shoes], performed before dialogue leading into their other duet "Milostné zvířatko." Jan Neruda (1834–91), the great Czech journalist, writer, and poet, attended the premiere and expressed his misgivings about the couplet to Smetana. Neruda also criticized the opera for having no national dances.

Second, most of the audience was middle-class, and were used to seeing aristocratic, historical, or mythological characters on the stage, not Czech village folk. Third, May 30 turned out to be one of the hottest days of the year, and the Provisional Theatre was notoriously uncomfortable in the heat. Many preferred not to attend the theater that evening. Fourth, May 30 was also an official holiday, traditionally reserved for society outings. Many people traveled to the countryside, and the theater was almost empty. Fifth, relations between Austria and Prussia were very strained. In this political climate, many feared the outbreak of war, which would certainly affect Bohemia. A light comedy was not on the minds of many. War did break out seventeen days later, and the main campaign was in Bohemia. Finally, there were issues with the cast.[11]

Most of the lead singers were not suitable for their parts. For Mařenka, Smetana had engaged Eleonora z Ehrenbergů (1832–1912), an outstanding coloratura soprano, who throughout her life would often state that the lyrical range of Mařenka's part was not suited to her type of voice. Interestingly, Smetana had employed her earlier for *Braniboři v Čechách*, hoping her involvement would help assure the opera's success. During the first piano rehearsal she threw down the score, exclaimed "And you expect me to sing that? Why, there's not a single coloratura passage in it," and stormed out. While Eleonora z Ehrenbergů only sang Mařenka twice, she did sing Háta in her later years, forty-four times.

The first Jeník, Jindřich Polák (1834–?) had a weak voice and was a bad actor. His physique and character were also the wrong type to portray the young, handsome Czech from the countryside. Although the first Kecal, František Hynek (1837–1905), had a strong, colorful voice, he was a terrible actor and had a prominent German accent. He went on to be a successful stage director, including for new productions of *Prodaná nevěsta* in the 1880s. His acting evidently improved, as he ended up singing Kecal more than one hundred times at the Prague National Theatre, including the 150th performance in 1886. Vašek, played by Josef Kysela (1833–1904), fared better. His acting was apparently better than his singing, and he performed the role some twenty times before leaving for Plzeň to be a director.

The smaller roles were much better cast. Krušina was sung by the bass Josef Paleček (1842–1915), who performed the role twice and then went on to become an outstanding Kecal. In 1869 he left for St. Petersburg to sing and direct. This included directing the 1871 Russian premiere of *Prodaná nevěsta* while also singing Kecal. The first Principál, Jindřich Mošna (1837–1911), ended up singing the role for ten years, 446 times! He was responsible for the lines ". . . polykati bude židl—é—vidličky a nože. . ." [he will swallow chairs—uh—forks and knives] and "Dluhů—é—peněz máme vždycky nazbyt. . ." [Debts—uh—money we always have a surplus of] in Act III, sc. ii. These lines were improvised during a rehearsal, and Smetana wrote them down into the piano score. After the *skočná* was added to the opera, Mošna, who loved the circus, did juggling, sword-swallowing, and somersaults. The first Esmeralda, Terezie Ledererová-Seifertová (1844–1914) was both a good actress and singer, successful in drama, operettas, and small opera roles. She performed the part sixty times. The first Indián, Josef Křtín (1830–84) was an actor and nonsinger—since recitative for the Indián was not written yet, this was no problem! He performed the role twenty-nine times and eventually became a stage manager.[12]

Smetana had the following to say about casting, after he was forced to relinquish his post because of the onset of deafness in 1874. He wrote to his replacement, Adolf Čech:

"Frankly, I was glad I no longer had to decide on those matters. Casting was always a bothersome and ungrateful task, where one was required to pay regard to all conceivable sides and parties whose number was legion. I feel really glad that I can now entrust that assignment to you *for ever* and, in doing so, I am convinced that you will ensure the best possible casting for the benefit of the work itself."[13]

The budding Provisional Theatre orchestra, with excellent Czech musicians, was made up of thirty-four players. (The principal violist was the young Antonín Dvořák [1841–1904], who played in the orchestra for nine years, from 1862 to 1871.) The chorus, mainly because of the small stage, consisted of ten women and eight men, possibly augmented by another eight choristers borrowed from the German theater. Most of the solo singers had dual contracts with the Provisional Theatre and the German Estates Theatre.[14]

When war was declared on June 16, Smetana and his family packed their bags and joined hundreds of others to flee Prague. As the composer of the supercharged nationalistic opera *Braniboři v Čechách*, he was afraid the Prussians would execute him or send him to a labor camp. Immediately after the Seven Weeks' War ended, attitudes toward the arts in Prague shifted, and Smetana was offered the post of music director of the Provisional Theatre after five years of petitioning. He threw himself into building a solid company, and his work included conducting the second production of *Prodaná nevěsta.*[15]

The second production opened on October 27, 1866 and lasted almost two years, with fourteen performances. The new Mařenka, Terezie Rückaufová (1846–?), was a much better choice than before. Twenty years old, she had a small but fresh and clear voice. Her character, both cheerful and serious, was ideal for the part, and she came across as a nice country girl, much different from the aristocratic Eleonora z Ehrenbergů. Halfway through this production, in 1867, Polák was replaced by Jan Ludevít Lukes (1824–1909) as Jeník. Even though the tenor was approaching the end of his career, he had the right combination of a beautiful voice, excellent acting, and the right character, so that he is considered to be the first real Jeník.

The opening of this production was very important for shaping the opera's ultimate form. It was announced that Emperor Franz Joseph I would attend the premiere. Protocol for such an occasion required a ballet. Not having time to compose one, Smetana took the energetic ballet music from Act I, sc. v of *Branibori v Čechách*, titled it "tanec cigánů" [dance of the gypsies], and placed it in Act II, just before the Esmeralda/Principál couplet. For the premiere, the couplet was omitted, as it was considered too frivolous for such an important occasion. For the rest of the run, however, the couplet was retained along with the interpolated ballet. Ironically, the emperor left after Act I and never heard the ballet or the couplet![16]

Second Version

The third production premiered on January 29, 1869, again with Smetana conducting. It ran for one month, playing four times. Although the work was still in only two acts with spoken dialogue, the composer had made significant changes. Besides altering some of the libretto, he wrote the men's beer chorus, placing it in Act I in between the Mařenka/Vašek duet and the Jeník/Kecal duet, while providing a change of scene to the village pub. Taking Neruda's advice, and having seen the effectiveness of a ballet, Smetana added the polka, along with its chorus. He did not place it where the gypsy dance had been, nor where it is today, but rather opened the second act with it, just before Vašek's aria. At first, the Esmeralda/Principál couplet remained, but then Smetana dropped it for good beginning with the February 7 performance. Finally, Smetana added Mařenka's second aria, "Ten lásky sen." The new aria, leaning more toward Wagner than any other music in the opera, added more depth to Mařenka's character, and grew naturally from its preceding accompanied recitative that had been written almost three years earlier.

Smetana was evidently happy with these changes, as he had the text translated into French in February, and sent the score to the Paris Opera in August, hoping for a performance there. Although nothing came of this in Smetana's lifetime, the prospects of a French production seem to have spurred Smetana on to his next revision.

Third Version

The fourth production of *Prodaná nevěsta* opened on June 1, 1869, and played nine times. There was still spoken dialogue, but Smetana added the *furiant*, *skočná* and the "pochod komediantů" [march of the comedians]. He also divided the opera into three acts. The *skočná* was preceded by the "pochod komediantů" and placed where it is today, where the gypsy dance and couplet used to be. Still, this version differed from the final version, even not counting the spoken dialogue. For whereas Smetana moved the beer chorus to the opening of Act II, and placed the polka at the end of Act I, he put the *furiant* immediately after the polka. This made for a spectacular ending to the first act, but a long dance scene. Otakar Hostinský (1847–1910), critic and founder of modern Czech musicology and aesthetics, wrote a review in the paper *Dalibor* stating that the opera would be greatly enhanced if the spoken dialogue were replaced by "short, light recitatives." This and another incident were to spur Smetana on to yet one more revision.[17]

Definitive Version

Bass Josef Paleček, who had sung Krušina in the very first production of *Prodaná nevěsta*, had moved to St. Petersburg in 1870 and changed his name there to Osip Osipovič Paleček. Together with Czech conductor Eduard Nápravník (1839–1916), he was mounting a Russian production of *Prodaná nevěsta* to open in 1871. Paleček both sang the role of Kecal and served as stage director. Nápravník and Paleček wrote to Smetana pleading for the composer to replace the spoken dialogue, which as a rule the Russian public did not like, with recitatives. The urgings of Hostinský, Nápravník, Paleček, and Smetana's own instincts, together with the prospects for an international performance, combined to create the impetus for the final addition of recitatives. In writing them, Smetana shortened some of the dialogue. He also repositioned the *furiant* into the second act after the beer chorus and before Vašek's opening aria. The exuberant male dance, coming after the men's lusty chorus, provided perfect dramatic contrast to the first entrance of the shy, stuttering Vašek. The work had achieved its definitive form.

The Czech was translated into Russian in August 1870, and a score was ready to send to St. Petersburg in September. However, Smetana decided to try out the new version first in Prague with the fifth production premiering on September 25. *Prodaná nevěsta* had been gaining more and more in popularity, and now it proved to be a complete success with both the Czech public and critics. By the early 1870s (and certainly by 1892, when the opera became a sensation in Vienna), both the *mladočechy* and *staročechy* parties began to acknowledge the work as a model for Czech national opera. The production ran for just under four years, with twenty performances. At this point, Sabina was purported to have said:

"Had I only guessed Smetana's treatment of that operetta of mine, I would have devoted much more effort to it and written a far better and more substantial libretto for him."[18]

The last performance, on June 22, 1874, was Smetana's last time to conduct the opera, as the onset of his deafness would then only allow him to compose. The next production was to be handed to Smetana's assistant, Adolf Čech.

The Russian premiere occurred on January 11, 1871, and was a failure. During rehearsals, Paleček had written to Prague begging for at least one picture of a rustic from Plzeň, saying:

". . . for the Russians have no idea what it means to be Czech, and they have even less idea about our peasants no matter how you try to explain it to them."[19]

International fame was to come via another route.

On August 10, 1872, the newspaper *Národní listy* shocked its readers with its front page disclosure "Mr. Karel Sabina has turned traitor to the nation." He had been exposed as an informer for the Prague Austrian police. The name so linked to *Prodaná nevěsta* was now omitted from theater posters. Only Sabina's initials were allowed to be shown on the title page of the first piano/vocal score, published in 1872 by the newly established Hudební matice. It was their first publication.[20]

Synopsis of the Opera

The entire opera takes place during one day in a Bohemian village. It is a day of celebration, probably May Day.

Act I

As the whole village rejoices, Jeník asks his beloved Mařenka why she is so sullen. She explains that in order to take care of a debt, her father had made a contract years ago with Mícha, a well-to-do landowner, promising her hand in marriage to his son. Her mother told her that Mícha and his son will come to the village today so he can court her. Jeník reassures her that all will be well—she need only trust him. Mařenka then questions Jeník's secretiveness—she knows little of his past. He explains how his mother died when he was young, his father remarried, and his stepmother made his life so miserable that he ran far away from home and lived among strangers. Jeník and Mařenka sing of their faithful love, and then leave separately.

Kecal, the marriage broker, enters with Mařenka's parents, Ludmila and Krušina. Dominating the conversation, Kecal assures them that he can convince Mařenka to honor the contract. While Krušina is satisfied, Ludmila wants to make sure of her daughter's feelings, and wants to know more about the groom.

Kecal glowingly proclaims all of Vašek's attributes, to the satisfaction of both parents.

Mařenka comes, and after hearing of Kecal's proposed groom, argues that she is already bound to Jeník. She refuses their designs and leaves. As the villagers gather to dance the polka, Kecal reassures the parents that he will deal with Jeník personally while they find Mícha and Vašek.

Act II

Inside the pub, men sing a song praising the virtues of beer. Jeník counters that love alone can bring happiness. Kecal sings that good counsel and money are the secrets to a good life. A passionate Bohemian *furiant* dance follows.

Vašek appears dressed as a bridegroom, stuttering and fearful of what will happen if he does not obey his mother and marry the chosen bride. Mařenka, who has been eavesdropping awhile, realizes that Vašek is her intended. After making sure that he does not know that she is Mařenka, she convinces him that Mařenka is a cruel woman who would cheat and then kill him. With gentle flirtation, she persuades the gullible boy to renounce Mařenka forever.

Kecal now tries to get Jeník to renounce Mařenka. First, he offers him another girl who has lots of money. Then, he offers to pay Jeník. Jeník agrees to a bribe of three hundred gold coins, on two conditions: Mařenka may only marry "the son of Mícha," and all of Krušina's debts to Mícha must be forgiven. Content, the jubilant Kecal leaves to write up the contract and obtain witnesses.

Jeník is left alone to contemplate how his love is so strong he would never renounce Mařenka for all the money in the world.

Kecal returns with the villagers and Krušina to witness the contract. The villagers rebuke Jeník when they learn he has sold Mařenka.

Act III

Vašek enters, distraught over the prospect of being forced to marry a girl who will poison him.

A travelling circus arrives, and the ringmaster introduces the star performers, Esmeralda and the Indian, with promises of a dancing bear. As a sample, the troupe presents a rousing short performance (during the *skočná*).

Suddenly, the Indian rushes in to tell the ringmaster that the person who plays the bear is too drunk to perform. Eyeing Vašek, they surmise that he would fit perfectly in the bearsuit. Seeing that Esmeralda and Vašek share a mutual attraction, the ringmaster joins Esmeralda in inviting Vašek to join their circus.

Vašek's parents, Mícha and Háta, enter with Kecal. They are stunned about Vašek's new perception of Mařenka. Kecal smells deceit, and vows to get to the bottom of it. Vašek runs away.

Mařenka enters with her parents. She is incredulous and angry that Jeník has sold her. Vašek is called in and points out Mařenka as the one he loves. After he leaves again, both sets of parents and Kecal urge Mařenka to consider well her future happiness.

Mařenka is left alone with little hope. When Jeník happily runs in to meet her, she is so livid she will not allow him to explain his actions. She decides to marry Vašek.

Kecal gathers the villagers together to finalize arrangements. Mícha and Háta are astounded to see Jeník. Jeník steps forward to declare himself "the son of Mícha," and asks Mařenka to choose her husband. Mařenka gladly chooses Jeník. The contract is honored, to the abhorrence of Háta, and to the dismay and humiliation of Kecal. Suddenly, two boys warn everyone that the circus bear has escaped. All are relieved—and amused—when Vašek reveals it is he in disguise. His irate mother leads him away. Seeing that Vašek is far from ready to marry, Mícha welcomes back his prodigal son, and gives his blessing to the couple. All rejoice over the triumph of true love and the impending wedding.

Musical and Other Matters

Again and again critics have praised *Prodána nevěsta* for its "naturalness" and its "Mozartian" qualities.[21] When a critic in St. Petersburg condemned the opera as being like Offenbach, only worse, Smetana himself retorted:

> "And none of those gentlemen noticed that my model was Mozart's light opera?"[22]

In its spirit (as well as canonic writing and rapid violin passages), the overture is often compared to Mozart's overtures to *Le nozze di Figaro* and *Die Zauberflöte*. Although Smetana's overture was uncharacteristically written months before the bulk of the work, it sets up the opera perfectly. Three themes from the overture occur later in a very natural way. The opening of the overture is heard at the beginning of the Act I finale, where Kecal calls the villagers together to witness the contract. Czech conductor Bohumil Gregor (see chapter 2) commented on his choice of tempo for the overture:

> "The tempo of the overture is always like the tempo of the finale. If it is different, it goes badly. I always sing to myself "Pojd'te lidičky, pojd'te," and then it works."[23]

After the series of runs in the strings, a second theme appears at m. 100 in the overture that is mirrored in the Act I finale, as well, soon after the first theme. Whereas the first theme was more associated with Kecal, the second is related to the communal witnessing of the marriage contract. A third theme enters in the overture at m. 189. This, too, appears in the Act I finale at m. 1160, just before Kecal reveals that Jeník sold Mařenka for three hundred gold coins. When Mařenka is outraged at Jeník about this, in Act II, sc. vii, just before their fight duet, the music returns. Brian Large describes other motives within the opera itself, used as simple, yet natural "musical reminicences" connected with faithful love (beginning in the Jeník/Mařenka Act I duet), or with Mařenka herself.[24]

Mozartian in spirit, too, are the many ensembles, which display a stunning variety of moods, compositional writing, and natural responses among the various characters. Quite a few of these can be excerpted for opera scenes programs, even the short Jeník/Mařenka fight duet, along with its recitative. That duet is so contrasting to most opera duets, and even features two high Cs for Mařenka. The Jeník/Kecal duet often had to be repeated in performances throughout the world. A real masterpiece is the sextet, in Act III. This ensemble allows us to see the minor characters of the parents as real human beings who truly have the welfare of their children as their utmost concern. Here, we even believe that Kecal, too, thinks that the role he plays as marriage broker truly helps to bring order and security, if not necessarily happiness, to troubled souls and families. Really a quintet until the last thirteen measures, the ensemble requires beautiful phrasing, a wide range of dynamics, and perfect intonation. Audience members at the Prague National Theatre might have noticed that when Zdeněk Košler conducted, the intermission before Act III was longer than usual—this was because he always took time then to rehearse the sextet one more time.[25]

Most Mozartian of all is the musical characterization that Smetana is able to achieve, giving depth and humanity to the characters that rise far above the limitations of the libretto. An overview of past performances (see chapter 2) shows that although audiences may still be entertained by comedy and the wonderful music, those performances that fail are the ones that play only for a laugh, falling short of illuminating relationships and the true depth of characterization that Smetana achieved.[26] The great Czech set designer Josef Svoboda (see chapter 2) also pointed out the danger, mostly for Czechs, of presenting the opera as a museum piece that tries to re-create the youthful memories of audience members. *Prodána nevěsta*, he stated, ". . . is a comedy, but it's also serious, not a decorative piece."[27]

In line with underestimating the depth of the work, another pitfall is to underestimate the difficulty of performing it. Leaving the singers for chapter 4, it can be noted that many a community production has been brought down by the shortcomings of the orchestra. For violinists, both the overture and the *skočná* are in the standard repertoire for orchestral auditions. This means that violinists should know these excerpts, but it also means that they are difficult! Winds are also featured prominently in the work. Some organizations would do well to consider performing the opera with piano. Besides the piano transcription of the overture in piano/vocal scores, the 1982 Supraphon score contains Smetana's own arrangement of the overture for piano four-hands (see appendix B).

Whereas Dvořák is often rightly hailed for bringing folk music into the concert hall, Smetana paved the way. Without quoting any folk music in the opera except for the *furiant* (see chapter 3), Smetana created a work that has consistently been hailed as "Czech," although it is impossible to pinpoint exactly what makes it so. Michael Beckerman and John Tyrrell attribute the musical Czechness to a combining of many elements, including, perhaps most of all, associations, such as the village setting and the character types.[28] Another strong ingredient, of course, is the Czech language—if the opera is sung in Czech, the spirit and "earthiness" of the opera are all the more enhanced. One obvious factor is the use of the three Bohemian dances—polka, furiant, and skočná—as well as dance rhythms that pervade sung numbers (see chapter 3). In any event, the opera is so thoroughly Czech that stage directors have a hard time changing the setting to anywhere else but a Czech village. Because the plot hinges on a marriage broker, it is difficult to change the time period, as well. (Plenty of cultures today arrange marriages, but they would probably not be dancing polkas or furiants!) When Daniel Pelzig staged *Prodána nevěsta* for Opera Boston in 2009, using English as the actual language of the characters, he decided to set it in an American Czech community (see chapter 2).

Jaroslav Smolka has shown how Smetana's beer chorus follows in the tradition of Czech men's beer choruses, including the raising of glasses on held notes. The choruses were traditionally mixed with an evening of dancing as well, so the *furiant* that immediately follows is right in line with the festivities.[29]

Costumes for the opera are traditionally from the Plzeň region, west of Prague. Each area of the Czech lands had its own unique wear, or *kroj* (the plural is *kroje*), that really reflected the region of the wearer. Bohemian *kroje*, for example, were distinctly different from Moravian *kroje*, and the areas within these regions all had unique types. The *kroje* for festive occasions would be particularly colorful, with beautiful, finely-worked embroidery. The women from the Plzeň region wore *holubičky*, which literally means "little doves." These were white bonnets with tail-feather shapes on each side. Kecal usually wore a short cylinder hat, and for decades always carried a red umbrella. Esmeralda often had a tambourine, especially in early productions where she was associated with Victor Hugo's Esmeralda. Maypoles are a common feature in productions, to reflect what was probably May Day. There was usually a small church in the back of the scenery somewhere, typical of Czech towns and villages. The first Czech productions did not completely begin this way, though, but evolved to embrace what became expected tradition for generations of Czechs. Later Czech productions, however, stylized many elements, so that, for example, different aspects of *kroje* were combined with modern dress; or *kroje* from different regions, even Moravia, were incorporated into the costumes. Esmeralda lost her tambourine, and Kecal lost his red umbrella, although from time to time they return. Designers outside of the Czech Republic, then, need not panic when it comes to capturing the right spirit of a Bohemian village in the midst of its celebrations.[30]

In *Prodána nevěsta*, Smetana stayed a good distance away from Wagner's chromaticism, nodding to the German composer only in Mařenka's second, added, aria. This explains some of the freshness and charm of the work, and how the composer is able to fuse so well elements of folk music with "high art." "Bringing folk music into the concert hall" partly means that the opera is both refined and rustic at the same time. We hear this right away in the overture, where listeners are swept away by the overflowing, infectious energy, most of them not realizing that a fugue has already begun in the ninth measure. The *furiant*, too, taken from an actual folk song, would have bewildered many a village musician in its middle section, where the cellos repeat a four-measure phrase note-for-note eight times, but each time with different harmonies (mm. 150–81). The dance is so vital, though, that this sophistication is a natural part of the work's fabric. The main thing that comes across is the earthiness of the dance.

While polish and finesse are definite requirements for performing *Prodaná nevěsta*, even professional opera companies have occasionally missed the mark exuding the earthy side of the work—too refined and too elegant have been occasional pitfalls in past performances, even for Czechs (see chapter 2). Listening to Czech folk music and watching videos of Czech folk dance groups can help instrumentalists and singers alike to loosen up and find the right spirit. For *Prodaná nevěsta*, an ideal group to consult is Mladina from Plzeň. Founded in 1954 under the name Škoda Plzeň, Mladina tours internationally and features mostly folk music and dancing from Southwest Bohemia, using *kroje* from several regions. Photos, videos, and CDs are available from their web site at http://www.mladina.cz/en-index.htm.

Quite a few English-language productions opted to dispense with Smetana's recitatives and use spoken dialogue instead. This was usually done with the justification that recitatives were added only in the final version. However, Smetana conducted that final version twenty times in a production that lasted just under four years, stopping only because of deafness. He was obviously satisfied with the results, as was the public. In the Czech lands, dialogue never replaced recitatives during Smetana's lifetime, or after. The opera is not an operetta, not a *Singspiel*, and not musical theater. It is a Czech comic folk opera, and the recitatives—which are not extensive—add weight, depth, and refinement to the work, blending with its wonderful mix of comic, serious, refined, and earthy elements.

Cuts

Cuts in the opera have been made in many professional productions, although probably never in the Czech lands. The following are some possibilities, mostly in recitatives, and mostly for Kecal and Jeník. None are necessary, but some may help to give young singers a needed break here and there.

Possible Cuts in the Recitatives

Act II, sc. iv:
M. 940, second beat, to m. 953. Jeník sings "Tak– tak–," thinks a little while, then the orchestra plays the D major chord and he sings "Nuže, staniž se!" This

works better if the orchestra adds a G to the A major chord in m. 939. The disadvantage is that we miss Kecal's great line implying that his own marriage is not a happy one.

M. 961, the orchestra plays its two D major chords, and then Jeník comes in on "Vyhradím si to ve smlouvě!" in m. 966.

M. 969, the orchestra plays the downbeat F major chord, but as a short quarter, and Kecal enters with "Ano, ano, ano, do smlouvy všecko dám."[31] Unfortunately, the audience then misses Jeník's condition that Krušina's debts to Mícha will be erased. Even though this is the only time that Krušina's debts are mentioned, it is still nice to see just how much is gained from Jeník's trick.

Act III, sc. ii:
M. 484, fourth beat, to m. 493, the orchestra plays fourth beat A major chord. The Principál sings ". . . a plnou svobodu," the orchestra plays the A major chord, and Esmeralda sings "Nuže, můj drahý." Despite the Principál's short part, he does have a lot of words!

Act III, sc. iii:
Kecal sings "No, a ty, Mařenko? Vezmeš si syna Míchova?," cut mm. 1154–57, except that the orchestra plays the last, G major, chord in m. 1157, then continue as written in m. 1158.

Possible Musical Cuts

None of these cuts are necessary!

Some cuts in repeats in the *skočná* could be worked out by the conductor.

Act II, opening, the second verse of the beer chorus.
Act II, sc. iv, Kecal, cut mm. 754–93, but only if the singer really needs it!
Act III, opening, Vašek, cut beat two of m. 57 through beat one of m. 71.

Notes

1. John Tyrrell, *Czech opera* (Cambridge: Cambridge University Press, 1988), 41–43; and see throughout: Jan Panenka, and Taťána Součková, *Prodaná nevěsta na jevištích Prozatímního a Národního divadla 1866–2004* (Prague: Gallery and Národní divadlo, 2004).

2. Gerald Abraham, "The genesis of *The Bartered Bride*," in *Slavonic and Romantic music: Essays and studies* (New York: St. Martin's Press, 1968), 28; and "*The Bartered Bride* mosaic," in English-language program booklet for the Prague National Theatre *Prodaná nevěsta*, ed. Helena Havlíková (Prague: National Theatre, 1992), 43.

3. Note especially the mordents used in each. Panenka and Součková, *Prodaná ne-*

věsta na jevištích Prozatímního a Národního divadla 1866–2004, 24; Brian Large, *Smetana* (New York: Praeger Publishers, 1970), 172; and Bedřich Smetana, *Wedding scenes* (Miami Lakes, Fla.: Masters Music Publications, 1989), 6–15.

4. František Bartoš, *Bedřich Smetana: Letters and reminiscences*, trans. from Czech by Daphne Rusbridge (Prague: Artia, 1955), 67–68; and Brian S. Locke, *Opera and ideology in Prague: Polemics and practice at the National Theater 1900–1938* (Rochester: University of Rochester Press, 2006), 20–21.

5. Petr Daňek and Jana Vyšohlídová, "Dokumenty k operní soutěži o cenu hraběte Harracha," *Miscellanea musicologia*, XXX (1983): 154.

6. See below. Tyrrell, *Czech opera*, 101–104; and Hans Heinsheimer, "An enemy of the people," *Opera News* 43, no. 6 (2 December 1978): 27–28.

7. In the opera, there are three themes heard previously in the overture. These are discussed later. Abraham, "The genesis of *The Bartered Bride*," in *Slavonic and Romantic music: Essays and studies*, 29; Large, *Smetana*, 161; and *Slavoj*, no. 11 from 1 December 1863, 203.

8. Smetana occupied Lažanský Palace from 1863 to 1869. Located straight across from the National Theatre opera house, this building now houses the famous café Slávia. Bedřich Smetana and Karel Sabina, *Prodaná nevěsta; první náčrtek*, facsimile of holograph sketches, preface and notes by Mirko Očadlík (Prague: Společnost Bedřicha Smetany, Melantrich, 1944), xii–xiii.

9. From a letter to Srb-Debrnov, October 16, 1880, in Bartoš, *Bedřich Smetana: Letters and reminiscences*, trans. from Czech by Daphne Rusbridge, 229.

10. Large, *Smetana*, 126, 145; and Panenka and Součková, *Prodaná nevěsta na jevištích Prozatímního a Národního divadla 1866–2004*, 22.

11. Large, *Smetana*, 165–66, 168, 399–408; and Panenka and Součková, *Prodaná nevěsta na jevištích Prozatímního a Národního divadla 1866–2004*, 33. The deleted duet is printed in the orchestral score, 627–35, as well as in Large, *Smetana*, 409–13. A piano reduction exists in: Bedřich Smetana and Karel Sabina, *Prodaná nevěsta*, piano/vocal score, English translation by Mark Herman and Ronnie Apter (Shepherd, Mich.: M. Herman and R. Apter, 2003), 276–79.

12. The dearth of coloratura soprano roles in Slavic music is adressed in chapter 4. Panenka and Součková, *Prodaná nevěsta na jevištích Prozatímního a Národního divadla 1866–2004*, 28–30, 48; and Large, *Smetana*, 144.

13. Written on December 12, 1878. "*The Bartered Bride* mosaic," in English language program booklet for the Prague National Theatre *Prodaná nevěsta*, Havlíková, 57.

14. Tyrrell, *Czech opera*, 28, 32, 33; Josef Bartoš, *Prozatímní divadlo a jeho opera* (Prague: Sbor pro zřízení druhého národního divadla v Praze, 1938), 25; and Hans-Hubert Schönzeler, *Dvořák* (London: Marion Boyars Publishers, 1984), 39–41.

15. Large, *Smetana*, 166–67.

16. Brian Large calls this production version *two* of the opera (Large, *Smetana*, 399–408), but the Prague National Theatre considers it part of the first version. Panenka and Součková, *Prodaná nevěsta na jevištích Prozatímního a Národního divadla 1866–2004*, 31–32, 34.

17. Large, *Smetana*, 168, 399–408; and "*The Bartered Bride* mosaic," in English-language program booklet for the Prague National Theatre *Prodaná nevěsta*, ed. Helena Havlíková, 52.

18. "*The Bartered Bride* mosaic," in English-language program booklet for the Prague National Theatre *Prodaná nevěsta*, ed. Helena Havlíková, 49.

19. Vladimír Procházka, ed., *Národní divadlo a jeho předchůdci: Slovník umělců divadel Vlastenského, Stavovského, Prozatímního a Národního* (Prague: Academia Praha,

1988), s.v. "Paleček, Josef;" and Panenka and Součková, *Prodaná nevěsta na jevištích Prozatímního a Národního divadla 1866–2004*, 35, 38–39.

20. Tyrrell, *Czech opera* (Cambridge: Cambridge University Press), 243. Hudební matice was the precursor of Supraphon. Smetana had written the piano/vocal score for the Russian production, dedicating it to Grand Duke Konstantin Nikolaevich (1827–92), who had been instrumental in liberating the serfs in 1861. *"The Bartered Bride* mosaic," in English-language program booklet for the Prague National Theatre *Prodaná nevěsta*, ed. Helena Havlíková, 55; and Heinsheimer, "An enemy of the people," *Opera News*, 30.

21. Besides countless reviews throughout the twentieth century, see Large, *Smetana*, 184.

22. Quoted by Otakar Hostinský in Bartoš, *Bedřich Smetana: Letters and reminiscences*, trans. from Czech by Daphne Rusbridge, 124.

23. Alena Martínková, *Bohumil Gregor: Chtěl jsem sloužit divadlu* (Prague: Jalna, 2006), 95.

24. Large, *Smetana*, 174–75. Also see his descriptions of various characters' music, 175–79.

25. Thanks to my wife, dancer Bohuslava Jelínková, who was in Košler's production.

26. Characters are discussed in chapter 4.

27. Josef Svoboda, with Milena Honzíková, *Tajemství divadelního prostoru* (Prague: Odeon, 1990), 155; and John W. Freeman, "The theater of Josef Svoboda," *Opera News* 43, no. 6 (2 December 1978): 43–46.

28. Tyrrell, *Czech opera*, 298.

29. Jaroslav Smolka, *Smetanova vokální tvorba: Písně, sbory, kantáta*, vol. 2 of *Dílo a život Bedřicha Smetany* (Prague: Editio Supraphon, 1980), 179. For much more on Czech men's beer choruses, both in Bohemia and in Moravia, see Jan Miroslav Krist and Jitka Matuszková, "Zpívání na pivo," *Národní ústav lidové kultury*, http://www.nulk.cz/Informace.aspx?sid=133 (24 October 2008).

30. The University of Michigan had beautiful *kroje* for its 2007 production. However, the costumes had to be obtained from several different sources, and they ended up being not only from different regions, but from different East European countries! While most audience members didn't notice, native Czechs found it odd that one character looked like he was from Hungary, while another was from Slovakia. The performance more than overrode this detail, however, so Czechs thoroughly enjoyed it. In her book, Lída Brodenová describes traditional productions of the opera: Lída Brodenová, *Notes on Smetana's opera Prodaná nevěsta*, edited by Judith Fiehler (Washington: K. Maier, 1990), 1–23.

31. These words are preferable to "Ano, ano, ano, to vše svoluji"—see chapter 7.

2

Performance History

Prodaná nevěsta is the most well-known and widely performed Czech opera in the world. After the pivotal 1892 production in Vienna by the Prague National Theatre, the work gradually entered the repertoire of opera houses everywhere, large and small, professional and amateur. English-language music schools, too, perform everything from English-language productions with piano to Czech-language productions with full orchestra. Praised as a thoroughly "Czech" opera, *Prodaná nevěsta* is enjoyed universally for its stunning, joyous music and its well-defined and well-loved characters that reach far beyond any borders. From time to time, however, its "Czechness" has taken the limelight in various political turning points throughout history, even outside of the Czech lands.

In the Czech Lands

Prodaná nevěsta was written for a striving Czech nation to be performed first in its own National Theatre, an opera house built by donations from the budding nation. When the theater was constructed, Czechs traveled from throughout the country to marvel at "their" theater. In the modern Czech Republic, many Czechs still journey to see their famed opera house and to partake of a Czech opera there. Many have memories of their first *Prodaná nevěsta*, seen in childhood with beloved family members. *Prodaná nevěsta* tops the list for the most performed opera in Prague. Since its inception it has never missed a year without being presented in the capital, not even in two world wars or the 1968 Russian invasion. At one point, 1958–59, there were even three different productions showing in Prague alone. In 2004, it was estimated that the opera had been performed by the Prague National Theatre (and its predecessor, the Provisional Theatre) 3,443 times.[1]

Like German opera houses, Czech companies are repertory houses. A large house like the Prague National Theatre (which today seats 996) has a ten-month season that maintains a full-time resident company of singers, chorus, dancers, and orchestra. Some opera productions (whether Czech, Italian, French, German, or Russian) may play continuously for several years, especially *the* Czech national opera *Prodaná nevěsta*, heard not only by Czech citizens but also by a steady stream of international tourists. The repertory system gives singers the opportunity to work as an established ensemble and to perform a variety of roles, often many times. For *Prodaná nevěsta*, there are quite a few examples of steady artistic work. In 1871, a new tenor, Adolf Krössing (1848–1933), joined the fifth production under Smetana as Vašek. He was ideal for the part, so Smetana was very satisfied. Krössing left the role in 1914 at sixty-six years old. The public did not seem to mind his age. He returned in 1923 at age seventy-five for one more performance. Eduard Haken (1910–96) sang Kecal at the National Theatre, and then ventured outside Prague to sing the role more than 1,000 times throughout Europe. His last Kecal was at the National Theatre in 1985 at the age of seventy-five. As Kecal, he can be heard on recordings and on a 1971 television broadcast. The great artist Karel Berman (1919–95) was known at the National Theatre for his portrayal of Leporello and other roles, including a stellar Kecal, which he sang from 1952 to 1985. The opera chorus was allowed to venture into small parts as well—Karel Hynek Lažanský (1878–1957), a member of the chorus since 1913, sang the role of the Indián 762 times from 1915 to 1940. Karel Hruška (1891–1966) sang the Principál from 1919 to 1957 a record 1,074 times. There are many more examples.[2]

From 1866 to 1874, Smetana had led *Prodaná nevěsta* through its four versions and beyond, covering five productions and forty-nine performances. Since then, productions in Prague have tended to be overseen by a team of a prominent leading conductor and stage director, one of whom was usually head of opera at the National Theatre. With such a revered opera led by renowned artistic figures of the day, these productions could not help but to reflect—and even to influence—the cultural, social, and political life of the times.

Into the Twentienth Century

Smetana's former assistant, Adolf Čech, was musically responsible for the sixth through tenth productions at the Provisional Theatre and the new National Theatre. These productions ran from 1874 to 1909, 441 performances. Čech died in 1903, so later performances were taken up by several other conductors, including Karel Kovařovic. Still, Čech's leadership amounted to the longest direct influence of any one leader involved with the opera. Whereas the duties of the first stage directors for *Prodaná nevěsta* were far removed from the role we see today, two directors involved with the Čech productions helped to usher in modern concepts. These were Edmund Chvalovský (1839–1934) and František Hynek (1837–1905). Hynek had sung Kecal in the very first performance of the opera. These directors sought to integrate the soloists and chorus into one dramatic unit, going beyond mere posturing, realistic scenery, and costumes. Costumes had gradually evolved to reflect the Plzeň region, west of Prague. Dance elements evolved significantly during this period, as well, under the work of groundbreaking choreographers (see chapter 3).

June 1878 saw the first foreign guest star in *Prodaná nevěsta* in Prague. She was the London-born Emilie Chiomi, twenty-four years old, from Her Majesty's Opera in London. She had arrived in Prague the year before, and performed Violetta and other roles. Chiomi sang the role of Mařenka in three performances in Italian, while everyone else sang Czech. Occasionally, however, she would throw in a Czech word, to the delight of the audience.[3]

The Prague National Theatre opened for good on November 18, 1883, with a performance of Smetana's festive opera *Libuše*. Five days later, *Prodaná nevěsta* played for the first time in the landmark theater, with the premiere of the ninth production. Smetana, whose health was quickly deteriorating, had been fêted at the celebration of the one-hundreth performance of the opera on May 5, 1882, and he was able to see the new premiere in the new theater, as well. Many people throughout the Czech lands and beyond traveled to see the comic opera in this production at the new theater. Bedřich Smetana died on May 12, 1884. His funeral was set for May 15, which by coincidence was the same day as a scheduled performance of the joyous *Prodaná nevěsta*. It was decided not to cancel the performance, but instead to perform the work in his memory.[4]

The tenth production opened on May 8, 1892, playing for a record seventeen years, 297 performances. With this production the chorus was fully integrated into the action. In the opening there appeared the village figures of a priest, teacher, gypsies, police who chase away the gypsies, and others. For the first time the whole village danced in the polka. The *kroje* (traditional folk wear, very distinctive from region to region) was now very authentic, clearly reflecting the Plzeň region. The orchestra was now at forty-five to fifty members (instead of thirty-four at the tiny Provisional Theatre), and the chorus at sixteen men and sixteen women (instead of usually eighteen total). The opera was primed for its first international tour, although some authorities were still not convinced of the opera's worth. Some argued that Dvořák's opera *Dimitrij* was a much better choice than "a piece of life from a Czech village in the middle of nowhere." *Prodaná nevěsta* won out, however, opening in Vienna on June 1, 1892.

Čech was able to push for an orchestra of sixty-four players for the landmark performance, in Czech, at the International Exhibition of Music and Theater in Vienna. The production was such a hit that scheduled performances of other Czech works had to be replaced with repeat performances of *Prodaná nevěsta*. The road to world fame had begun. Vienna staged its own production the following year, in German, with a translation by Max Kalbeck that was to find its way to the New York Metropolitan Opera in 1909. The opera quickly spread to country after country, year after year. After Vienna came Berlin, Chicago, and Budapest, all in 1893; Ljubljana and Stockholm in 1894; Strasbourg, London, Antwerp, Warsaw, and Riga in 1895; and so on, until it soon became a staple of every German opera house and a delight throughout Europe and the Americas.[5]

The Birth of Czechoslovakia

Karel Kovařovic (1862–1920) was opera director of the National Theatre from 1900 to 1920. A composer himself, he is most known for his battles with Janáček over *Jenůfa*. Kovařovic led the eleventh and twelfth productions of *Prodaná nevěsta* from 1909 to 1923, 367 performances. Other conductors joined in, including Otakar Ostrčil, taking over after Kovařovic's death in 1920.

Kovařovic was the first conductor after Smetana to truly work conceptually with stage directors, singers, and designers. The eleventh production of *Prodaná nevěsta* opened on the twenty-fifth anniversary of Smetana's death, May 12, 1909. (This was three months after the historic performance of the opera at the New York Metropolitan Opera.) Kovařovic immediately set about restoring discipline to the company, which had languished after so many years under Čech. The seventeen-year run of the previous production of *Prodaná nevěsta* had especially led to text liberties, cheap laughs, and sloppiness in intonation, apparent from critiques and early recordings.

August 8, 1909, saw the 500th Prague performance of *Prodaná nevěsta*. In 1913, the opera was performed outdoors in Šárka, a Prague park named after the legendary warrior Šárka, who supposedly threw herself off a cliff there. With seats for over 9,000 people, and room for 8,000 more standing, the production inspired further outdoor operas. Live goats were used in the performance, and a circus caravan was bought from a real Komediant for the occasion. During World War I, 1914–18, the comic opera was performed as part of national dem-onstrations. On October 28, 1918, the independence of Czechoslovakia was proclaimed, and Tomáš Garrigue Masaryk was elected the new nation's first president. Kovařovic proclaimed "Well, on our first day of freedom, there must be a *Prodaná*," and the opera was performed on the evening of October 29 as a welcome to the new nation.[6]

Days before Kovařovic's death on December 6, 1920, *Prodaná nevěsta* became entangled in a political incident between Czech-speaking and German-speaking citizens. A group of Czech speakers had decided that the historic Es-tates Theatre (the Stavovské divadlo), built in 1783 and mainly used for the performance of plays in German, should become part of the Prague National Theatre. On November 16, 1920, a Czech-speaking mob entered the theater and forcibly removed its German director from his office. A decision was made to perform *Prodaná nevěsta* on the "new" stage that very evening. Even with such short notice the performance was sold out. The remainder of Kovařovic's twelfth production of *Prodaná nevěsta* shared performances between the Na-tional Theatre and the Estates/Stavovské Theatre. Otakar Ostrčil, who would soon be the new head of opera at the National Theatre, disapproved of the ag-gressive takeover and distanced himself from the Estates Theatre during his tenure.[7]

"Modern" Controversy

Conductor Otakar Ostrčil (1879–1935) and stage director Ferdinand Pujman (1889–1961) created the thirteenth and fourteenth productions, from 1923 to 1936, 454 performances. Other conductors led some reprises, taking over after Ostrčil's death. A formidable composer himself, Ostrčil was opera director at the National Theatre from 1920 to 1935. Pujman produced eighty-eight operas collaborating with Ostrčil. His precise and detailed stage directing led to a new Czech word in vogue at the theater for a time, "vypujmanovat," "to follow through to perfection." Singing and acting became wonderfully synthesized, characters had greater depth, and the dances were more integrated with the opera.

These two productions reflected well the highly creative and experimental time between the two world wars. They also brought to the fore the antagonism between the conservative and liberal factions that had arisen with the *staročechy* and the *mladočechy*. Ostrčil and Pujman had teamed up with set designer František Kysela (1881–1950) to create a more modern, stylized concept of *Prodaná nevěsta*. Up to now, the opera had seen a steady progession of realistic elements, building on portrayals, costumes, and scenery that had become part of an expected tradition. For the new concept, Kysela took twentieth-century fashion elements to create modern stylized *kroje*. Scenery was less literal and more stylized. Dances, partly choreographed by Pujman, were less about being authentic and more about integrating movement with the overall stylized conception (see chapter 3). Although by today's standards the new productions were far from radical, for the time they caused such a stir that heated arguments reached as far as the strata of parliamentary debate. As Czechs searched for their voice in European modernism, there was much talk now about "tradition." Historically, the timing for this debate was ripe.

The International Society for Contemporary Music (ISCM) had just been founded in Salzburg in 1922. In 1924, Prague was set to host an orchestral showcase as part of that year's ISCM festival, along with a cycle of Smetana's operas to celebrate his one-hundredth birthday. With a "modern" production of the "traditional" *Prodaná nevěsta* opening in May 1923, leading up to the international festival, few things could have sparked such an explosion of controversy. By late November, a senator spoke in Parliament denouncing the production and hoping that audiences would boycott it. In December, another senator diplomatically stated that such decisions about the direction of modern theater were best left to the Ministry of Education and National Culture, or to the artists themselves. This latter view meant victory for Ostrčil, and set up a tolerant attitude for the ISCM event. This was only the beginning of a debate, however, which has persisted in Prague to the present day—how best to balance the tradition represented by the Czechs' national opera with the new visions of succeeding generations of artists.

In 1925, *Prodaná nevěsta* was performed for the first time at the Neues Deutsches Theater (now the Státní divadlo) in Prague, in German under Alexander Zemlinsky (1871–1942), conductor and head of opera. From 1925 to 1938, *Prodaná nevěsta* (*Die verkaufte Braut*) was one of the most loved works in the repertory of the then German house, and was performed 105 times. Back at the Czech National Theatre, *Prodaná nevěsta* celebrated its 1,000th performance on May 30, 1927, with president Masaryk, other dignitaries, and celebrities from past performances of the opera in attendance.[8]

World War II

The great conductor Václav Talich (1883–1961) became the next head of opera from 1935 to 1945 and 1947 to 1948, and presided over three productions of *Prodaná nevěsta*, from 1936 to 1949. These productions—*despite* and *because of* adverse conditions—amounted to a record total of 492 performances. These were shared by a handful of other conductors who took over completely after World War II.[9] The stage director for the first two productions was Hanuš Thein (1904–74), who also sang the role of Kecal in 1937, and continued singing up until 1966. For his concept of the opera, Thein returned to traditional folk elements. At first, this was probably as a reaction to the previous productions. Very soon, however, with Hitler's occupation of Czechoslovakia on March 15, 1939, the folk elements served as a manifestation of national pride and defiance, so that folk elements were even strengthened in the third production.

The set designs for the first production in 1936 were by Josef Lada (1887–1957), the famous Czech painter and writer who had just written and illustrated the still-famous children's book *Kocour Mikeš* [The cat Mikeš]. He was already renowned as the illustrator of Jaroslav Hašek's novel *The Good Soldier Švejk* in the 1920s. Lada's setting contributed a fairytale atmosphere to the opera, and when Talich decided to have children sing in the opening chorus, the result was an expression of joy and innocence. A new invention, the revolving stage, added to the wonder of this production. It opened on October 24, 1936, with a special performance on October 27 to help celebrate the establishment of Czechoslovakia, with the former President Masaryk in attendance.

Lada's sets and costumes, however, proved too idealistic for the times, so that in 1938 Vincenc Beneš (1883–1979) replaced Lada for the second production, using a more realistic concept. On March 15, 1939, Czechoslovakia was occupied by Nazi Germany. Whereas the Germans banned performances of the historical *Braniboři v Čechách* and *Libuše*, they strangely allowed *Prodaná nevěsta* to be performed, labeling it as "art originating in German lands." While Talich performed the opera every chance he had as a way of asserting Czech national identity, the Germans tried to use the opera for their own purposes. Talich had performed the opera in December 1938 in honor of the new president Emil Hácha (1872–1945). The Germans ordered a performance in 1939 to celebrate their entry into Czechoslovakia (which Talich did not conduct), and another in 1940 for the visit of their propaganda minister Joseph Goebbels (1897–1945) (which Talich did conduct). When the Germans took over the Estates Theatre in 1939 to perform German works there once again, they had the theater in Karlín (in Prague) renovated as a replacement for the Czechs. The Czechs responded by naming it the "Prozatímní divadlo" [Provisional Theatre], and it opened with Talich conducting *Prodaná nevěsta*. By this time, Thein, who was of Jewish descent, had left. His name had had to be omitted from programs and posters, and Pujman was brought back to assist with the new venue.

The third production opened on September 25, 1943. The new stage director was Luděk Mandaus (1898–1971), and the new set designer was Karel Svolinský (1896–1986). They created a classic folk-inspired production, even using women's *kroje* purchased from private collections of authentic wear from the Plzeň region. Mandaus was to return in the 1960s to direct two new productions, and Svolinský would return for several productions, the last one in 1982, when he was eighty-six years old.

After *Prodaná nevěsta* was heard at the National Theatre on August 27, 1944, it was not performed for almost a year. Goebbels ordered all theaters in the country closed as of September 1 in order to concentrate on the war effort. On Februray 14, 1945, American forces bombed the city as part of the attack on Dresden. Holding on in vain, the Nazis ordered a performance of *Prodaná nevěsta* on Hitler's birthday, April 20, 1945, at the Provisional Theatre. Performances continued on April 22 and 28. General Patton's American troops had entered Czechoslovakia on April 22, and came very close to Prague, liberating Plzeň on May 6 as Czech citizens were in the middle of a standoff with German soldiers in Prague. Patton had been ordered to let the Russians liberate the capital. VE Day was heralded on May 8, and the Red Army poured into Prague on May 9. *Prodaná nevěsta* reopened on May 13 to celebrate liberation by the Red Army. With victory and newfound freedom, the opening chorus of *Prodaná nevěsta*, "Proč bychom se netěšili" [Why shouldn't we be happy] took on a deeper meaning. Talich, however, was denounced as a Nazi collaborator by the influential Zdeněk Nejedlý (1878–1962) and removed from his post. The authoritarian critic and musicologist Nejedlý had absorbed *staročech* policies into his socialist beliefs, and was soon to become the new Czech regime's Minister of Culture and Education from 1948 to 1953. Nejedlý and his family had fled to the Soviet Union during the Nazi occupation, following Nejedlý's policy of total noncollaboration with the Nazis in Czech cultural life. On June 27, 1945, Talich was cleared of any misdeeds and lauded for his promotion of Czech culture under the worst circumstances. However, he was to have several confrontations with the upcoming communist government.[10]

The Communist Era

By 1948, a socialist—soon to be communist—government took hold, and *Prodaná nevěsta* was upheld as the perfect "people's opera." Nejedlý frequently influenced scenery and casting at the National Theatre. The new eighteenth production, premiering on May 28, 1949, was dedicated to the Ninth Congress of the Communist Party of Czechoslovakia, and played until January 4, 1953, 193 performances. Jaroslav Krombholc (1918–83), a former student and assistant of Talich, conducted, while Jaroslav Vogel (1894–1970), a young Zdeněk Košler, and others led some of the performances.

With the next, nineteenth production, the concept of Socialist Realism was clearly realized. Opening on February 9, 1953, the 2,000th performance of the opera, President Klement Gottwald (1896–1953) was in attendance, and the performance celebrated the seventy-fifth birthday of Nejedlý. It ran until 1959, with 188 performances. Critics praised the typical Plzeň *kroje*. Krombholc led again, with Bohumil Gregor and others conducting some of the performances. Set design (but not costumes) was by Josef Svoboda (1920–2002), who was soon to bring a different type of artistic vision to the world.

While the nineteenth production was still playing, a new twentieth production opened in 1955, and the two productions overlapped for about four years. Under the tutelage of the new head of opera, Jiří Pauer (b. 1919), the new production was created especially for a tour to Moscow in 1955. It ran at the National Theatre until 1963, with 159 performances. The great conductor Zdeněk Chalabala (1899–1962) led, and Svoboda again served as the set designer. On April 17, 1955, a performance was broadcast on television—the first live performance from the National Theatre. It must have come as a blow to Nejedlý that Moscow criticized the production, steeped in Socialist Realism, as being too old-fashioned and conservative.

With Moscow's pronouncement, the twentieth production was not canceled, but a new production soon arose with the intent of being presented at Expo 58, the Brussels World's Fair. The premiere was on July 17, 1958, and was conducted by Zdeněk Košler (1928–95), playing 117 times. For about a year, Prague audiences had quite an opportunity for being entertained or confused, as there were now three productions of *Prodaná nevěsta* playing from 1958 to 1959! Svoboda again was the set designer. In 1950, he had become the chief designer and technical director at the National Theatre, overseeing fifteen new productions each season. Svoboda, whose name means "freedom," was allowed to use a stylized approach for the latest production that would have an international showing. His work, which included Laterna Magika, won three gold medals at the World's Fair. In Prague, however, it was felt that he had gone too far, and his latest concept of *Prodaná nevěsta* was adjusted after the tour to add more realism. Looking back twenty years later at the performance that was booed in Prague, Svoboda said:

> "People have their own conceptions, naturally, but so do I. The traditional approach would be a betrayal of the work, of the audience, of my own intentions, since I don't believe in it. . . . I don't believe in realism or non-realism. I don't accept this distinction. Look, the theater is not everyday reality to begin with. It has its own reality, which on the stage becomes a question of artistic conception. That's the reality I'm working with."[11]

It is no wonder that for the next, twenty-second production, there was a return to tradition, although it was gently stylized. Opening in 1963, this production ran a relatively meager four years, playing 150 times into 1967. Krombholc was back to conduct, as well as Luděk Mandaus and Karel Svolinský from the Talich days.

Anticipating a European tour within the relaxed political climate of Slovak politician Alexander Dubček (1921–92), the twenty-third production soon arose. It was basically a variation of the previous production, however, and again ran for only four years, from 1967 to 1971, 126 performances. Josef Kuchinka

(b. 1925) was the main conductor, with Mandaus returning (and even Hanuš Thein back with a "revision" of the staging!), and Svolinský using the same scenery as before. Despite the harsh period of Normalization after the Soviets invaded Czechoslovakia on August 20, 1968, the theater was able to carry on with its planned agenda, largely due to the new leadership in 1969 of director Přemysl Kočí (1917–2003). However, the tours throughout most of western Europe and Poland in 1967, 1969, and 1970 brought many bad reviews for the staging, acting, and sets. Some critics wrote that it looked like the Czechs were trying to re-create the original 1866 production.[12]

For the twenty-fourth production, the Czechs seemed to hit on the right balance of traditional and stylized elements. The successful production ran for eleven years, from 1971 to 1982, playing 239 times. Krombholc returned to lead the production, which Přemysl Kočí himself staged. The costume designer, Jarmila Kalašová (b. 1927) had studied southern Czech and other *kroje* to give a folk feeling to the nonexact, stylized costumes. One major development was to erase acting stereotypes while infusing young blood into the opera. The stellar cast included the young Slovak soprano Gabriela Beňačková (b. 1947) singing Mařenka at twenty-four years old; a young Jana Jonášová (b. 1943), (who joined the production soon after its premiere) performing Esmeralda at twenty-two years old; and the experienced Jaroslav Horáček (b. 1926), who at forty-five years old was perfect as Mícha.

The twenty-fifth production had another long run. Playing 197 times for ten years, from 1982 to 1992, Zdeněk Košler, now head of opera, was back as conductor, with quite a few other conductors leading subsequent performances, including Oliver Dohnányi. Ladislav Štros (b. 1926) was the stage director, and Svolinský returned for the last time as set designer and costumer. A wonderful Kecal, Bohuslav Maršík (b. 1937), performed at the premiere, and the production toured to Moscow, Japan, and Vienna in 1985 and 1986. Košler's slow tempi seemed to help give depth to the opera, but were dangerous when added with the simple conventional staging, sets, and still often lackluster acting. Critics were unimpressed.[13]

A Democracy Once More

With Czechoslovakia back to a democratic nation in 1989, stage director Jiří Nekvasil (b. 1962) and set designer Daniel Dvořák (b. 1954) submitted a plan for a modern production of *Prodaná nevěsta*. Its colorful Chagall-like sets and other elements would help to reenergize the opera and reflect the vibrant new era. Their ideas were too radical for the administration, however, and they had to wait until 2004 before their chance came. Instead, conductor Bohumil Gregor (1926–2005) and choreographer/stage director Pavel Šmok (b. 1927) teamed up with set designer Jan Dušek (b. 1942) to create a lively, artistically successful new production that ran for seven years, from 1992 to 1999, playing 155 times. Although Šmok had certainly shown himself to be a great choreographer (for example, with the Met's *Prodaná nevěsta* in 1978), he had never staged an opera before. The singers' movements proved to be natural and logical, the chorus well integrated with the drama, and, of course, the dances spectacular. Dušek's simple wooden sets—even wooden clouds—revealed themselves to be very effective. Soprano Dana Burešová (b. 1967), chosen by Gregor to sing Mařenka, soon joined the cast, as did bass Miloslav Podskalský (b. 1944) as Mícha. Bohuslav Maršík portrayed Kecal many times. Even after seven years, this production remained very fresh.

Czechoslovakia peacefully split into Slovakia and the Czech Republic in 1993. Stage director Josef Průdek (b. 1944) became head of opera from 1996 to 2002, and scored a huge success with a world-class production of *Jenůfa* at the National Theatre in 1997. It toured to Japan in 1999, and played at the National Theatre until 2004. For the twenty-seventh production of *Prodaná nevěsta*, he teamed with conductor Bohumil Kulínský (b. 1959) and costume designer Jan Skalický (b. 1929), who had designed the costumes for the Met's 1978 production. Initially triple-cast, singers included Slovak tenor Miroslav Dvorský (b. 1960) and the Belorussian tenor Valentin Prolat (b. 1958) as Jeník; as well as baritone Ivan Kusnjer (b. 1951) as Krušina. Despite the talent and the ambitions of the directors, the production only played eighty-two times, from 1999 to 2004. Průdek moved the opera's setting to the early 1900s, so that, for example, the Indián phoned his first line to the Principál. Prague critics found the circus scene to lack humor because it was too professional. Costumes were too modern, provocative, and insensitive. The dances were uninteresting. When the opera toured to Salzburg in 2002, it again met with foreign disapproval, but for opposite reasons—costumes were too old-fashioned, and the dances were lively, helping to revive the languor of the staging!

Becoming head of opera in 2002, Jiří Nekvasil was now poised to carry through his thwarted plans with Daniel Dvořák from 1989 for a fun, playful, new staging of *Prodaná nevěsta*. The Slovak conductor Oliver Dohnányi (b. 1955) conducted this twenty-eighth production. It suffered a worse fate than the previous one, playing only forty-nine times, from 2004 to 2007.

The twenty-ninth production brought several new milestones. The year 2008 marked the 125th anniversary of the National Theatre. Despite this, for the first time in its history, the National Theatre's *Prodaná nevěsta* had its premiere outside of Prague. The new production opened on June 20, 2008, in Litomyšl, Smetana's birthplace, as part of their annual international festival, before moving to Prague in September. With this production, Magdalena Švecová (b. 1977) became the first female stage director of *Prodaná nevěsta* for the Prague National Theatre. Slovak conductor Ondrej Lenárd (b. 1942) led musically. The Czech Republic's Divadlo Continuo, with their circus acrobatics and life-size puppetry, provided entertainment in Act III. Playfulness mixed with bitter-sweetness were the keys to this production. Critic Peter Freestone was very positive:

> "The ensemble worked together to provide a true slice of Czech life in a way that no amount of international stars flying in for performances could ever give."[14]

In English-Speaking Lands

United States

After the landmark performance by the Prague National Theatre at the international exhibition in Vienna in 1892, *Prodaná nevěsta* quickly made its way to opera houses throughout Germany and Austria. By 1894, the *Washington Post*, via the *New York Sun*, featured an article titled "*Die verkaufte Braut*: Smetana's posthumous opera creating furore in Germany and Austria," and proclaimed that only *Cavalleria rusticana* and *I pagliacci* were more popular the past two years. The article further mentioned a promise of having the opera that winter in New York. That promise was not to materialize until 1909. In the meantime, *Prodaná nevěsta* had already had its American premiere on August 20, 1893, in Czech.[15]

Premiere

On May 1, 1893, the World's Fair ("Columbian Exposition") opened in Chicago. Illuminated by electric lights, it was the largest fair the world had ever seen, and was represented by almost fifty nations. František Ludvík (1842–1910), head of a Czech theater society, had traveled from Europe with his group to tour America and perform at the fair. Czech-Americans in Chicago seized on the opportunity and asked Ludvík for help with mounting *Prodaná nevěsta*. They offered him the assistance of their Sokol group for the dances, and their Lada and Lyra singing societies for the chorus. For the orchestra, members of conductor Theodore Thomas's group were recruited. Thomas (1835–1905) conducted his last performance at the fair on August 11, and none other than Antonín Dvořák took over the Exposition orchestra the next day for a "Bohemian Day" concert that included the overture to *Prodaná nevěsta*. Selected players were then free to perform the opera the following week.

Ludvík provided the Czech singers from his theater society. Among them were Rudolf Innemann (1861–1907) as the Principál, a role he had just performed in the famed 1892 Prague/Vienna production; and his wife, the opera singer Ludmila Innemannová, daughter of the famous Czech baritone Josef Lev (1832–98).[16] For stage director, Ludvík was able to enlist Josef Šmaha (1848–1915), the director of the 1892 Prague/Vienna production, who quickly traveled from Prague to Chicago to take part. The conductor was the acclaimed Czech-born violinist Josef Horymír Čapek (1860–1932), who would soon become first violinist of the newly formed Chicago Symphony Orchestra under Thomas. Čapek had already presented concerts in 1883 and 1885 in Milwaukee that featured orchestral, choral, and sung selections from *Prodaná nevěsta*. Audiences were so enthusiastic that each selection had to be repeated.

Prodaná nevěsta premiered on August 20, 1893, at the Haymarket Theater on Madison Street in Chicago, and was performed three times. Despite the possibilities, the orchestra was small and under-rehearsed, and the cast was overall not very strong. Still, audiences and critics were very enthusiastic, and awaited "a proper presentation."[17]

New York Metropolitan Opera

The "proper presentation" came on February 19, 1909, at the New York Metropolitan Opera (Met). The premiere was touted in the *New York Times* as "given for the first time in America." Scenery and costumes were made in Vienna. The opera was performed in German, and it was conducted by Gustav Mahler (1860–1911), who continued with six more performances that season. Mahler had seen performances of *Prodaná nevěsta* in Prague, and had already conducted the work in Hamburg and Vienna. He knew well the Max Kalbeck German translation, and it was the language of default for most of the cast. Mahler was in fact a German-speaking Czech, born in Kaliště and raised in Jihlava. The star was the legendary Czech soprano Ema Destinnová (Emmy Destinn) (1878–1930) as Mařenka. Destinnová had first sung in *Prodaná nevěsta* at the Prague National Theatre in 1903. She would sing Mařenka there a total of thirteen times as well as on many stages around the world. Soon, she would star in the world premiere of Puccini's *La fanciulla del West* at the Met.

Alma Mahler wrote that the production was marvelous, but "did not catch on and was dropped." Still, New York critics praised the production, which also toured to Chicago, Philadelphia, and Cincinnati, and was performed every year for four years, a total of twenty-five times.

One unusual feature of the performances was that the overture was not played at the beginning, but between the first and second acts. This was not done to accommodate latecomers, but rather to keep latecomers from disturbing the overture! "Tradition" dies hard in opera—the overture was still played as an entr'acte for the second production at the Met that premiered in 1926, conducted by Artur Bodanzky (1877–1939), and the second production was also in German. A highlight of performances was the singing of the German bass-baritone Michael Bohnen (1887–1965). A consummate actor with a beautiful voice, his portrayal of Kecal was one of the best. On March 5, 1928, Bohnen suffered a severe attack from gallstones just before a performance, so Czech Met singer Pavel Ludikar (1882–1970) stepped in at the last moment. Ludikar managed to sing in German throughout except for Kecal's aria "Každý jen tu svou, má za jedinou," which he sang in Czech, bringing immense applause.[18]

A successful, but short-lived 1933 production followed, with only three performances. The overture finally was performed as an overture. The language was still German, with the legendary German soprano Elizabeth Rethberg (1894–1976) as Mařenka.[19]

A fourth production at the Met arose in 1936, playing for two years, twelve performances, and sung to an English translation (see appendix A). Muriel Dickson, from D'Oyly Carte, sang impeccably clear English, and the opera set records at the Met for being performed more times than any other opera that season, and to near-capacity or capacity audiences. George Rasely (1889–1965) was singled out for both his singing and his funny but sincere and charming portrayal of Vašek. For all the excellent diction, and for all the laughs, though, the English translation strayed considerably from the original, and the performance by other cast members deteriorated into farce, putting "a final damper on the gentle charm of Smetana's music."[20]

Anticipating the arrival of the great Czech soprano Jarmila Novotná (1907–94) in 1939, the Met planned a new production of *Prodaná nevěsta* for her Met debut. The Met was slated to return to a German-language production of *Prodaná nevěsta*, for although she spoke English very well, Novotná only knew the role of Mařenka in German and Czech, and there was not enough time for her to learn it in English. However, with the occupation of Czechoslovakia by the Nazis on March 15, Czech-Americans and Czech sympathizers protested the mounting of the national Czech opera in German. Unable to perform the work in Czech, the Met considered having Novotná sing in Czech while everyone else sang in English. Instead, it was decided to postpone the work for a year, and have Novotná debut as Mimì in *La Bohème*. Finally, the fifth production of *Prodaná nevěsta* premiered in 1941, with Bruno Walter conducting. It lasted only two seasons, with seven performances. Appearing as Kecal in the first two performances was the great Italian bass Ezio Pinza (1892–1957). Novotná's English was very good, but Pinza's was mostly unintelligible. Moreover, Pinza was miscast, playing Kecal as a complete caricature. Walter conducted with refined beauty and warmth, but missed the earthiness of the opera. Similarly, Novotná sang with artistry, but overall came off as too aristocratic and elegant.[21]

The next Met production did not come until October 25, 1978. It played a year and a half, with seventeen performances, including tours. It was revived in 1996, with eight performances. This production achieved a true match to the 1909 classic under Mahler. James Levine conducted, overseeing a star-studded cast that originally included Canadian Teresa Stratas (b. 1938) as Mařenka, Swede Nicolai Gedda (b. 1925) as Jeník, Canadian Jon Vickers (b. 1926) as Vašek, and Finn Martti Talvela (1935–89) as Kecal. Englishman John Dexter (1925–90) was the stage director, while Czechs Josef Svoboda designed the sets, Jan Skalický designed the costumes, and Pavel Šmok (see "Debuts" and chapter 3) choreographed. A new English translation was written by the English poet and playwright Tony Harrison (b. 1937) (see appendix A).

Levine's goal was to present the opera as a real folk opera, avoiding "superficial operetta treatment:"

> "Smetana's characters and their problems are universal. These are not stereotyped, fun-loving peasants—the action takes place on a springtime feast day, but most of the year is spent working the land in a struggle to survive. We tried to show this reality and the natural humor."[22]

Much was made of the "sometimes radically unadorned production," referring to Svoboda's spare sets consisting of a couple of facades, a few chairs, and a blue cyclorama. They were in stark contrast to the colorful costumes of Skalický. However, Patricia Craig, who made her Met debut covering Stratas, explained that Svoboda's original plan was to project slides and films onto the cyclorama. The Met ran out of money, so the slides and films were omitted.[23]

Director Dexter and the cast worked hard to focus on the relationships among the characters, and the results were remarkable. When the high-powered Stratas sang the premiere, no one would have known that she had a black eye, hidden by makeup, brought on by fighting off a would-be mugger or rapist outside her apartment building. Her energy was just as formidable on stage as her five-foot frame stood up to the six-foot-eight Kecal, played by Talvela.[24]

New York City Opera and Other Venues

The Met was not the first to perform *Prodaná nevěsta* in English in New York. That distinction came with the semiprofessional New York Opera Comique/Little Theatre Opera Company in 1931, playing at the Heckscher Theatre. Known for Risë Stevens' solo debut, as Ludmila (see "Debuts"), the production was often sold out and had to be extended.[25]

During the thirty-six years that the Met had no performances of *Prodaná nevěsta*, the New York City Opera helped fill the gap with two productions. Founded in 1943, New York City Opera mounted an English-language *Prodaná nevěsta* in 1945–46, eight performances, using the Cross/Crozier translation (see appendix A). Another followed in 1955. In both, spoken dialogue was opted for instead of recitatives. In both, singers, dancers, and conductors were praised, but performances were denounced for bad acting that brought the Czech folk opera into the realm of American slapstick and burlesque.[26]

Another gap was admirably filled by Bronx Opera in 1993, using the Met's Harrison English translation. The production by the small company, founded in 1967, was well received, although some singers were cited for falling into the trap of "comic mugging." Linda Mohler proved to be an excellent Mařenka, and would go on to reprise the role in Czech with Sarasota Opera in 1994. Bronx Opera repeated *Prodaná nevěsta* in 2003, premiering a new English translation by Mark Herman and Ronnie Apter (see appendix A).[27]

Chicago

After the American premiere in 1893, Chicago had to wait until the Met's visit in 1909 to hear *Prodaná nevěsta* again. Two operas were performed on one day—while the press allotted barely three sentences to *La Bohème*, starring Geraldine Farrar, the response to Smetana's opera, with Ema Destinnová as Mařenka, stretched to almost two glowing pages.[28]

To the dismay of many, Chicagoans were forced to wait until 1930 for more performances, but they were rewarded that year with two different homegrown productions. Just outside Chicago in Highland Park, the Ravinia Festival is a world-class summer festival that from 1912 to 1931 boasted the Ravinia Opera. When Ravinia mounted three performances of *Prodaná nevěsta* in 1930, it was the capital of American summer opera, and Smetana's comic opera was the hit of their season. As in 1909, the opera was performed in German, and sung by a great cast headed by Elizabeth Rethberg. Ruth Page was an equal colleague in the dances. The other production that year was at Chicago Civic Opera, where the opera was also performed in German three times. With a completely different cast, conductor, and others, the production was highly successful. Shortly after, with the Great Depression, the Civic Opera closed its doors in 1931.[29]

With no opera company in Chicago, the new "American Operetta corporation" was formed in 1933, debuting at the Garrick Theater with *Prodaná nevěsta*. Although the new company was very short-lived, the production was excellent, and was highlighted by a new English translation, a first for Chicago. Libushka Bartusek, who had danced in the Civic Opera's German performances (see chapter 3), wrote the translation (see appendix A) and choreographed the dances.[30]

Also in 1933, two performances in Czech were presented at the Auditorium Theatre opera house under the auspices of Chicago Czech-American societies, again as a way of making up for the dearth of opera in the city. Notable leads were hired from Prague, including tenors Richard Kubla (1890–1964) and Mirko Štork (1880–1953), as well as the Czech Met/National Theatre singer Pavel Ludikar as Kecal. Frank Kubina led the Chicago Symphony Orchestra in this excellent, fully staged production.[31]

The new Chicago City Opera Company produced exceptional performances of *Prodaná nevěsta* in 1936 (using some of the Met's cast) and again in 1939 before closing its doors for good. It was a long time before the city could witness the opera again. The Chicago Park Opera guild produced an English concert version of the opera at Grant Park in 1948. Chicago's Hull-House Opera Workshop put on a performance in Chicago in 1950. Finally, Chicago Opera Theater gave a wonderful production of the opera in 1984, using the Cross/Crozier English translation. Audiences could catch the opera again in 1987—in Lithuanian—at the Lithuanian Opera Company of Chicago. Although the Lyric Opera of Chicago had been founded in 1954, and audiences had requested the opera for years, the Lyric did not perform it until 1992–93. Using an American cast, the disappointing production was cited for a bad English translation. However, "the real fault was that the distinctive Czech spirit of the work was lost."[32]

California

Conductor Alfred Hertz (1872–1942) took over Mahler's performances of *Prodaná nevěsta* at the Met from 1909 to 1912 before leaving for San Francisco. There, in 1934, he led the San Francisco Opera's first performance of the opera, in German. Several of the cast were from the Met's 1933 production, including Elizabeth Rethberg as Mařenka. SFO repeated the opera in 1942, this time with Bartusek's English translation. Their sparkling new 1958 production, in the Met's English translation, starred Elizabeth Schwarzkopf (1915–2006) as Mařenka and Giorgio Tozzi (b. 1923) as Kecal. SFO's 1964 production, again in English, starred Mary Costa (see "Debuts") as Mařenka and the great Welsh baritone Geraint Evans (1922–92) as Kecal.[33]

For years, San Francisco Opera traveled to Los Angeles to share its performances there, including *Prodaná nevěsta*. Los Angeles produced its own performances, too, at the outdoor Hollywood Bowl, beginning in 1936, with the English Met translation. This was the Southern California Symphony Association's first foray into opera. With audiences of around 20,000, the performances had to be miked, but were very successful artistically and financially, and were repeated in subsequent years.[34]

In 1948, Carl Ebert (1887–1980), famed German opera director and co-founder of the Glyndebourne Opera, moved to Los Angeles to create and head an opera department at the University of Southern California (USC). In 1950, he became the head of what was soon to become the Los Angeles Guild Opera. Insisting on productions sung in English, he was able to showcase local talent, some coming from his department at USC. This included a production of *Prodaná nevěsta* staged by Ebert that year, with a new English translation by Henry Reese. In 1951, *Prodaná nevěsta* immediately took on a different role. Guild Opera's new mission was to produce opera for thousands of schoolchildren aged nine to eleven years old at the huge Shrine Auditorium. Students were prepared ahead of time by their teachers. Since no child was allowed to attend for more than three years, a repeating cycle of three operas was created—*La cenerentola* [Cinderella], *Hansel and Gretel*, and *The Bartered Bride*. The young Marilyn Horne, Marni Nixon, Mary Costa (see "Debuts"), and others got important stage experience, while tens of thousands of children enjoyed opera for the first time, in English. Ebert's son Peter (b. 1918) took over his father's productions, adding *The Magic Flute* to the cycle, so that *The Bartered Bride* continued in its new role through 1966.[35]

Other Cities

Only a handful of other productions can be cited here. *Prodaná nevěsta* quickly premiered across the country: Minneapolis (1910), Cincinnati (1911), Cleveland (1930), St. Paul (1936), Philadelphia (1940?), Syracuse (1947), Baltimore (1950), Montgomery (1955), etc.[36] Central City performed the work in 1940 and 1977. Sarasota Opera performed the opera in Czech in 1994 with a fine cast of American singers. Baltimore Opera offered a rousing Czech production in 2007 led by the Slovak conductor Oliver Dohnányi, and featuring Czech soprano Dana Burešová (see "Debuts"), Belorussian tenor Valentin Prolat, and a remaining strong cast of Americans.

Boston has an interesting history with *Prodaná nevěsta*. Chicago Civic Opera toured to Boston with the work in 1931, as did the Met in 1979. The Opera Company of Boston produced it in 1973, in English. Founder Sarah Caldwell (1924–2006) both conducted and directed the production, which included Mary Costa (see "Debuts") as Mařenka; the legendary clown Emmett

Kelly, Sr. (1898–1979) of the Ringling Brothers and Barnum and Bailey Circus; Alan Crofoot as the Principál (see "Debuts"); and even performing dogs. Czechs from the Prague National Theatre were bass Jaroslav Horáček (b. 1926) as Kecal (see "Debuts"), costume designer Jan Skalický (b. 1929), choreographer Vlastimil Jílek (1925–96) (see chapter 3), and tenor Miroslav Švejda (b. 1939), who played Jeník. Caldwell inserted a long pantomime after the overture depicting Czechoslovakia's oppressive history, and storm troopers attacked the village during the furiant. The next production came with Opera Boston in 2009, both directed and choreographed by Daniel Pelzig (b. 1955) (see chapter 3). After deciding to perform the opera in English (with the Met's Harrison translation), Pelzig set it in the Czech-American community of Spillville, Iowa, in 1934. In this setting, he had chorus members occasionally sing verses in Czech as a way of celebrating their heritage.[37]

Schools and Community Theater

As in the UK and other English-speaking countries, the United States has created countless productions of Smetana's beloved opera in nonprofessional venues. It is impossible to list the numerous countrywide performances, mostly in English, that have graced community theaters and music departments. A few examples that demonstrate the wide range of possibilities are: New York City's School of Music and Art—a high school—in 1949, with orchestra and seventy-five chorus members; Juilliard American Opera Center, conducted by the Czech-born American Peter Herman Adler (1899–1990), with costumes by Jan Skalický, 1973; University of Puget Sound, Washington, two performances with piano accompaniment, 1982; and everything in between!

Oberlin College, Ohio, opened the Oberlin Opera Theater for the first time in 1952 with *Prodaná nevěsta*, and performed the opera again in 2002 to celebrate its fiftieth birthday.

The University of Michigan produced the opera in 1937, 1946, 1968, and 2007. In the 1968 cast was a young master's student, soprano Jessye Norman (b. 1945) as Ludmila. She would win the Munich International Music Competition that year, and debut with the Berlin Deutsche Oper in 1969. The 2007 production, consisting of four double-cast performances, was performed in Czech with English supertitles. This was certainly not done as an academic exercise, but because the students were able to absorb the flavors and inflection of the language and sing communicatively, expressively, and very naturally. Stage director Joshua Major focused on illuminating the relationships among the characters in the most believable, honest manner. The true spirit of the folk opera was able to shine through in these very special performances. Diction instruction and all-around instruction for singers has come a long way![38]

THE BARTERED BRIDE

A COMIC OPERA
in three acts

Librette by KAREL SABINA
English translation by JOSEF BLATT

Music by
BEDRICH SMETANA

CHARACTERS
(in order of appearance)

JENIK, a young farm hand .... Jerry Langenkamp
MARENKA, his sweetheart .... Lynda Weston (Thurs., Sat.)
                                              Nancy Seabold (Fri.)
                                              Lynn Utzinger (Sun.)
KECAL, marriage broker .... Robert Schneider
KRUSHINA, Marenka's father .... Franklin Dybdahl
LUDMILLA, her mother .... Jessye Norman
VASHEK, a rich farmer's son .... Jim Bryan
MANAGER of a strolling circus .... Howard Travis
ESMERELDA, a dancer .... Nancy Hall (Th., Fri., Sat.)
                                              Catherine Grimshaw (Sun.)
AN INDIAN .... Daniel Berry
HATA, Vashek's mother .... Susan Harris
MICHA, his father .... John Hein
TWO BOYS .... David Krimm, Tad Langenkamp
CIRCUS MUSICIANS .... Joel Behrens, Donald Grosz,
                                              John Suba, David Reed

VILLAGERS, WAITRESSES: Diane Borgus, Andonea Chronopulos, Linda Deater,
Francine Deschambault, Nancy Goeboro, Rosemarie Gore, Karel Ann Kooistra,
Mary Kovar, Janice Lent, Laureen McPherson, Terry Niles, Andrea Odle, Sandra
Pfister, Margaret Priest, Nancy Shafer, Diane Turner, Karen Upton, Susan Wepfer,
Robert Armstrong, Daniel Berry, Alexander Chmil, John Englert, Charles Gara-
brant, Randy Lambert, Cyrus Lutz, Don Renz, James Robbins, J. Mark Rottschafer,
Mark Thomas, Robert Weibel, Robert Zajac.

DANCERS: Polka: Robert Borgen, Elleva Davidson, Jeanne Dettor, Diane Elliot,
Edward Faust, Lee Overholser, Jack Perry, Janet Pollack, Philip Stamps.
FURIANT: Elleva Davidson, Edward Faust, Jack Perry, Philip Stamps, Ellen
Winkler.

CIRCUS SCENE: Acrobats: Charles Fuller, Stanley Goldblatt; Arabian Girls:
Jeanne Detter, Janet Pollack; Cossack: Philip Stamps; Ponies: Elleva Davidson.
Diane Elliot, Ellen Winkler; Strong Man: Lee Overholser.

The scene is a Bohemian village in the first half of the nineteenth century.

MUSIC DIRECTOR AND CONDUCTOR .... Josef Blatt
STAGE DIRECTOR .... Ralph Herbert
DESIGNER AND TECHNICAL DIRECTOR .... John Sheldon Murphy
CHOREOGRAPHER .... Elizabeth Weyl-Bergmann
ASSISTANT TO MR. BLATT .... *John Landis
STAGE MANAGER .... Priscilla Travis
MAKE-UP .... Sophie Farah, Amy Wuolo, Dorothy Barnes
PROPERTIES .... Marsha Blum
OPERA PROGRAM AND POSTER DESIGN .... Sandra Crossette
OPERA FLYER DESIGN .... Carol Hack
COSTUMES .... The Chicago Lyric Opera Company

* Mr. Landis will conduct Sunday's performance

University of Michigan program from March 21–24, 1968, showing Jessye
Norman as Ludmila.[39]

Canada

Edmonton, Alberta, first staged *Prodaná nevěsta* in 1930. Another production, sung in Czech, came in 2007 as part of the Canadian summer program Opera Nuova. The young double-cast Canadian performers sang and acted both beautifully and naturally in this delightful production staged by Opera Nuova founder Kim Wannat.[40]

In Toronto, the Royal Conservatory Opera School's first full production was *Prodaná nevěsta* in 1947. This was led by the school's music director Nicholas "Niki" Goldschmidt (1908–2004), born and raised in Moravia. Goldschmidt went on to teach singers such as Teresa Stratas and Jon Vickers, and co-founded the Royal Conservatory Opera Company. Together with the Opera Festival Association, they mounted *Prodaná nevěsta* in 1952, conducted by Goldschmidt. The company later became the Canadian Opera Company, which mounted Czech productions of the opera in 1992–93, 1999–2000 (with Slovak tenor Miroslav Dvorský [b. 1960] and Czech soprano Eva Urbanová in the leads, and choreography by Bengt Jörgen), and in 2007–08.

The Vancouver Academy of Music performed *Prodaná nevěsta* in English in 2004, while the University of British Columbia Opera School performed the opera in Czech in 2003. The UBC Opera School had maintained a relationship with noted Czech conductor Norbert Baxa and stage director Josef Novák that included a summer opera program in the Czech Republic.[41]

United Kingdom

Prodaná nevěsta began its life in the United Kingdom sung in German. The first performance was in 1895 in London, by the Ducal Court Company of Saxe-Coburg and Gotha, with a nondescript cast. The Carl Rosa Company followed in 1905 with a performance in English and tours throughout England, Scotland, and Ireland into 1906. (Performances by the company also spread throughout the world in British colonies before and after World War I.) Next came another German production at Covent Garden in 1907. The Esmeralda was Minnie Nast (1874–1956), who in 1911 would create the role of Sophie in *Der Rosenkavalier* in Dresden. The public took their opera so seriously that they were afraid to laugh, and critics proclaimed the opera not great enough for Covent Garden.

An English production followed at the Oxford University Opera Club in 1929, borrowing *kroje* from Prague and even keeping the original Czech names of the characters. Another English performance opened the season at Covent Garden in 1931, conducted by Sir John Barbirolli (1899–1970). *Prodaná nevěsta* first became part of Sadler's Wells repertoire in their 1935–36 season, and quickly spread from London to tours throughout the country, using spoken dialogue instead of recitative. A new production at Covent Garden came in 1939. Opening the season on May 1, it had disastrous results. Hitler had just marched into Czechoslovakia on March 15. A trip to London by the Prague National Theatre with Václav Talich performing Dvořák's *Rusalka* had been canceled because of the Nazi takeover. Sir Thomas Beecham (1879–1961) led an international cast that deliberately included "Nazi, Jew, Teuton, Briton and Slav," but that ended up heightening tensions more than promoting unity. The Met had postponed its own production to avoid performing the Czech opera in German, but Covent Garden's three performances were in German, the language the whole cast could most easily sing. Several of the cast, who can be heard on a recording, were refugees. These included the great Austrian tenor Richard Tauber (1891–1948), who sang Jeník, and Marko Rothmüller (1908–93), a Croatian baritone who was debuting at Covent Garden as Krušina. Rothmüller suddenly became ill a few hours before the last performance, and was replaced by two different baritones in Act I and Act III who quickly learned the part in German backstage. Besides the ill-chosen language, the performances suffered from the singers portraying empty caricatures.[42]

Sadler's Wells presented a wonderful production of the opera in 1943, under the direction of Eric Crozier (see "Debuts") and Joan Cross. Because this production, along with others in 1945 and 1947, depended on the artistry of Czech choreographer Saša Machov, it is discussed in chapter 3.

The Covent Garden Opera Company presented a new production, sung in English in 1955, using the Cross/Crozier translation, and performed fourteen times. This marked the company debut of Czech conductor Rafael Kubelík (1914–96). The Australian soprano Elsie Morison (b. 1924) sang Mařenka, and became Kubelík's wife in 1963. English tenor Peter Pears (1910–86) was a delightful Vašek. The American baritone Jess Walters (1908–2001), who sang more than 650 times at Covent Garden, was Krušina. The Czech/British baritone Otakar Kraus (1909–80) (the first Nick Shadow in *The Rake's Progress*) sang Mícha.[43]

The Royal Opera, performing at Sadler's Wells Theatre, produced a Czech version of *Prodaná nevěsta* in 1998, conducted by Bernard Haitink (b. 1929), and directed by the American stage director Francesca Zambello (b. 1956). English tenor Ian Bostridge (b. 1964) sang the role of Vašek. Zambello returned to stage the work at Covent Garden in 2001 with conductor Sir Charles Mackerras (b. 1925), this time with an English translation by Kit Hesketh-Harvey, who played the Indián. The wonderful production was revived in 2006 with almost the same cast, and Mackerras recorded the English version shortly beforehand in 2005 (see appendix B).[44]

As much as director Carl Ebert loved *Prodaná nevěsta*, he did not produce it during his tenure at the Glyndebourne Festival. That came in 1999 with a Czech production, revived in 2005, directed by Nikolaus Lehnhoff.[45]

As with the United States, it is beyond the scope of this book to even list the countless other productions in England, Wales, Scotland, Ireland, and in nonprofessional venues across the United Kingdom.

Australia, South Africa

After World War I, music schools led the way for Smetana's opera in Australia, with the Sydney Conservatory mounting *Prodaná nevěsta* in 1936, and the Melbourne Conservatory following in 1947. The opera also quickly made its way with tours across the country through the Elizabethan Trust Opera Company, 1957–70. The Australian Opera, 1971–95, mounted a significant Czech production in 1981 utilizing important figures from Prague's National Theatre. František Vajnar (b. 1930), head of opera at the National Theatre from 1985 to 1987, conducted the first performances; Šárka Hejnová (b. 1949) designed the costumes; and Přemysl Kočí (1917–2003), head of the National Theatre from 1969 to 1979, and stage director of their 1971 production of *Prodaná nevěsta*, served as stage director. The opera was performed in Sydney, Melbourne, and Brisbane in 1981 and 1982.[46]

In South Africa, *Prodaná nevěsta* debuted in Johannesburg in 1937 as part of celebrations of the coronation of British King George VI (1895–1952). In 1948, the opera was performed in Cape Town at the South African College of Music. When the Cape Performing Arts Board Opera was established in 1965, *Prodaná nevěsta* was the first opera to be mounted. Bass-baritone Angelo Gobbato (b. 1943) (see "Debuts") debuted as Kecal, and Gobbato staged the work for Cape Town Opera in 2003.[47]

Elsewhere

In its early history, *Prodaná nevěsta* had a few isolated performances in Europe that were sung in Czech outside the Czech lands. Since then, Czech-language performances have become much more common in the larger companies, even in Germany, where the opera is so well-known in German. In Europe, besides the United Kingdom, one example is a production at the Opéra national de Paris in 2008–09. Conductor Jiří Bělohlávek (b. 1946) and Aleš Briscein were the only Czechs among the international cast. The performance was also recorded and released on CD (see appendix B).[48]

Debuts

A number of distinguished singers, conductors, librettists, dancers, and choreographers either had their professional debuts with *Prodaná nevěsta*, or debuted in an important opera house with this opera. Below is a sampling of some of these artists, while others are discussed elsewhere. When appropriate, each section below begins with Czech singers and ends with native English-speakers.

Singers

Sopranos

Ella Tvrdková (1878–1918) had a formidable career, mostly at the Munich Hofoper under the name Ella Tordek, even making several important historical recordings. At twenty years old, she debuted professionally as Mařenka in 1898 as a special guest at the Prague National Theatre, joining their tenth production conducted by Adolf Čech. Tvrdková later appeared in the premiere of Dvořák's *Rusalka* at the National Theatre as a Lesní žínka. Under the name Tordek, she sang the lead in the premiere in 1909 of Wolf-Ferrari's *Il segreto di Susanna*, which was performed at first in German at the Munich Hofoper.[49]

The remarkable Bulgarian singer Christina/Kristina Morfová (1889–1936) began her career as Mařenka in 1909 at the State Opera in Brno. Known as the "Bulgarian nightingale," she had a distinguished career singing in major theaters in the Czech and Slovak lands, as well as in Bulgaria, singing everything from Queen of the Night to Lakmé to Mařenka to Libuše. In 1912, Morfová mounted the first production of *Prodaná nevěsta* in Bulgaria, singing the title role while also serving as stage director.[50]

Although Ema Miřiovská (1891–1974) officially debuted at the National Theatre in Prague with the role of Lidunka in Blodek's *V studni* in 1912, she was a guest at the time, invited by head Karel Kovařovic. She then guested as Esmeralda in *Prodaná nevěsta*, officially joining the company with this role soon after. Esmeralda, then, marked her debut role as a member of the company, in late 1912. Her teacher was the legendary Ema Destinnová. Miřiovská continued at the National Theatre for more than twenty-five years, singing one hundred roles, including Mařenka. It was not uncommon for young singers in Prague to begin as Esmeralda, progress to Mařenka, and even sometimes end their careers singing Ludmila. Miřiovská had the further distinction of singing in the premiere of Janáček's *Výlety páně Broučkovy* in 1920 as Málinka/Etherea/Kunka.[51]

Czech soprano Běla Rozumová (1903–1962) debuted professionally as Mařenka in 1923, beginning her career in Ljubljana. She then went on to join the State Opera in Brno 1925–1936, and married the legendary Czech conductor Zdeněk Chalabala (1899–1962) in 1927. After joining the roster of the National Theatre in Prague 1936–1942, she dedicated the remainder of her career to teaching.[52]

Czech soprano Jarmila Novotná (1907–1994) made her solo debut at the Prague National Theatre as Mařenka in 1925 at the age of seventeen. Within days, she joined the company, singing Violetta. Novotná was a student of Ema Destinnová. Besides singing at the Vienna Staatsoper for five years, she was on the Met roster from 1940 to 1956. She last sang Mařenka at the National Theatre in 1947. Novotná appeared in a number of films, most notably the first opera film, *Die verkaufte Braut*, directed by Max Ophüls in 1932; *The Search*, winner of two Academy Awards, with Montgomery Clift, in 1948; and *The Great*

Caruso, with Mario Lanza, in 1951.[53]

Milada Musilová (1912–1996) debuted in Ostrava as Mařenka in 1936 before embarking on an illustrious career. Besides singing Mařenka in the 1949 Prague National Theatre production, she sang the role in the Albanian premiere of the opera in Tirana in 1960. She can be heard on several recordings, including the wonderful Supraphon 1952 recording of *Prodaná nevěsta* under conductor Jaroslav Vogel, reissued as a CD in 2009.

Jadwiga Wysoczanská (b. 1927), born and raised in Prague, debuted in 1946 as a soloist with Mařenka at the Smetana Theater in Prague. Mařenka was to be one of her most popular roles. She also sang the role of Kosinská in the premiere of Janáček's opera *Osud* in 1958. Wysoczanská's voice gradually developed from lyric to dramatic, so that she sang everything from Pamina to Donna Anna and Aida, as well as the dramatic soprano Smetana roles. Ending her career at the Prague National Theatre in 1989, she fondly remembered singing Mařenka with the legendary Beno Blachut as Jeník.[54]

After singing several roles while still a student at the Prague Conservatory, such as Esmeralda in České Budějovice, and Mařenka in Plzeň, Dana Burešová (b. 1967) had the distinction of winning a very competitive audition to debut as a company member in the role of Mařenka at the Prague National Theatre in 1992, immediately after her graduation in 1991. This was the Bohumil Gregor/Pavel Šmok production. She also appeared frequently in the following two productions. Burešová had a triumphant American debut, as well, as Mařenka in the Lyric Opera of Baltimore's Czech production—Baltimore's first *Prodaná nevěsta*—in 2007.[55]

German soprano Ute Vinzing (b. 1936) debuted in Lübeck in 1968 as Mařenka. She has sung throughout the world in roles such as Brünnhilde, Isolde, and, in her Met debut in 1984, Elektra. She can be heard on the 1988 CD with Cheryl Studer of *Die Frau ohne Schatten*.[56]

Scottish soprano Muriel Dickson (1903–90) was lauded at her Metropolitan Opera debut as Mařenka in 1936. Dickson had been at the D'Oyly Carte Opera Company from 1928 to 1935, and her excellent English diction was one reason she was offered the role. According to her memoirs, she found the planned translation to be appalling, and refused to sing it. So she, other members of the cast, and the "dialogue coach" (Madeleine Marshall [1900–93]) rewrote it (see appendix A). Dickson also starred as Amelia in the Met's first performance of Menotti's *Amelia Goes to the Ball*, in 1938.[57]

American soprano Mary Costa (b. 1932) debuted with the lead role of Mařenka in 1958, following in Marilyn Horne's footsteps (see below) at Shrine Auditorium with the Los Angeles Guild Opera. The cast included American soprano Marni Nixon (b. 1930). Costa continued with the role throughout her career, singing Mařenka with the San Francisco Opera in 1964—the same year as her New York Metropolitan Opera debut as Violetta in *La Traviata*—and with the Opera Company of Boston in 1973. Despite her operatic fame both in America and in Europe, she is most well known as the voice of Princess Aurora in Walt Disney's *Sleeping Beauty*, made in 1959.[58]

After serving as cover for Teresa Stratas, American soprano Patricia Craig (b. 1947) debuted with the Metropolitan Opera in 1978 as Mařenka, under James Levine. Craig had just come from critically acclaimed performances with the New York City Opera and in Europe. She went on to perform for twelve seasons in leading roles at the Met, specializing in Puccini and Verdi heroines.[59]

After studies with Hans Hotter and Phyllis Curtin, American soprano Cheryl Studer (b. 1955) began her career as Mařenka in 1980 at the Munich Staatsoper. An illustrious career at all the major opera houses in the world and a legacy of recordings has followed.[60]

Mezzo-sopranos

The great German mezzo Christa Ludwig (b. 1928) made her first recording in 1954, singing Háta in the Act III sextet of *Prodaná nevěsta* (in German). This was one year before her engagement with the Vienna Staatsoper, and world fame, began.[61]

American mezzo (and soprano) Lucielle Browning (Lucille Brown Somers) (b. 1913) debuted at the Metropolitan Opera in 1936 as Ludmila. She continued at the Met until 1951, singing in 558 opera performances there.[62]

The great American mezzo Risë Stevens (b. 1913) debuted as Ludmila in *The Bartered Bride* in 1931 with the semiprofessional Little Theatre Opera Company (later changed to the "New York Opéra Comique") in Brooklyn and Manhattan. That performance also marked the first time the opera had been heard in English in New York. Stevens' formal debut came in Prague in 1936, singing the lead in Thomas' *Mignon*. Stevens had a phenomenal career in opera, and performed in movies and on radio as well. She revisited *The Bartered Bride* for the European release of the 1944 film *Going My Way*, where she appeared as Mařenka. The movie won seven Academy Awards, including best picture. Stevens is probably best known for her portrayal of Carmen.[63]

Superstar American mezzo Marilyn Horne (b. 1934) made her professional opera debut as Háta in 1954 with the Los Angeles Guild Opera, produced by the great German theater and opera producer Carl Ebert (1887–1980). The Guild Opera performed in the mammoth Shrine Auditorium to an audience of about six thousand children. While she sang the mezzo role of Háta, Horne at the time considered herself a soprano. Needless to say, Horne went on to become one of the greatest singers of all time.[64]

Tenors

The great Czech tenor Karel Burian (in the USA known as "Carl Burrian") (1870–1924) made his professional debut as Jeník in Brno in 1891. In 1900 he joined the roster of the National Theatre in Prague, singing quite a few major lead roles before quickly leaving for Dresden and joining the international circuit. He sang the role of Herod alongside Ema Destinnová in the premiere of Richard Strauss's *Salome* with the Dresden Opera in 1905. This was soon followed by many Wagner roles sung at the Met, Bayreuth, and Covent Garden.[65]

True to his name, Miloslav Jeník (1884–1944) debuted at the Prague National Theatre in 1914 with the role of Jeník. After service in WWI, he continued at the National Theatre as a permanent member from 1918 to 1941, singing one hundred roles more than two thousand times. The role of Jeník was his mainstay, with 154 performances, including in the premiere of the National Theatre's thirteenth production in 1923 under Ostrčil and Pujman. With Miřiovská (see above), he sang in the premiere of Janáček's *Výlety páně Broučkovy* in 1920, as Blankytný.[66]

The legendary Czech tenor Beno Blachut (1913–85) made his debut as Jeník with the Olomouc Opera in 1939. He joined the roster of the Prague National Theatre in 1941 at the invitation of Václav Talich, and soon went from lyric to dramatic tenor. Thanks to his many recordings, his portrayals of Dalibor and Janáček roles serve as artistic models to this day. Jeník did remain a staple of his repertoire throughout most of his career, however. Blachut's performances of Jeník spanned eight different productions of *Prodaná nevěsta* at the National Theater from 1941 through 1970.[67]

Czech tenor Miroslav Frydlewicz (1934–2002), born in Plzeň, made his professional debut as Jeník with the Opava Opera in 1957. After fulfilling contracts with the Opava and Plzeň Operas, he sang at the Prague National Theatre from 1965 to 1992. There, among an extensive list of roles, Frydlewicz performed Jeník in the Krombholc/Mandaus production in the 1960s. The years 1966–68 brought guest appearances as Pinkerton and Jeník at the Berlin Staatsoper. Frydlewicz's long singing career continued at the Prague Státní Opera 1992–98, with even further engagements afterwards. His singing can still be enjoyed on Supraphon and Panton recordings today.[68]

With Belgian tenor Octave Dua (1882–1952) came several "firsts." His professional debut was as Vašek in *Prodaná nevěsta*, singing in the first performance in French of the opera. This was on Feburary 23, 1907, at La Monnaie opera house in Brussels. Dua went on to perform in the main houses of the United States and the United Kingdom. He sang in the premiere of Prokofiev's *The Love for Three Oranges* as Truffaldino, given in Chicago in French in 1921, and conducted by the composer. In 1930, he sang Vašek again, in German, in Chicago Civic Opera's first performance of the opera.[69]

Swedish tenor Nicolai Gedda (b. 1925) made his American television debut before an audience of millions on the Bell Telephone Hour singing the Jeník/Kecal duet, in exquisite English, with Giorgio Tozzi in 1959. His long, illustrious career included singing Jeník in the 1978 Met production.[70]

Bulgarian tenor Nikola Nikolov (b. 1925) made his La Scala debut as Jeník in 1955. Based at the Sofia National Opera, Nikolov sang all over the world. His Metropolitan Opera debut was in 1960 as Don José, a role he repeated at the age of seventy with the Sofia National Opera.[71]

The German lyric tenor Christoph Prégardien (b. 1956) made his professional debut as Vašek with the Frankfurt Opera in 1984, where he performed for five years. His many lauded recordings and live appearances span music from the early Baroque to the twentieth century.[72]

American tenor George E. Rasely (1889–1965) made his Metropolitan Opera debut in 1936 as Vašek, along with Muriel Dickson and Lucielle Browning (see above). Well known as a radio singer, Rasely continued at the Met through March 1944, mostly singing comprimario roles.[73]

Canadian tenor Alan Crofoot (1929–79) made his Metropolitan Opera debut as the Principál in their 1978 production of *Prodaná nevěsta*, singing in eleven performances. Crofoot is fondly remembered by many in Canada and the United Kingdom as the Pied Piper in the 1963 children's television series *Mr. Piper*.[74]

British lyric tenor Paul Charles Clarke (b. 1965) made his Metropolitan Opera debut as Jeník in 1996. He can be heard singing the role on the 2005 CD of *The Bartered Bride*, sung in English, with Sir Charles Mackerras.[75]

The New Zealand tenor Simon O'Neill (b. 1971) made his Covent Garden debut as Jeník in 2006, under Sir Charles Mackerras. Firmly rooted in lyric, *bel canto* singing, O'Neill quickly became renowned for his Wagner roles.[76]

Basses, bass-baritones, and baritones

Czech bass Vilém Heš (in Germany "Wilhelm Hesch") (1860–1908) made his solo debut as Kecal in 1880 at the State Opera in Brno. He first sang Kecal at the Prague National Theatre in 1885, where he was engaged from 1882 to 1894. His interpretation served as a model for generations, so that his influence can even be seen in one of the more recent Prague Kecals, Bohuslav Maršík (b. 1937). Even Heš's idea to blacken one of his front teeth was copied by numerous basses. In 1892 he toured with the Prague company to appear as Kecal in the historic Vienna performance of *Prodaná nevěsta* that launched the opera's international fame. In 1894 he left for the Hamburg Opera, where he performed under Gustav Mahler. When Mahler took up his position at the Vienna Hofoper in 1896, he took Heš with him, and the singer performed Kecal there as well, with Mahler conducting. Heš amassed a long list of opera roles and numerous awards before his death at the age of forty-eight. Besides being a wonderful actor and excelling in *buffo* roles, he possessed one of the most beautiful bass voices of his generation. Fortunately, we can hear his singing on an extensive collection of early recordings.[77]

The wonderful Czech bass Jaroslav Horáček (b. 1926) made his solo debut as Kecal in 1945 with the Opava Opera. From there, he joined the Ostrava Opera in 1951, and then appeared for the first time at the Prague National Theatre as a guest in 1952, singing Kecal. A consummate artist, Horáček joined Prague's roster in 1953 and performed a long list of roles well into his seventies. Altogether, he sang in seven different productions of *Prodaná nevěsta* at the Prague National Theatre. Kecal alone he sang for thirty years, from 1952 to 1982. He added the role of the Indián with the premiere of the 1955 Chalabala/Kašlík production. Mícha came at the premiere of the 1971 Krombholc/Kočí production. He can be heard as Mícha in the 1980/81 definitive Supraphon recording conducted by Zdeněk Košler (see appendix B). Horáček has the distinction of being the only singer to have sung *four* roles in *Prodaná nevěsta*—on October 20, 1958, he filled in for the ill Rudolf Vonásek (1948–78), singing the tenor part of the Principál!

Another first for Jaroslav Horáček was his American debut as Kecal with the Opera Company of Boston on January 27, 1973. The opera was performed in English. Horáček related to the author that when he learned he would be singing Kecal in English, a language he didn't know, he searched the Prague libraries for an English singing translation, and memorized it. Upon arriving in Boston, he said, the company was aghast at the antiquated English.[78] He then had to quickly learn another translation. To his (and tenor Miroslav Švejda's) credit, according to the New York Times, "Their English was quaint, but usually understandable." Still, it is no wonder that in the patter of the Kecal/Jeník duet, ". . . the Czechoslovak artists lapsed into their native language." Horáček returned to Boston to sing Kecal again in 1977, while also directing the opera.[79]

Hungarian bass-baritone Zoltán Kelemen (1926–79) began his opera career in Augsburg in 1959 as Kecal. He is known mostly for his Wagner roles—he debuted in Salzburg, Covent Garden, and in 1968 at the Metropolitan Opera as Alberich in *Das Rheingold* under Herbert von Karajan (1908–89).

South African bass-baritone Angelo Gobbato (b. 1943) debuted as Kecal in 1965 in Cape Town, at CAPAB (Cape Performing Arts Board) Opera. *The Bartered Bride* was also the first opera to be mounted by the newly established CAPAB. Best known for his *buffo* roles, Gobbato also began directing operas in 1966, becoming the resident stage director for CAPAB operas in 1976, and eventually staging *The Bartered Bride* for the Cape Town Opera in 2003. He was director of the world-renowed Opera School at Cape Town University from 1982 to 1988, and then in 1989 artistic director of CAPAB Opera, now Cape Town Opera.[80]

The warm-voiced and warm-hearted American bass Ara Berberian (1930–2005) made his Metropolitan Opera debut as Kecal in April 1979. This was in Cleveland as part of a Met tour, with Stratas, Gedda, Levine, and others from the premiere six months earlier. (He was to have debuted in the house, but the Met orchestra had been on strike, considerably delaying the season.) His repertory included more than one hundred roles, and he sang all over the world. At the Met, Berberian appeared in more than three hundred performances, ending in a 1997 *La Bohème*. Another notable performance was his 1964 studio recording of Jud Fry in *Oklahoma!*[81]

The versatile American baritone Timothy Nolen (b. 1941) made his Metropolitan Opera debut as Krušina in 1996. This was a revival of the 1978 production, conducted by Levine. Nolen's career has included a wide range of roles in most of the major opera houses in America and Europe. His characters cover not only the standard repertory, but also recent works such as *McTeague* and *A View from the Bridge* by William Bolcom (b. 1938). With his exceptional acting ability, he has been equally successful in musical theater. A perfect example of this is Nolen's singing of the lead role in *Sweeney Todd* on Broadway as well as at New York City Opera, both to critical acclaim.[82]

Conductors

Walter Ducloux (1913–97) conducted *Prodaná nevěsta* at the Prague National Theatre on October 24, 1945, becoming the first American to conduct there. An assistant to Toscanini, Ducloux was also a lieutenant and language interpreter under Patton, serving at the liberation of Plzeň. Ducloux was a regular participant of the Metropolitan Opera Quiz for twenty-five years, and an English translator of a long list of operas.[83]

For conductor James Levine (b. 1943), his first encounter with *Prodaná nevěsta* was not with the Met's 1978 production. Rather, this came at the age of nine when he played the child who shouted "The bear is loose!" in a Cincinnati Summer Opera performance in 1953. Passionate for Smetana's music, Levine was awarded the Smetana Medal by the Czechoslovak government in 1986 following his performance of *Má vlast* in Vienna.[84]

Librettist

English author, director, and librettist Eric Crozier (1914–94) produced *The Bartered Bride* as his first opera at Sadler's Wells, in 1943. Along with singer and producer Joan Cross (1900–93), Crozier made his first English translation of a libretto with this opera (see appendix A). Crozier went on to create quite a few other opera singing translations, and to write outstanding librettos for several of Benjamin Britten's operas.[85]

Choreographers

The pioneering American ballet dancer and choreographer Ruth Page (1899–1991) made her Metropolitan Opera debut in 1927 dancing in the polka and furiant in *Prodaná nevěsta*, with choreography by Augustin Berger (1861–1945). With this performance, in fact, Page became the first American guest ballet soloist with the Metropolitan Opera. Her "firsts" in the world of ballet are many. Besides performing with Anna Pavlova's classical ballet company, Page was the first American ballerina to dance with Diaghilev's Ballet Russe, in 1925, and the first American to commission a ballet from George Balanchine, the *Polka Mélancholique*. She also danced in the world premiere of Stravinsky's *Apollo* in 1928, and arranged the American debut of Rudolf Nureyev in 1962. A proponent of opera ballet, she created a string of "opera into ballet" choreographies. Her legacy continues at the Ruth Page Center for the Arts in Chicago.[86]

Ballet dancer and choreographer Paul Godkin (1914–85) made his stage debut in 1935. He was one of thirty dancers in a Hollywood Bowl concert produced by Agnes De Mille (1905–93) in a work she titled *May Festival*, using music from *The Bartered Bride*. The dancers, including De Mille, were joined by thirty singers from a Los Angeles Bohemian society wearing Czech *kroje*, and singing one of the opera's choruses in Czech. After Godkin toured with the Ballets Russes de Monte Carlo, he joined the American Ballet Theater in 1949, and then became one of the pioneers of television and movie choreography.[87]

The great Czech choreographer Pavel Šmok (b. 1927) first choreographed the dances in *Prodaná nevěsta* for the 1978 Metropolitan Opera production, his debut at the Met. Šmok had first danced in the opera himself as a member of the Prague Army Opera ballet from 1952 to 1955. He debuted as an opera stage director in 1992 with the twenty-sixth Prague National Theatre production of *Prodaná nevěsta*, conducted by Bohumil Gregor (1926–2005). Šmok, of course, also served as the choreographer. This vibrant production ran until 1999, with 155 performances.[88]

Notes

1. Jan Panenka and Tat'ána Součková, *Prodaná nevěsta na jevištích Prozatímního a Národního divadla 1866–2004* (Prague: Gallery and Národní divadlo, 2004), 147, 199. While many of the author's notes are from this wonderful book, Panenka and Součková's work is largely based on the book by Přemysl Pražák, *Smetanova Prodaná nevěsta* (Prague: Lidová demokracie, 1962), which goes into more detail up to 1962.

2. Panenka and Součková, *Prodaná nevěsta na jevištích Prozatímního a Národního divadla 1866–2004*, 37, 90, 101, 122, 139.

3. When British soprano Lorna Haywood sang the lead role in the 1969 *Jenůfa* production at the Prague National Theatre under Bohumil Gregor, she sang in English while everyone else sang in Czech. Mixing languages was not uncommon at the New York Metropolitan Opera and elsewhere, either, especially with Slavic opera. Panenka and Součková, *Prodaná nevěsta na jevištích Prozatímního a Národního divadla 1866–2004*, 39–42, 45–46, 50; and Josef Bartoš, *Prozatímní divadlo a jeho opera* (Prague: Sbor pro zřízení druhého národního divadla v Praze, 1938), 351–53.

4. Brian Large, *Smetana* (New York: Praeger Publishers, 1970), 385.

5. John Tyrrell, *Czech opera* (Cambridge: Cambridge University Press, 1988), 28, 33; Panenka and Součková, *Prodaná nevěsta na jevištích Prozatímního a Národního divadla 1866–2004*, 52, 54; and Alfred Loewenberg, *Annals of opera 1597–1940*, 3d ed. (Totowa, N.J.: Rowman and Littlefield, 1978), 983–84.

6. Panenka and Součková, *Prodaná nevěsta na jevištích Prozatímního a Národního divadla 1866–2004*, 59, 71, 92–93.

7. *Dráteník* [The tinker], a *Singspeil* by František Škroup (1801–62), had debuted at the Estates Theatre in 1826. Czechs of 1920 certainly considered *Dráteník* to be the first Czech opera. Josef Kajetán Tyl (1808–56), dramaturg of the Estates Theatre, also wrote his play *Fidlovačka* (the name of a traditional spring fair) in 1834 to be performed in the theater. Incidental music was by Škroup, and included the song "Kde domov můj" [Where is my homeland], which became the official Czech national anthem in 1918. When the Provisional Theatre had opened in 1862, the Estates Theatre was dedicated to a German ensemble and named the "Deutsches Landestheater." Brian S. Locke, *Opera and ideology in Prague: Polemics and practice at the National Theater 1900–1938* (Rochester: University of Rochester Press, 2006) 140–42; and John Tyrrell, *Czech opera*, 23, 63–66.

8. Ostrčil and Kysela had actually already worked together on a modern, stylized *Prodaná nevěsta* much earlier, in 1915, with stage director Karel Hugo Hilar (1885–

1935), at the Vinohrady Theatre in Prague. Brian S. Locke, *Opera and ideology in Prague: Polemics and practice at the National Theater 1900–1938*, 150–51; Pamela Tancsik, *Die Prager Oper heißt Zemlinsky: Theatergeschichte des Neuen Deutschen Theaters Prag in der Ära Zemlinsky von 1911 bis 1927* (Vienna: Böhlau, 2000), 187, 234; and Panenka and Součková, *Prodaná nevěsta na jevištích Prozatímního a Národního divadla 1866–2004*, 87, 95, 97, 101.

9. Immediately after World War II, one of these conductors was Walter Ducloux (1913–97), the first American conductor to conduct at the National Theatre (see "Debuts," below).

10. Panenka and Součková, *Prodaná nevěsta na jevištích Prozatímního a Národního divadla 1866–2004*, 106–109, 114, 117–18, 120, 123, 211; Brian S. Locke, *Opera and ideology in Prague: Polemics and practice at the National Theater 1900–1938*, 334; and "Václav Talich," *Národní divadlo*, http://archiv.narodni-divadlo.cz (5 May 2009).

11. John W. Freeman, "The theater of Josef Svoboda," *Opera News* 43, no. 6 (2 December 1978): 43–46; Panenka and Součková, *Prodaná nevěsta na jevištích Prozatímního a Národního divadla 1866–2004*, 126–27, 129, 133–34, 141–42, 145, 148.

12. Panenka and Součková, *Prodaná nevěsta na jevištích Prozatímního a Národního divadla 1866–2004*, 155–56, 160–61.

13. Panenka and Součková, *Prodaná nevěsta na jevištích Prozatímního a Národního divadla 1866–2004*, 162–64, 166, 170–71.

14. Peter Freestone, "Czech Republic," *Opera* 60, no. 2 (February 2009): 172; Panenka and Součková, *Prodaná nevěsta na jevištích Prozatímního a Národního divadla 1866–2004*, 179, 182, 186–87, 191, 195; "*Prodaná nevěsta*," *Národní divadlo*, http://archiv.narodni-divadlo.cz (8 May 2009).

15. "*Die verkaufte Braut*," *Washington Post*, 23 September 1894, 16.

16. Their son was an important film director, Svatopluk Innemann (1896–1945), who made a sound film of *Prodaná nevěsta* in 1933. "Rudolf Innemann," *Národní divadlo*, http://archiv.narodni-divadlo.cz (20 May 2009); and Panenka and Součková, *Prodaná nevěsta na jevištích Prozatímního a Národního divadla 1866–2004*, 102–103.

17. Thomas had conducted the American premiere of the overture to *Prodaná nevěsta* at a New York summer concert in 1887. Theodore Thomas, *Theodore Thomas: A musical autobiography*, vol. 2, ed. by George P. Upton (Chicago: A.C. McClurg & Co., 1905), 287, 377, 381; Jan Löwenbach, *Hudba v Americe* (Prague: Hudební matice, 1948), 46; "Music at the fair," *Chicago Daily Tribune*, 13 August 1893, 2; "Music and drama," *Chicago Daily Tribune*, 21 August 1893, 4; and Přemysl Pražák, *Smetanova Prodaná nevěsta*, 309–13.

18. For the 1903–04 season, Met head Heinrich Conried (1855–1909) had announced his hopes to produce *Prodaná nevěsta* with an English translation by the English critic and pioneering libretto translator Charles Henry Meltzer (1853–1936). "*Parsifal*, $10 a seat," *New York Times*, 21 August 1903, 9; "*Bartered Bride* at Metropolitan," *New York Times*, 20 February 1909, 7; Panenka and Součková, *Prodaná nevěsta na jevištích Prozatímního a Národního divadla 1866–2004*, 75. Alma Mahler, *Gustav Mahler: Memories and letters*, 3d ed., translated by Basil Creighton, edited by Donald Mitchell (Seattle: University of Washington Press, 1975), 6, 131, 154; Irving Kolodin, *The Metropolitan Opera 1883–1966: A candid history* (New York: Alfred A. Knopf, 1966), 204, 330; and Ladislav Hájek, *Paměti Augustina Bergra: Choreografa a baletního mistra národního divadla v Praze a několika světových scén* (Prague: Orbis, 1942), 323.

19. "*Bartered Bride*," *MetOpera Database*, http://archives.Metoperafamily.org/archives/frame.htm (16 May 2009).

20. "Fifth performance of *Bartered Bride*," *New York Times*, 3 June 1936, 26; Olin

Downes, *"Bartered Bride* is well received," *New York Times*, 26 December 1936, 14; and Irving Kolodin, *The Metropolitan Opera 1883–1966*, 402.

21. Olin Downes, *"Bartered Bride* at Metropolitan," *New York Times*, 1 March 1941; and Irving Kolodin, *The Metropolitan Opera 1883–1966*, 427, 433.

22. Gary D. Lipton, "Czech mates," *Opera News* 43, no. 6 (2 December 1978): 41.

23. Met performances of the opera were even cut short because of a strike. Richard Dyer, "Patricia Craig profile," *Opera Boston* http://www.operaboston.org/operas_ bride_ specialfeatures.php (21 May 2009), 2; and John Rockwell, "Patricia Craig sings title role in *Bartered Bride* at the Met," *New York Times*, 27 November 1978, C16.

24. Donal Henahan, "Teresa Stratas is what she is—and will always be so," *New York Times*, 24 December 1978, D13.

25. Pavel Ludikar, famed baritone Lawrence Tibbett (1896–1960), and Deems Taylor (1885–1966) of *Fantasia* fame attended the premiere. W.B.C., "Opera," *New York Times*, 24 March 1931, 31; and "Extends run of opera," *New York Times*, 27 March 1931, 34.

26. Olin Downes, *"Bartered Bride* heard in English," *New York Times*, 4 October, 1945, 26; and Howard Taubman, "Music: *Bartered Bride* at City Center," *New York Times*, 27 October, 1955.

27. Allan Kozinn, "Smetana's long-absent *Bride* is back in town," *New York Times*, 11 January 1993, C13.

28. W.L. Hubbard, "Two operas sung to big audiences," *Chicago Daily Tribune*, 18 April 1909, 6.

29. Edward Moore, *"Bartered Bride*, forgot 20 years, wins at Ravinia," *Chicago Daily Tribune*, 9 August 1930, 7; Edward Moore, *"The Bartered Bride* becomes triumph at first presentation," *Chicago Daily Tribune*, 26 December 1930, 19.

30. Edward Moore, "Opera you can understand gets enthusiastic welcome," *Chicago Daily Tribune*, 4 December 1933, 21.

31. Přemysl Pražák, *Smetanova Prodaná nevěsta*, 324.

32. Robert C. Marsh, *150 years of opera in Chicago*, completed and edited by Norman Pellegrini (DeKalb, Ill.: Northern Illinois University Press, 2006), 197; John von Rhein, *"Bride* escapes handmaiden status," *Chicago Tribune*, 2 April 1984, D C4; and Algimantas Kezys and Ada Sutkus, "Posters by Ada Sutkus," *Lituanus* 42, no. 2 (Summer 1996), from http://www.lituanus.org/1996/96_2_04.htm (22 May 2009).

33. *"Bartered Bride," San Francisco Opera performance archive*, http://archive. sfopera.com/qry1operalist.asp (22 May 2009).

34. *"Bartered Bride* heard by throng," *Los Angeles Times*, 13 August 1937, 15.

35. Peter Ebert, *In this theatre of man's life: The biography of Carl Ebert* (Sussex: The Book Guild, 1999), 193–94; and Martin Bernheimer, "Opera for students at Shrine," *Los Angeles Times*, 11 May 1966, C11.

36. These are taken from a poster listing premieres hanging in the Smetana Museum in Prague, 2008. Some dates are incorrect—the poster lists Philadelphia as 1946, but Frances Greer (1917–2005) sang Mařenka in an English production at the Philadephia Opera Company in 1940. See "Opera in English," *Time* 36, no. 23 (2 December 1940), at http:// www.time.com/time/magazine/article/0,9171,772496,00.html; the poster lists San Francisco as 1959, but it was 1934 (see above). Some information is through personal correspondence with the author.

37. Raymond Ericson, "Opera: *Bartered Bride* fascinates and maddens," *New York Times*, 28 January 1973, Special to the *New York Times*, 49; and Richard Dyer, "Daniel Pelzig profile," *Opera Boston*, http://www.operaboston.org/operas_bride_ specialfeatures.php (18 May 2009), 1–2. Jan Skalický defected while in the USA in 1965. He al-

so helped create *Prodaná nevěsta* at Juilliard in 1973, and after returning to the Czech Republic, worked in the National Theatre's 1999–2004 production. Panenka and Součková, *Prodaná nevěsta na jevištích Prozatímního a Národního divadla 1866–2004*, 187–88; and "Swatches and splashes," *Time* 85, no. 10 (5 March 1965), at http://www.time.com/time/magazine/article/0,9171,839323,00.html (15 May 2009).

38. See preface. Some information is through personal correspondence with the author, or through the author's own experiences. Also see Harold C. Schonberg, "Opera: *Bartered Bride* at Juilliard," *New York Times*, 16 December 1973, 75; Leonard Buder, "City students sure of profit on opera," *New York Times*, 14 December 1949; and Laura Macy, ed., *The Grove book of opera singers* (Oxford: Oxford University Press, 2008), s.v. "Norman, Jessye."

39. University of Michigan School of Music, *School of Music programs* (Ann Arbor: University of Michigan School of Music, 1967–68), March 21–24.

40. See preface. The 1930 date comes from the poster listing premieres of *Prodaná nevěsta* throughout the world, hanging in the Smetana Museum, Prague, 2008.

41. "3D opera festival starts in Toronto," *New York Times*, special to the *New York Times*, 22 February 1952, 14; "Nicholas Goldschmidt, Tavikovice, Moravia, December 6, 1908—Toronto, February 8, 2004," *Opera News* 69, no. 1 (1 July 2004): 69; Joan Wellwood, "*The Bartered Bride*," *The Point*, University of British Columbia's weekly activities and events guide (26 February 2003): 3; and personal correspondence with author.

42. Harold Rosenthal, *Two centuries of opera at Covent Garden* (London: Putnam, 1958), 269, 321, 474, 544; and Přemysl Pražák, *Smetanova Prodaná nevěsta*, 280–82.

43. "*Bartered Bride*," *Royal Opera House: Collections online*, http://www.rohcollections.org.uk/performances.aspx (13 February 2009); Harold Rosenthal, *Two centuries of opera at Covent Garden*, 643.

44. "*Bartered Bride*," *Royal Opera House: Collections online*, http://www.rohcollections.org.uk/performances.aspx (13 February 2009).

45. "Productions," *Glyndebourne*, http://www.glyndebourne.com/archive/productions/ (25 May 2009).

46. Přemysl Pražák, *Smetanova Prodaná nevěsta*, 328–29; "Gateway to the Australian Performing Arts," *AusState*, http://www.ausstage.edu.au/ (25 May 2009); Vladimír Procházka, ed., *Národní divadlo a jeho předchůdci: Slovník umělců divadel Vlastenského, Stavovského, Prozatímního a Národního* (Prague: Academia Praha, 1988), s.v. "František Vajnar" and "Přemysl Kočí;" and "Šárka Hejnová," *Národní divadlo*, http://archiv.narodni-divadlo.cz (25 May 2009).

47. Přemysl Pražák, *Smetanova Prodaná nevěsta*, 328–29; and Macy, ed., *The Grove book of opera singers*, s.v. "Gobbato, Angelo."

48. "2008–2009 season: *The Bartered Bride*," *Opéra national de Paris*, http://www.operadeparis.fr (26 May 2009).

49. Procházka, *Národní divadlo a jeho předchůdci*, s.v. "Tvrdková, Ella."

50. Panenka and Součková, *Prodaná nevěsta na jevištích Prozatímního a Národního divadla 1866–2004*, 89; and Procházka, *Národní divadlo a jeho předchůdci*, s.v. "Morfová, Christina."

51. Procházka, *Národní divadlo a jeho předchůdci*, s.v. "Miřiovská, Ema."

52. Václav Věžník, "Divadelní jubilea—vzpomínky," *Zpravodaj* (February 2009): 1.

53. Macy, ed., *The Grove book of opera singers*, s.v. "Jarmila Novotná;" and Panenka and Součková, *Prodaná nevěsta na jevištích Prozatímního a Národního divadla 1866–2004*, 102.

54. Procházka, *Národní divadlo a jeho předchůdci*, s.v. "Musilová, Milada;" K.J. Kutsch and Leo Riemens, *Großes Sängerlexikon*, 3d ed. (Bern: K.G. Saur, 1997) s.v.

"Wysoczanská, Jadwiga;" and email from Wysoczanská to the author, 8 June 2009.

55. Timothy Cheek, CD notes for recording *Vítězslava Kaprálová: Songs* (Prague: Supraphon, 2003), 13.

56. Gerhart Asche, "Retrospektive: Die Macht des Schicksals," *Opernwelt* 46, no. 8 (Aug. 2005): 69. Thanks also to Rita Richter of the Lübeck Opera for validating this.

57. The translation she refused to sing was by Libushka Bartusek, published in Chicago in 1934. See appendix A. Muriel Dickson, *There and back: A light-hearted, sentimental autobiography* (Billingham, U.K.: The Gaiety, 2004) 18–19; Irving Kolodin, *The Metropolitan Opera 1883–1966* (New York: Alfred A. Knopf, 1966), 396; and "Muriel Dickson," *MetOpera Database*, http://archives.metoperafamily.org/archives/frame.htm (10 April 2009).

58. Kutsch and Riemens, *Großes Sängerlexikon*, s.v. "Costa, Mary;" "Children to hear opera," *Los Angeles Times*, 23 February 1958, E6; Albert Goldberg, "S.F. Opera to Light Shrine on Friday," *Los Angeles Times*, 1 November 1964, N1; and "Mary Costa to sing Violetta in *Traviata* at Met debut Jan. 6," *New York Times*, 30 December 1963, 16.

59. John Rockwell, "Patricia Craig sings title role in *Bartered Bride* at the MET," *New York Times*, 27 November 1978, C16; and Kutsch and Riemens, *Großes Sängerlexikon*, s.v. "Patricia Craig."

60. Macy, ed., *The Grove book of opera singers*, s.v. "Studer, Cheryl."

61. Christa Ludwig, *In my own voice*, trans. by Regina Domeraski (New York: Limelight, 1999), 34.

62. "Lucielle Browning," *MetOpera Database*, http://archives.metoperafamily.org/archives/frame.htm (21 March 2009).

63. The American release has a scene from *Carmen* instead of one from *The Bartered Bride*. The Smetana was used in Europe because *Carmen* was still under copyright there. John Pennino, *Risë Stevens: A life in music* (Fort Worth: Baskerville Publishers, 1999) 18–19, 160–61, 177, 358; and W.B.C., "Opera," *New York Times*, 24 March 1931, 31.

64. A total of 40,000 children attended performances of *The Bartered Bride*, performed at 10:30 a.m. Unfortunately, the opera in the huge auditorium was miked and amplified so loud that the critic was unable to successfully evaluate the distorted performance of the premiere. Albert Goldberg, "The Sounding board: Electronics sound out over music of opera," *Los Angeles Times*, 6 April 1954, A11; and Marilyn Horne, with Jane Scovell, *Marilyn Horne: My life* (New York: Atheneum, 1983), 69–70.

65. Dalibor Janota, and Jan P. Kučera, *Malá encyklopedie České opery* (Prague: Paseka, 1999, s.v. "Burian, Karel."

66. Janota and Kučera, *Malá encyklopedie České opery*, s.v. "Jeník, Miloslav;" Procházka, *Národní divadlo a jeho předchůdci*, s.v. "Jeník, Miloslav;" and Panenka and Součková, *Prodaná nevěsta na jevištích Prozatímního a Národního divadla 1866–2004*, 95.

67. Macy, ed., *The Grove book of opera singers*, s.v. "Blachut, Beno;" and Panenka and Součková, *Prodaná nevěsta na jevištích Prozatímního a Národního divadla 1866–2004*, 122.

68. Procházka, *Národní divadlo a jeho předchůdci*, s.v. "Frydlewicz, Miroslav."

69. "Octave Dua," *The digital opera archives of La Monnaie*, http://carmen.demunt.be (2 April 2009); Macy, ed., *The Grove book of opera singers*, s.v. "Dua, Octave" (the role of Jeník is incorrectly listed); and Edward Moore, "*The Bartered Bride* becomes triumph at first presentation," *Chicago Daily Tribune*, 26 December 1930, 19.

70. Gary D. Lipton, "Czech mates," *Opera News* 43, no. 6 (2 December 1978): 41.

71. Kutsch and Riemens, *Großes Sängerlexikon*, s.v. "Nikolov, Nikola."

72. Macy, ed., *The Grove book of opera singers*, s.v. "Prégardien, Christoph."

73. "George E. Rasely, opera singer, 74," *New York Times*, 5 January 1965, 33; and "George Rasely," *MetOpera Database*, http://archives.metoperafamily.org/archives/frame.htm (10 April 2009).

74. Tragically, Crofoot committed suicide while in Dayton, Ohio, to direct *Salome*, after his fiancée broke off their engagement. "Alan Crofoot," *MetOpera Database*, http://archives.metoperafamily.org/archives/frame.htm (7 April 2009); and "Met tenor kills himself; cite broken engagement," *Chicago Tribune* (6 March 1979), B4.

75. Kutsch and Riemens, *Großes Sängerlexikon*, s.v. "Clarke, Paul Charles."

76. Rebecca Paller, "Sound Bites: Simon O'Neill," *Opera News* 70, no. 3 (September 2005): 14.

77. Kutsch and Riemens, *Großes Sängerlexikon*, s.v. "Hesch, Wilhelm;" and Panenka and Součková, *Prodaná nevěsta na jevištích Prozatímního a Národního divadla 1866–2004*, 48, 55.

78. The Prague City Library owns no English version of the score, but the Klementinum National Library in Prague owns two British English translations—the well-known one translated from the Czech by Rosa Newmarch, published by Boosey & Hawkes in 1934 (see appendix A); and one translated by Felix Goodwin, published in London by Evans Brothers 1942–1962. It was probably the latter that Horáček learned, although it seems as though he might have found the 1934 translation by Libushka Bartusek.

79. Raymond Ericson, "Opera: *Bartered Bride* fascinates and maddens," *New York Times*, 28 January 1973, Special to the *New York Times*, 49; Janota and Kučera, *Malá encyklopedie České*, s.v. "Horáček, Jaroslav;" Panenka and Součková, *Prodaná nevěsta na jevištích Prozatímního a Národního divadla 1866–2004*, 142, 163, 172; and personal interview with author, Prague, July 1996.

80. Macy, ed., *The Grove book of opera singers*, s.v. "Kelemen, Zoltán," and "Gobbato, Angelo."

81. Anne Midgette, "Ara Berberian, 74, a bass in opera and musical theater," *New York Times*, 24 February 2005, B11; and Ginny Berberian, email to author, 4 February 2008.

82. Kutsch and Riemens, *Großes Sängerlexikon*, s.v. "Nolen, Timothy."

83. "In memoriam: Walter Ducloux," *The University of Texas at Austin*, http://www.utexas.edu/faculty/council/1999-2000/memorials/Ducloux/ (27 May 2009).

84. Gary D. Lipton, "Czech mates," *Opera News* 43, no. 6 (2 December 1978): 41; and "James Levine," *The Metropolitan Opera*, http://www.metoperafamily.org/metopera/about/whoweare/levine.aspx (10 April 2009).

85. J.M. Thomson, "Crozier, Eric." *Grove Music Online. Oxford Music Online*, http://www.oxfordmusiconline.com/subscriber/article/grove/music/45792 (11 April 2009).

86. Jack Anderson, "Ruth Page, dancer, is dead at 92; proudly American choreographer," *New York Times*, 9 April 1991, D19; and Irving Kolodin, *The Metropolitan Opera 1883–1966: A candid history*, 336–37.

87. Larry Billman, *Film choreographers and dance directors: An illustrated biographical encyclopedia, with a history and filmographies, 1893 through 1995* (Jefferson, N.C.: McFarland & Co., 1997), 338; Agnes De Mille, *Speak to me, dance with me* (Boston: Little, Brown and Co., 1973), 317–18; and Isabel Morse Jones, "New concerto and dances features of Bowl program," *Los Angeles Times*, 26 July 1935, A11.

88. Pavel Šmok, "My meetings with *The Bartered Bride*," in English-language program booklet for the Prague National Theatre *Prodaná nevěsta*, ed. Helena Havlíková (Prague: National Theatre, 1992), 68; and Panenka and Součková, *Prodaná nevěsta na jevištích Prozatímního a Národního divadla 1866–2004*, 182.

3

Dance in *Prodaná nevěsta*

One of the wonderful qualities of *Prodaná nevěsta* is how well integrated the dances are with the rest of the opera—even though Smetana added them in different revisions. (There is a simple reason they fit so well into the fabric of the opera, discussed below under "Sung Dances.") Moreover, because they are so vital to the communal spirit and the national flavor of the opera, and because they are so well known in the concert hall, the dances simply cannot be cut. The opera, then, has served as a showcase for choreographers and dancers almost as much as for singers.

Polka

Even though the polka has been cultivated by Polish-American societies for generations, the Poles in Poland do not consider it one of their national dances. The polka originated in Bohemia around 1830 and quickly became popular, spreading throughout Europe and into America. The etymology of its name has several explanations. "Polka" is possibly derived from the Czech work *půlka*, meaning "half," referring to the half step in the dance. Literally, though, *polka* means "Polish woman." This could pay homage to its roots, which are indirectly Polish. The dance originated in the Czech Bohemian city of Hradec Králové, not far from Smetana's home town of Litomyšl. After Prague, Hradec Králové was the largest center of new Czech societies during the Czech revival period of the early nineteenth century. In some of these upper middle-class organizations of intellectuals, artists, and musicians, there was dancing. There was dancing of new and old aristocratic European dances, along with regional Czech folk dances. It just happened that during this time, young, nationalistic Czechs found much inspiration in the 1830–31 Polish revolution. They wore Polish hats and Polish national colors. They read Polish poems and Polish novels. And they sang, and later danced, the Polish *krakowiak*. They took the words from the *krakowiak* dance-songs, translated them into Czech, and sang them to the melodies of Czech folk songs and Czech folk dance-songs. They did this mostly with the *schottische*, another dance of Bohemian origin, that could be described as a kind of slow polka. Somehow, out of all this intermingling of dances, folk texts, and (inter)national fervor, the polka came into existence, and so the word *polka* could have arisen to pay homage to the Poles. It is amazing that out of this spirit of revolution and nationalism by upper middle-class Czech groups, the polka was born and spread to every strata of society, including the peasants. It was truly a dance for everyone, a dance for the whole nation, and so a source of national pride. Countless people wrote polkas, but Smetana was its main proponent.[1]

Smetana composed many polkas, including *Lousina polka* [Lousina's polka] (1840); *Jiřinková polka* [Dahlia polka] (1840); *Ze studentského života* [From student life] (1842); *Vzpomínka na Plzeň* [Memory of Plzeň] (1844); *Bettina polka* [Betty's Polka] (1859); and polkas that appear within works, such as the second movement from his autobiographical first string quartet (1876); or the fourth song, "Hej, jaká radost v kole" [Hey, what joy to dance in a circle], from his song cycle *Večerní písně* [Evening songs] (1879). He wrote many more! Smetana wrote polkas that were stylized, in the manner of Chopin's *mazurkas*; he wrote *salonní polkas*, meant to be danced by urbanites; and he wrote a polka that could be danced by villagers.

With its duple meter, moderate tempo, eight-measure phrases, and rhythms characterized by two sixteenth notes followed by an eighth note—not to mention its warm spirit—the polka from *Prodaná nevěsta* defines the dance beautifully. The moderate tempo is key to the Czech spirit—Czech polkas are not like the polkas of Johann Strauss, Jr., for example, many of which are really *galops*. On the other hand, a village polka was not as slow as a typical Czech *salonní polka* (such as Smetana's *Jiřinková polka*), which had to be slower to accommodate the long, puffy skirts of the women. (The *salonní polka* has only one subtle hop in the middle of the step, while the village polka has a hop in the beginning and in the middle.) The Czech dance master Karel Link (1832–1911) worked with the great writer Jan Neruda (1834–91) (who was a very good dancer), and the musician Ferdinand Heller (1824–1912), friends of Smetana, to create the Czech national *beseda* ballroom (*salonní*) dances, in 1863. These were refined versions of the Czech folk dances, based on their fundamental steps. Karel Link wrote the first dance manual describing the *beseda* dances, and suggested a tempo of ♩ = 92 for the steps of the *salonní* polka.[2] The *village* polka in *Prodaná nevěsta* works better around ♩ = 104 or 106. The tempo is usually a little faster when the chorus enters, and faster again the measure before "Basa bručí." Conductor Bohumil Gregor would begin the polka slower than 104 to make a greater contrast of tempi when the chorus entered. Zdeněk Košler, on the other hand, would perform the polka proper around 104 to 106, make a less noticeable increase in tempo when the chorus entered, and then really go quickly at "Basa bručí."

In its early history, the setting of *Prodaná nevěsta* quickly took on that of the Plzeň region, west of Prague. For those who wish to re-create authentic dance steps, the difference between a polka from the Plzeň region and one from Hradec Králové is that the Hradec polka is danced on the front part of the foot, while the Plzeň polka is danced on the whole foot, but not leaning back on the heel, with the knees gently bent.[3] This brings up the question of "authenticity" in Smetana's opera, as not only are there various types of polkas from country to country, but some stylistic differences within the Czech lands. The great thing about the polka, though, is that the basic pattern of "step-together-step" is the same everywhere, with couples dancing in a circle, and there is a great variety of movements possible based on these fundamental steps. Certainly, it is crucial that none of the dancers should be on pointe, as these are village dancers! When Augustin Berger had the chorus join the dancers in the polka in the 1892 Prague/Vienna production, he not only added realism, but he also bridged the gap between singers and dancers that is often an obstacle in opera. When directors at the Prague National Theatre asked dancers to learn the words of the chorus, so that they would not be the only ones not singing, the dancers, too, became integrated with the action.[4]

Furiant

With *Prodaná nevěsta*, Smetana made the Bohemian *furiant*, one of the most typical of the Czech folk dances, world renowned. Other composers quickly followed with their own versions, most notably Dvořák. (Remember that Dvořák played the viola under Smetana in all the early performances of *Prodaná nevěsta*!) This was the only music in the whole opera that Smetana borrowed from Czech folk song:

There are several versions. The above comes from Klatovsko, in the Plzeň region in west Bohemia. The words mean:

> "Farmer, farmer, farmer, once again farmer, farmer, farmer, he's a big shot: he has a belt on his belly, and on his fur coat he has a tu-, tu-, tu-, tu-tulip."

A second verse goes:

> "See, see, see, how the farmer is stupid: he goes in the field with two watches, see, see, see, how stupid he is." [5]

Reminiscent of the Kecal/Jeník duet, another verse has:

> "His Mařena, she has lots, lots, lots, of dukats [money]." [6]

Quick and fiery, with its characteristic hemiolas, the *furiant* was definitely a village dance (although Link did come up with a tame version for the *beseda*). Attendance today at folk dance concerts in the Czech Republic, or at the graduation concert of conservatory folk dance majors in Prague, reveals just how virtuosic, colorful, and earthy folk dance can be. The fast, virtuosic *furiant* was danced by couples, but featured the men. In fact, the word *furiant* has two meanings in Czech—besides being the name of the dance, *furiant* can mean "a proud, swaggering, conceited man." In 1887, Ladislav Stroupežnický (1850–1892) wrote the first Czech realist play, *Naše furianti*, which the Prague National Theatre translates as "Our uppish and defiant fellows." [7] Here lies part of the interpretation of the dance—finding the virile, one-upmanship, "macho" character of the dance, which grows out of the men's beer chorus. The more macho, the better, as who shows up right after this but the poor, stuttering, scared Vašek! (And Kecal had just sung in the Act I trio that Vašek is no *furiant*.) Some recent Czech solutions have been to choreograph a fight among the men, with the women intervening (see "Choreographers").

Skočná

Very fast, loud, and in duple meter, the *skočná* was one of the most difficult and virtuosic of the Bohemian folk dances. It was only danced by peasants, and like the polka and furiant, it was danced by couples. The word *skočná* means "jumping," and the steps involve a sharp jump and fast spinning. No matter how elaborate the *kroje*, they did not hinder the dancers, however, but added to the color and excitement. The *skočná* also often had fun or funny texts. One example from the Plzeň region is:

> "Our man can't go to bed without a stool, our man can't get on the couch without a stool: our woman jumps up and pushes him a stool—climb up, old man, I'll help push your leg." [8]

A stylized, virtuosic *skočná* by Smetana can be heard in his second set of *České tance* [Czech dances] for piano, from 1879. It ends the set. Fast, loud, exciting, virtuosic, fun, funny—these are all words to describe the *skočná*, which in *Prodaná nevěsta* is soon taken over by the antics of the Komedianti.

Sung Dances

During staging rehearsals for the twenty-seventh production of *Prodaná nevěsta* at the Prague National Theatre in May 1999, conductor Bohumil Ku-línský pointed out how the wonderful fight duet between Jeník and Mařenka is very much like a *csárdás*. The dance had made its way from Hungary to the Czech lands via Slovakia. The opera duet, with its duple meter and alternating slower and faster tempi, does sound much like the dance.

In 1864, a famous French dancer of the *cancan*, Marguerite Bedel (stage name "Rigolboche," also known as "Corilla") performed at the Prague Novo-městské divadlo, and caused a sensation. Sabina's original libretto to *Prodaná nevěsta* had the Principál describing how Esmeralda would dance the *cancan* in the manner of the world-renowned "Miss Rigolboche."[9] Smetana deleted those words, but he seems to have paid homage to the dance in Esmeralda's duet with the Principál. With its rhythmic pattern of ♪♪♪♪ ♩ ♩ , singing of how Vašek will dance in his bear suit, the duet is a slowed-down, gentle, charming version of the *cancan*.

Even if particular sung numbers cannot be labeled specifically with a dance name, they are still often suggestive of dances. The *sousedská* was a common Bohemian dance similar to the Austrian *Ländler*, in a moderate tempo in triple meter. A couple's dance, it was predominantly lyrical, free, and bound with its sung words, which could be cheerful or sorrowful.[10] The opening of Mařenka's first aria, then, or the beginning of Jeník's "Utiš se, utiš se" are suggestive of the *sousedská*. John Tyrrell points out how even before Smetana added the polka, furiant, and skočná to the opera, there was an underlying dance element throughout much of the work already. This, he says, consists of frequent types of motion of the *beseda*—slow to moderate triple time, and moderate to fast duple time. Some extended numbers, like the Kecal/Jeník duet, alternate the two, also typical of *beseda*. It is near the end of the opera, where events turn darker—and Sabina accordingly changed verse meters—that the dance element breaks off. All this explains why the added dances worked so well:

> "When Smetana added dances to later versions of *The Bartered Bride*, he was not weakening an operatic structure but consolidating one based essentially on dance."[11]

Choreographers

Augustin Berger, Otakar Bartík, and Achille Viscusi

The staged dances of *Prodaná nevěsta* that we enjoy today are a far cry from what audiences experienced in 1869. After the Provisional Theatre opened in 1862, opera, drama, and orchestra all had independent Czech companies to carry out the Czechs' artistic goals. The ballet company, however, was very much in its infancy, and had to be shared between Prague's Czech theater and its German one. It was not until 1860 that Prague even had a Czech-born ballet master, Václav (also known as "Julius Wentzel") Reisinger (1828–92), head at the German theater. The whole period of the Provisional Theatre was ruled by ballerinas, who, if need be, disguised themselves as men simply because male dancers were even more scarce than they are today.

When *Braniboři v Čechách* premiered in 1866, the paper *Národní listy* remarked how the ballet "offended the eyes." After Smetana assumed leadership at the Provisional Theatre a few months later, he oversaw both opera and ballet. The next year one of the top solo dancers, the German-speaking Marie Hentz, was appointed as the new ballet mistress, and in 1868 she became the head of a new ballet school for theaters. When Smetana added the dances to *Prodaná nevěsta* in 1869, twelve women danced, all wearing short ballet skirts—no men, no *kroje*. This continued throughout the 1870s. The strongest folk elements in the whole opera looked the least folk on the stage!

By 1877 the ballet company consisted of four soloists and twelve corps dancers who served operas, operettas, plays, and ballets. They were often getting bad reviews. The ballet school had twenty-four students. One of Hentz's handpicked students was Augustin Berger (1861–1945), who would soon become instrumental in developing the national ballet.

In 1882, Reisinger returned to Prague from almost twenty years of international work that had included choreographing the first *Swan Lake*, in Moscow in 1877. He quickly assumed many duties as ballet master again, one of which was to take over the choreography of the dances in *Prodaná nevěsta*. His work was an instant hit with artists, critics, and the public. In 1883, Berger also returned from outside work in Germany, Italy, and even a circus. He, too, was quickly engaged to work at the theater, first as a dancer. By now it was traditional to have a *paňáca*—a clown much like Pierrot—performing in the Komediant scene in *Prodaná nevěsta*. The *paňáca* had always been danced by a woman, but Berger convinced Reisinger to let him dance it. He asserted, too, that a male should be dancing in the polka and furiant, and he soon joined these dances. By late in the year, Berger was collaborating with Reisinger in choreographing the dances, and soon Berger had the women replace their ballet skirts with beautiful traditional *kroje*. When *Prodaná nevěsta* played for the first time in the new National Theatre on November 18, 1883, the ballet members had more than doubled to twenty-two corps dancers, three female soloists, and Berger; and the choreography had finally caught up to the rest of the staging—even though Berger was still the only male in the polka and furiant. In his biography, Berger movingly recalled meeting the ailing Smetana, who had seen a performance, given his approval, and complimented Berger's work. In 1884, Berger was appointed the new ballet master of the National Theatre and head of the ballet school. He was to serve twice, the first time from 1884 to 1900.[12]

As Berger built up his company, he hired a young Czech male dancer, Otakar Bartík (1868–1936). Quite ambitious, Bartík soon grew bored with his modest role in the corps de ballet and left to dance as a soloist in Munich for five years. Berger's and Bartík's paths would cross again in about forty years in New York City, where they would find themselves working together on *Prodaná nevěsta* at the Metropolitan Opera. Joining them would be a young Ruth Page making her debut at the Met.

Bartík's journey from Munich to the Met reads like an adventure novel. From Munich, he worked for a short while in Bayreuth, and then was hired as ballet master and choreographer at the German theater in Prague. Unsatisfied, he left there after only one year and became ballet master and choreographer in Zagreb, where one of his dancers was Achille Viscusi. Bartík soon found a better opportunity in Amsterdam, worked for a circus, and then found work again in Germany. He then joined Brettschneider's "flying ballet," and toured Russia, Asia, Africa, Australia, and America. In America, he worked for a troupe performing on a showboat down the Mississippi River, and then stayed for a while in Chicago, where there was a large Czech community. There, in 1905, he founded the "First Czech Vaudeville Theater," and joined Anna Pavlova's company. Still not content, Bartík moved to New York City where he finally put down roots for more than a few years.[13]

Meanwhile, Berger had given even more meaning to the dances in *Prodaná nevěsta*, so that, for example, the polka was now danced by the whole village. His choreography certainly contributed to the success of the opera at the National Theatre's tour to the International Exhibition of Music and Theater in Vienna in 1892. That pivotal National Theatre production ran from 1892 to 1909. Berger found himself in great demand choreographing the dances again as the opera premiered in houses in Vienna, Berlin, and Warsaw soon after the famous performance.[14]

The Italian dancer Achille Viscusi (1869–1945), trained at La Scala, replaced Berger as ballet master of the National Theatre from 1900 to 1912. When Viscusi choreographed the 1909 Prague production of *Prodaná nevěsta*, he was praised for how quickly and "better than his predecessor" he understood the style and character of Czech folk dance. Breaking Italian tradition, he replaced the straight quadrille with the circle dance, thus adding to the folk quality, and inserted more men in the dances.[15]

In New York, Bartík was approached by Gustav Mahler to choreograph the dances for the Met's first performance of *Prodaná nevěsta* on February 19, 1909. Bartík, known as "Ottokar Bartik" in America, imported six couples of dancers from Prague and blended them with Czech-American girls from Sokol societies to dance the polka. The virtuosic furiant was danced by six soloists— five women and Bartík. When the Met toured to Chicago with *Prodaná nevěsta* in April, the polka was applauded for so long that it had to be repeated. With this success, Bartík was engaged for other productions at the Met through 1928. True to his nature, he soon, however, branched out into other ventures in between engagements. He became a manager to Czech artists, even gaining Ema Destinnová (Emmy Destinn) as a client soon after her Met *Prodaná nevěsta* performance. Czech-American dancer and writer Libushka Bartusek Brown (1896–

1999) recalled how as a teenager she introduced herself in Czech to Destinnová after the opening night of *La Gioconda* (November 15, 1909), and Destinnová introduced her in turn to her manager, Bartík. Bartík then invited Bartusek to his hotel the next day with an offer to join the ballet of the Ringling Brothers Circus. Bartusek declined, and would go on to receive acclaim herself for *Prodaná nevěsta* (see below), and as a translator of the opera libretto (see appendix A). Bartík, like Berger before him, had joined the circus in Europe, and became ballet master for both Barnum and Bailey and the Ringling Brothers in the United States. He also performed with William Cody's combined Buffalo Bill and Pawnee Bill shows.[16]

Berger returned to the National Theatre in Prague to replace Achille Viscusi as ballet master from 1912 to 1922. Berger had had much success in Dresden, Milan, and even occasionally guesting in Prague. With *Prodaná nevěsta*, he took to revising Viscusi's choreography, and then served as choreographer for the next 1915–23 production with Kovařovic. After Berger left, the infamous Ostrčil/Pujman stylized production that ran from 1923 to 1934 (see chapter 2) was mounted, with choreography by Pujman himself. One critic stated that Pujman had "laid the foundations of a new Czech ballet," while another denounced the dancing as "sheer childish twirling." It was revised by the new ballet master, Remislaw Remislawský (1897–1973), who served his post from 1923 to 1927.[17]

Berger was next hired by the New York Metropolitan Opera as ballet master, working from 1923 to 1932. His tenure was highly successful, cut off only by illness that led to his retirement. After his arrival in New York, Berger was looking forward to seeing Bartík again after so many years, but they did not meet again until 1925, when the Met was preparing a new production of *Prodaná nevěsta*. The Met head Giulio Gatti-Gasazza (1869–1940) explained to Berger that he wanted Berger to choreograph the new production, using the Met's corps de ballet this time instead of girls from Czech-American societies. However, Gatti-Gasazza's soon-to-be bride, prima ballerina Rosina Galli (1906–69), had pointed out how well known Bartík was to Czech-Americans and others from the previous famous production. Gatti-Gasazza asked Berger to allow Bartík to choreograph one of the dances, preferably the circus scene. Berger sacrificed his fond memories of being the *paňáca*, and agreed. For the 1926 premiere, Berger thought Bartík had gone too far in his choreography, even using dancers on the high wire. Olin Downes of the *New York Times*, who had seen the Prague Ostrčil/Pujman production two years earlier (probably the revised version), criticized Berger's dances as being

> ". . . devitalized, with girls dressed as men, and as incapable as they were unaware of the virility and sweep of the movements of the Czech folk dances."

Downes was more enthusiastic the next season, when Ruth Page made her Met debut in the polka and furiant. For the new, short-lived production in 1933, Rosina Galli took over with her own choreography.[18]

Also in 1926, Berger was hired to choreograph the *Prodaná nevěsta* dances for a production at Covent Garden. He chose a corps of twenty-four dancers and two female soloists, one of whom danced as a man, and staged the dances "like everywhere before." He had no *paňáca*, though. After thoughts of reenacting the part himself, he decided to use two acrobats instead.[19]

Bartík enjoyed attending one last New York performace of *Prodaná nevěsta* on March 26, 1931, before returning to his native Czechoslovakia. It was not at the Met, but at New York's Heckscher Theatre with the Little Theatre Opera Company, performed in New York for the first time in English. In the production, a young Risë Stevens was making her solo opera debut as Ludmila.[20]

Joe Jenčík and Saša Machov

At the Prague National Theatre, the progressive choreographer Joe (Josef) Jenčík (1893–1945) staged the dances of *Prodaná nevěsta* for a string of productions that played from 1932 to 1949. Jenčík, who had studied with Achille Viscusi, brought more drama to the dances. For example, he contrasted graceful women with rough men in the polka and furiant; he began the polka with an elderly couple who yielded to more and more youthful dancers; he had a single "farmboy" dance the furiant, with all the drinkers in the pub joining in, etc. The circus scene was either a showcase for acrobats, the *paňáca*, and jugglers, or a ballet pantomime. Because of his leftist leanings, Jenčík's name was omitted from programs and posters for a while during the Nazi occupation, and he was only allowed to work as a guest at the National Theatre. He was soon reinstated as ballet master, however, until 1943.

Following Jenčík's death, the great Czech choreographer and stage director Saša Machov (František Mat'ha) (1903–51) choreographed the 1949 postwar production of *Prodaná nevěsta* at the National Theatre, also dancing in the polka and furiant in the production. The opera ballet company had just been formed in 1948, splitting off from the ballet company. For *Prodaná nevěsta*, however, Machov is more well known for his work in 1943 at Sadler's Wells in London under head Joan Cross (see appendix A). The opera probably would not have been presented then were it not for Machov. The theater's misgivings about producing the opera had hinged on the dances, which the administration considered to play a fundamental role, and which they wanted to be as authentic as possible:

". . . [Edward Joseph Dent] had constantly warned against attempting it unless there was an absolutely first class ballet, and the Czech Government in London released from the army Sasha Machow, their best ballet-master, to help the back row from the Wells ballet; the result had been thrilling."[21]

At the time, Machov was in the army, and had been sent to London to recuperate from malaria, which he had contracted in Africa while fighting Rommel's troops. The Czechoslovakian president-in-exile, Edvard Beneš (1884–1948) was in attendance at the London premiere. The dances were a great success, and the entire production was hailed for capturing the spirit of the work, and for never descending into caricature or "burlesque." Machov had helped considerably with the entire production, opening the door for his development as an opera stage director. He returned to Sadler's Wells to direct as well as choreograph wonderful productions of *Prodaná nevěsta* in 1945 and 1947, along with directing other operas there, in Brno, and in Prague. Machov played a pivotal role in developing the ballet company at the Prague National Theatre as choreographer in 1946 and head of ballet in 1948 until his suicide in 1951. For their English edition of *Prodaná nevěsta*, Joan Cross and Eric Crozier wrote:

> "This version is dedicated with affection and gratitude to the memory of Saša Machov, dancer, choreographer, soldier and friend."[22]

Ruth Page and Libushka Bartusek

After her 1926 New York Met debut in *Prodaná nevěsta*, the great dancer and choreographer Ruth Page (1899–1991) took over the Ravinia ballet the same year. In 1930, she choreographed and danced in the polka and furiant in *Prodaná nevěsta* presented by the Ravinia Opera, to great acclaim. In December of the same year, a different production of *Prodaná nevěsta*, with a completely different cast, opened at Chicago's Civic Opera. Singled out by critic Edward Moore for her exceptional dancing in the furiant was ballet mistress Libushka Bartusek (1896–1999). The Czech-American Bartusek had been inspired as a child to become a dancer when she saw the prima ballerina Anna Korecká (1880–1938) in *Prodaná nevěsta* at the Prague National Theatre around 1905. She went on to choreograph the dances in a 1933 production at Chicago's Garrick Theatre that utilized her own English translation.[23]

George Balanchine and Boris Romanoff

The legendary George Balanchine (1904–83) choreographed the dances for the first English-language production of *Prodaná nevěsta* at the Met in 1936, using members of his newly-formed American Ballet. In the production was the dancer and choreographer Ruthanna Boris (1919–2007), who would leave the Met in 1942 to join the Ballet Russe de Monte Carlo. The conservative critic Olin Downes stated that the ballet's dancing was

> ". . . better than has usually been the case, though dancing which remained a long way from the goal of professional finish or from a style indubitably Bohemian."[24]

He thought the entire production, though commendable in many respects, had fallen short of capturing the Czech spirit of the work, and he asked why Bartík's original 1909 choreography, "a famous feature of the production," had not been used instead.[25] Balanchine and his company had teamed up with the Met to bring "freshness, youth and novelty" to the opera house, but for several reasons their marriage did not last long. Composer and critic Virgil Thomson (1896–1989) thought it was due to a basic incompatibility between the dancers' movements and those of the singers—Balanchine's ballet style was full of explosive energy, tension, and vigor, inherited from Russia, while the singers used slow, broad, soft gestures, inherited from France and Italy. Furthermore, the Met had never allowed dancers to rehearse with the orchestra, in order to save money and time. For *Prodaná nevěsta*, the conductor had made cuts in the dances, but no one had bothered to tell Balanchine. The performance, then, was chaotic for the dancers, and critics responded accordingly.[26]

Both Downes and Thomson gave overall bad reviews for the 1941 Met production of *Prodaná nevěsta*, which unarguably failed to capture the spirit of the work (see chapter 2). This included the choreography by Russian-American Boris Romanoff (1892–1957), ballet director at the Met from 1938 to 1950:

> ". . . their atrocious unfitness and ineptitude should be pointed out. . . It was quickly evident yesterday that neither the dancers or the ballet master had the faintest ideas of what they were all about. . . As it turned out, one witnessed an ensemble and solo dancers in coy and silly posturings. . . . It wasn't even technically sound."[27]

Other American Choreographers

The Russian-American Adolf Bolm (1884–1951) had entered the United States in 1916 as director of the original Ballet Russes. After choreographing at the Met from 1918–26, he moved to the West Coast and successfully choreographed the dances in *Prodaná nevěsta* when the San Francisco Opera presented the work for the first time in 1934.[28]

As much as Olin Downes condemned New York City Opera's first performance of *Prodaná nevěsta* in 1945, he did praise the choreography by Carl Randall (1898–1965) as "strong and so redolent of the Czech soil." The next year, the work of the Russian-American Igor Schwezoff (1904–82) was singled out for greatly enlivening the production. Similarly, the opera company's next production in 1955 was soundly denounced except for the choreography of Ray Harrison (1917–81), where "the Czech spirit was most convincing."[29]

Noted American dancer and choreographer Todd Bolender (1914–2006) choreographed the dances in *Prodaná nevěsta* for the Juilliard American Opera Center in 1973. He seemed to have succeeded in conveying a folk character, even though his dancers were often on pointe![30]

For the 1984 production of *Prodaná nevěsta* at Chicago Opera Theater, the audience appears to have been transported back to the work's early history as the critic asked:

"Are qualified male dancers so scarce in the city that girls must be enlisted to partner other girls *en travesti*?"[31]

The wonderful artist Daniel Pelzig (b. 1955) served as resident choreographer for the Boston Ballet from 1995 to 1999, and began choreographing at the Met in 2007. He served as both choreographer and stage director for the Opera Boston 2009 production of *Prodaná nevěsta*. Setting the opera in Spillville, Iowa, in 1934, Pelzig enlisted six dancers, and had the polka begin as part of an impromptu baseball game. Said the inspired Pelzig:

"The dancing is folkloric, which is where my own dance history began. I loved the *weight* of that kind of movement, and I still do; it comes from people's guts."[32]

Pavel Šmok and Other Czech Choreographers

Just as the Czech nation's national opera was usually musically prepared in Prague by the head of opera, or dramatically by the head of the National Theatre, so were the dances usually prepared by the head of the National Theatre ballet. Vlastimil Jílek (1925–96) became head of ballet from 1951 to 1953 after Machov's death, and choreographed the 1953–59 production of *Prodaná nevěsta*. He also danced in four productions at the National Theatre. For the Opera Company of Boston's performance under Sarah Caldwell in 1973, Jílek both choreographed and appeared as the leading male dancer.[33]

Antonín Landa (1916–95) danced in three productions of *Prodaná nevěsta* choreographed by Jenčík, Machov, and Jílek before becoming head of ballet from 1953 to 1957. Landa choreographed both the 1955 production that embodied Socialist Realism and toured to Moscow, and the 1958 stylized production that toured to Brussels.

Jiří Němeček (1924–91) next took over as head of ballet from 1957 to 1970, and again from 1979 to 1989. During his long tenure, the ballet became a truly equal partner to the other ensembles at the National Theatre. Němeček was choreographer for the 1967 and 1982 productions of *Prodaná nevěsta*.

Emerich Gabzdyl (1908–93) took over as head of ballet from 1970 to 1974, and choreographed the 1971 production (starring Gabriela Beňačková). The highly successful production, which ran for eleven years, 239 performances, definitely succeeded in evoking a folk quality, even though Gabzdyl's choreography tended more toward ballet than folk dance.[34]

The great Miroslav Kůra (b. 1924) was next head of ballet from 1974 to 1978. He had danced as the *paňáca* in the 1955 *Prodaná nevěsta* choreographed by Landa. Kůra then choreographed the 1963 production, while also performing in all three dances.

Dancer and choreographer Petr Zuska (b. 1968) was appointed head of ballet in 2002. He choreographed the short-lived 2004 production with Dohnányi and Nekvasil.[35]

Remaining recent productions were choreographed by non-heads of ballet. Pavel Šmok (b. 1927) both choreographed and directed the highly successful 1992 production with Bohumil Gregor. One example of how well Šmok integrated the dancers and the singers occurred in the furiant—the dance began with the men quarreling over money that Kecal had just thrown on the table after extolling the virtues of money over love. The women dancers then entered, taking the men's minds off the money and on to love, a virtue that Jeník had argued to Kecal. This was also the only production in which the character of Franta, the Komediant too drunk to play the bear, appeared in the flesh. He is only mentioned by the Indián, but Šmok played the character himself in one or two performances early in the run. Šmok had first choreographed *Prodaná nevěsta* for the 1978 New York Met production. Although one critic denounced his work in New York as "mostly dull filler,"[36] the overwhelming majority of critics and opera-goers were swept away by Šmok's ebullient natural fusion of movement and music.[37]

Libor Vaculík (b. 1957), a highly successful and versatile dancer and choreographer, choreographed the 1999 production of *Prodaná nevěsta*. He presented a joyous, traditional polka, and had a different take on the furiant as a fight among the men with the women intervening.

Ladislava Košíková (b. 1957) became the first woman since the early history of *Prodaná nevěsta* to stage the opera's dances at the Prague National Theatre. This was for the twenty-ninth production, in 2008, in which Magdalena Švecová became the actual first female stage director of the work in Prague. Košíková, whose inspiration has come mainly from folk dance and culture, has been lauded internationally for her work.[38]

Notes

1. Josef Štefánek, ed., *O lidovém tanečním umění* (Prague: Orbis, 1954), 89–90.

2. Karel Link, *Beseda, český salonní tanec*, 2nd ed. (Prague: A. Storch Syn, 1882), 1–3, 18–19.

3. František Bonuš, *Tance, písně a hudba Plzeňského kraje* (Prague: Státní nakladatelství Krásné literatury, hudby a umění, 1955), 76.

4. To be sure, some just lip-synch! Many thanks to my wife, Bohuslava Jelínková, who danced in three productions of *Prodaná nevěsta* over a ten-year period at the National Theatre, for her insights.

5. The *furiant* was more typically known as the *sedlák* [farmer] among villagers. Bonuš, *Tance, písně a hudba Plzeňského kraje*, 117. The folk song is from the nineteenth-century collection by Karel Jaromír Erben, *Nápěvy písní národních v Čechách*, vol. 2 (Prague: J. Hoffmann, no date), 112.

6. Karel Link, *Beseda, český salonní tanec*, 2nd ed., 51.

7. The play depicts life in a South Bohemian village, including rivalry over who will be "first farmer." "*Our uppish and defiant fellows*," *Národní divadlo*, http://www.narodni-divadlo.cz (29 May 2009).

8. Bonuš, *Tance, písně a hudba Plzeňského kraje*, 78–79, 81.

9. Jan Panenka, and Taťána Součková, *Prodaná nevěsta na jevištích Prozatímního a Národního divadla 1866–2004* (Prague: Gallery and Národní divadlo, 2004), 25.

10. Bonuš, *Tance, písně a hudba Plzeňského kraje*, 94.

11. John Tyrrell, *Czech opera* (Cambridge: Cambridge University Press, 1988), 228–29.

12. In the 1890s, Berger also hired a young Czech pianist for the ballet company, the famous operetta composer Rudolf Friml (1879–1972), whom he would also meet later in New York. Ladislav Hájek, *Paměti Augustina Bergra: Choreografa a baletního mistra národního divadla v Praze a několika světových scén* (Prague: Orbis, 1942), 19, 123–24, 199–200; Božena Brodská, *Dějiny českého baletu do roku 1918* (Prague: Akademie múzických umění, 1983), 56–57, 61–62, 69–71, 74, 77; and Panenka and Součková, *Prodaná nevěsta na jevištích Prozatímního a Národního divadla 1866–2004*, 35, 44.

13. Ladislav Novák, *O těch, kteří odešli* (Prague: Máj, 1940), 127–28.

14. Hájek, *Paměti Augustina Bergra*, 176, 184–199; and Panenka and Součková, *Prodaná nevěsta na jevištích Prozatímního a Národního divadla 1866–2004*, 49.

15. Brodská, *Dějiny českého baletu do roku 1918*, 113, 137; and Panenka and Součková, *Prodaná nevěsta na jevištích Prozatímního a Národního divadla 1866–2004*, 76.

16. Novák, *O těch, kteří odešli*, 131–32; Libushka Bartusek Brown, *Everything but circus and burlesque* (Oak Park, Ill.: Libushka Bartusek Brown, 1994), 10 (Bartusek had written 1915 for the premiere of *La Gioconda*, but it was in 1909.); "Two operas sung to big audiences," *Chicago Daily Tribune*, 18 April 1909, 6–7; "Ottokar Bartik," *MetOpera Database*, http://archives.metoperafamily.org/archives/ frame.htm (11 May 2009); and Alma Mahler, *Gustav Mahler: Memories and letters*, 3d ed., translated by Basil Creighton, edited by Donald Mitchell (Seattle: University of Washington Press, 1975), 131.

17. Panenka and Součková, *Prodaná nevěsta na jevištích Prozatímního a Národního divadla 1866–2004*, 71, 88, 95, 97.

18. Hájek, *Paměti Augustina Bergra*, 319–20; Olin Downes, "Opera," *New York Times*, 29 January 1926, 18; Olin Downes, "Opera," *New York Times*, 8 February 1927, 20; "Bartered Bride," *MetOpera Database*, http://archives.metoperafamily.org/archives/ frame.htm (16 May 2009).

19. Hájek, *Paměti Augustina Bergra*, 320–21.

20. "Extends run of opera," *New York Times*, 27 March 1931, 34.

21. Hugh Carey, *Duet for two voices: An informal biography of Edward Dent compiled from his letters to Clive Carey* (Cambridge: Cambridge University Press, 1980), 177; and Panenka and Součková, *Prodaná nevěsta na jevištích Prozatímního a Národního divadla 1866–2004*, 101, 106, 122, 123.

22. Bedřich Smetana and Karel Sabina, *Prodaná nevěsta*, piano/vocal score, English translation by Joan Cross and Eric Crozier (London: Boosey & Hawkes, 1945, rev.1978), ii; and Vladimír Vašut, *Saša Machov* (Prague: Panorama, 1986), 97–103, 250–51.

23. For the Ravinia Festival, see chapter 2. Also see "Debuts" in chapter 2 for more on Ruth Page. Bartusek, who died at the age of 103, saw the famous tenth production at the Prague National Theatre that played until 1909, and that had toured to Vienna in 1892. Kopecká had been a student of Berger, who choreographed the production. Bartusek Brown, *Everything but circus and burlesque*, 53–54; Edward Moore, "*The Bartered Bride* becomes triumph at first presentation," *Chicago Daily Tribune*, 26 December 1930, 19; Robert C. Marsh, *150 years of opera in Chicago*, completed and edited by Norman Pellegrini (Dekalb, Ill.: Northern Illinois University Press, 2006), 102; and Edward Moore, "Opera you can understand gets enthusiastic welcome," *Chicago Daily Tribune*, 4 December 1933, 21.

24. Olin Downes, "*Bartered Bride* delights audience," *New York Times*, 16 May 1936, 10.

25. Olin Downes, "*Bartered Bride* is well received," *New York Times*, 26 December 1936, 14.

26. Bernard Taper, *Balanchine*. (New York: Harper & Row, 1960), 178–79, 180, 181.

27. The quote is by Olin Downes, "*Bartered Bride* at Metropolitan," *New York Times*, 1 March 1941, 8. See Virgil Thomson, "Czechish merry-go-round," *New York Herald Tribune*, 1 March 1941, at *MetOpera Database*, http://archives.metoperafamily. org/ archives/frame.htm (14 May 2009).

28. "San Francisco Opera begins new season," *New York Times*, special to the *New York Times*, 15 November 1934, 24; "Adolf Bolm, 67, a ballet dancer," *New York Times*, 17 April 1951, 29; and "Adolf Bolm," *MetOpera Database*, http://archives.metopera family.org/archives/frame.htm (16 May 2009).

29. Olin Downes, "*Bartered Bride* heard in English," *New York Times*, 4 October 1945, 26; R.L., "Miss Manners sings in *Bartered Bride*," *New York Times*, 12 May 1946, 42; and E.D., "*Bartered Bride* sung," *New York Times*, 4 November 1955, 23.

30. Harold C. Schonberg, "Opera: *Bartered Bride* at Juilliard," *New York Times*, 16 December 1973, 75.

31. John von Rhein, "*Bride* escapes handmaiden status," *Chicago Tribune*, 2 April 1984, D C4.

32. Richard Dyer, "Daniel Pelzig profile," *Opera Boston*, http://www.operaboston. org/operas_bride_ special features.php (18 May 2009), 1, 3; and Iris M. Fanger, "Daniel Pelzig: New kid in town," *Dance Magazine* 70, no. 10 (October 1996): 54–57.

33. "Vlastimil Jílek," *Národní divadlo*, http://archiv.narodni-divadlo.cz (14 May 2009); Raymond Ericson, "Opera: *Bartered Bride* fascinates and maddens," *New York Times*, 28 January 1973, Special to the *New York Times*, 49.

34. "Antonín Landa," "Jiří Němeček," and "Emerich Gabzdyl," *Národní divadlo*, http://archiv.narodni-divadlo.cz (18 May 2009); and Panenka and Součková, *Prodaná nevěsta na jevištích Prozatímního a Národního divadla 1866–2004*, 162.

35. "Miroslav Kůra," and "Petr Zuska," *Národní divadlo*, http://archiv.narodni-divadlo.cz (18 May 2009).

36. Allan Kozinn, *New York Times*, 7 October 1996, C12.

37. See, for example, John W. Freeman, "In review," *Opera News* 61, no. 7 (28 December 1996): 41.

38. "Libor Vaculík," and "Ladislava Košíková," *Národní divadlo*, http://archiv. narodni-divadlo.cz (18 May 2009).

Ta naše písnička česká, ta je tak hezká jako na louce kytička.
(That Czech song of ours is beautiful like a flower on the meadow.)
Song by Karel Hašler (1879–1941)

4

Characters (Osoby)

Czech opera—and Slavic opera in general—is not about high notes. Singers must have a wide range, but it is their *middle* that should be full. As an example, take the tenor role of the Prince in Dvořák's *Rusalka*, surely one of the most wonderful tenor parts in all of opera. The Prince has only one high C near the very end of the whole opera. That high C is only a quarter note, and Dvořák marks it *nekřičet*, "don't scream!"[1]

To be sure, Janáček can make huge demands on the upper ranges of his singers. His approach is not typically Italianate, however. The Slavic operatic repertoire is especially lacking in high coloratura sopranos, and Smetana rarely used coloratura for any voice type. (This is not to say that there are not some wonderful Slavic coloratura sopranos. They just usually sing other repertoire.) On the other hand, despite the fact that many Czech singers in the nineteenth and twentieth centuries found ready work in German opera houses, their training was mainly rooted in the Italian tradition, so that Smetana's writing was more Italian than German. What eventually evolved from singing in the Czech language and portraying distinctly Czech figures—founded largely on the achievements of Smetana—was really a unique, Czech lyrical style. Again, though, it is a style and sound—especially with its bright, Italianate vowels, and unaspirated consonants—that rests on a firm foundation of beautiful singing in the Italian tradition.

Style in *Prodaná nevěsta*

Smetana clearly marks optional notes. No extra ornaments, cadenzas, or high notes should be added.

Being music of the Romantic period, there is plenty of opportunity for expressive *portamenti*, especially for Mařenka. Similarly, *rubato* is part of the style, mainly in the arias.

As discussed earlier, *Prodaná nevěsta* is not an operetta, but a comic folk opera. Except for most of the circus performers, the characters have depth, even in the short roles. Avoid caricatures and mugging, and aim for honest acting—real people in real situations. Writing in 1941, critic Olin Downes described the opera well:

"For this opera is a human comedy. Much of its appeal lies in this reality, in the

71

sympathy, the love, the understanding that the musician and librettist have for their Czech folk. It should not raise merely a laugh. There is more than that in the play and the music. There is tenderness in the composition. . ."[2]

And in 1936:

"In fact all the people in Smetana's comedy feel; they do not merely caper; they are human beings, and not mere farcical puppets or dolls of operetta. Their humanity should be perceived as well as conveyed by the music."[3]

Roles

The roles are presented in the order that Smetana listed them, which is the two families first.

Mařenka's Family

Mařenka's parents do give their daughter a choice, singing that she can kick out the chosen bridegroom if she doesn't like him. Ludmila, especially, shows her concern for her daughter's happiness, and is not as easily persuaded by Kecal. Still, they go along with Kecal when Mařenka protests. The sextet reveals how much they want their daughter to make the right decision for her future happiness. At that point, given Jeník's apparent betrayal, they are doubly sure that marrying Vašek is best.

[kruʃɪna]

Krušina, sedlák [farmer]   baryton

As Smetana marks, Krušina is a baritone. He has the same range as the bass Mícha, but Krušina's high Es must be pianissimo in the sextet.

[ludmɪla]

Ludmila, jeho manželka [his wife]   soprán

[mařɛŋka]

Mařenka, jejich dcera [their daughter]   soprán

"Mařenka" is the diminutive of "Marie." Mařenka is not a soubrette. Apparently, she was played that way enough that Smetana had to protest, saying that hers was not a soubrette role, but a "dramatic" role.[4] The singer needs a decent-sized lyric voice, *full in the middle*. She has two high C's that come in the fight duet with Jeník, and an optional high C at the very end of the opera. All are strong, but none are held very long.

Mařenka is passionate and strongwilled. Her stubborness is an asset when it allows her to stand up to Kecal and her parents, but a weakness when it does not allow her to listen to Jeník's explanation for selling her off. The latter happens, however, because she feels betrayed and not treated as an equal partner. Mařenka reveals her charm and fun-loving nature in the duet with Vašek, where her trickery is not out of malice—it's certainly obvious to her that if she and Vašek were married, they would both be miserable.

Vašek's Family

It is curious that Mařenka and Vašek had never met before. Even if Vašek's doting mother had kept him at home most of the time, everyone would have seen one another in church. We do learn right away that Mícha and his son will be coming to the village to court her, meaning that they live outside the village, probably in some kind of manor by their farm. Somehow, they never saw one another in church. . .

[miːxa]

Mícha, gruntovník [farm owner]   bas

In nonprofessional productions, if Mícha is more of a bass than Kecal, Mícha can trade some of his higher phrases with Kecal's lower ones in the ensembles (see below).

Mícha is the owner of a *grunt*, a "plot of land." This made him fairly well off, in contrast to the *sedlák*, "farmer," who worked the land but didn't own any. (Mařenka calls Mícha a *sedlák* in Act I, sc. ii, but Mícha owns his own farm.)

Because he possesses substantial property, working with a marriage broker to safeguard his wealth would have been common. As small as his part is, we still see Mícha as having his own personality—he is not completely henpecked by Háta, he does head the farm and its assets, and he does welcome his son Jeník back.

[ɦaːta]

Háta, jeho manželka [his wife]   mezzosoprán

Háta is really the only villian in the opera. She loves her son Vašek, but she smothers and controls him—the true reason for his fear and stuttering. She wants a wife for her son, but she knows she can bend any daughter-in-law to do her bidding. For her many faults, we still see her as a complicated human being through the Act III sextet.

[vaʃɛk]

Vašek, jejich syn [their son]   tenor

"Vašek" is the diminutive of "Václav." Kecal makes his name even more endearing when he uses "Vašíček," in the vocative case "Vašíčku." Vašek may have the hardest part musically, as he is constantly singing on off-beats that must sound like stuttering. In the recitatives, the stuttering does not have to be exactly as written.

Vašek is one of the few people in the opera who is not trying to fool someone else. His shyness and stuttering come from his domineering mother. He is, then, an innocent, charming, and likable victim. We both laugh at his pitiful situation and sympathize with him at the same time. He has a simple, warm, innocent humanity and a good-natured character that makes us like him and hope that he and Esmeralda will end up together.[5] Vašek is *not* the town idiot. Though it may be tempting to play him for an easy laugh, Vašek must not be a fool. His quandary is real and touches us all.

[jɛɲiːk]

Jeník, Míchův syn z prvního manzelství
[Mícha's son from his first marriage]   tenor

"Jeník" is the diminutive of "Jan." Mařenka likes to call him by the even more endearing "Jeníček," using the vocative case "Jeníčku." Very self-assured, Jeník seems to have found stability after his wanderings through his love for Mařenka. At first glance, it is difficult to explain his cruelty for not letting Mařenka in on his trick. However, the whole story of the opera takes place in only one day—when we first see Mařenka and Jeník together, he has not yet come up with his plan. Later, she is too outraged to let him explain. Also, given that Jeník has had to fend for himself because of his mean stepmother, he cannot rely on any economic assistance from his family, and he has no way of knowing how his father will react. So, his trick can only safely be revealed in front of witnesses. We know how much he loves Mařenka through his aria. Another side to his personality is his strong need to be trusted—he asks Mařenka several times to trust him.

A full lyric tenor voice and a good actor who can portray the confident, handsome, country boy (but certainly not a bumpkin!) are the ideals for Jeník.

Kecal

[keʦal]

Kecal, vesnický dohazovač
[village marriage broker]   bas

(optional)

With Kecal comes probably the hardest role to cast, both musically and in terms of character. The part begins as a bass-baritone (a term that Smetana never used) and then descends to the bass range. Vocally, he must be as self-assured as his character—all his crazy trills, wide leaps, and constant repetitions are an exact expression of his overblown opinion of himself, and his need to completely convince others to share that opinion. He has more words than anyone else, and they are often in patter.

For nonprofessional productions where it may be difficult to cast a Kecal with a strong low range, it is possible to switch some lines in the ensembles with Mícha, assuming Mícha is more of a true bass. This will also help Mícha:

Act III, sc. iii, quartet:
M. 580 (first measuure) through m. 603, Kecal and Mícha switch parts, including the solo line "Copak, copak se přihodilo?"
M. 632, beat three ("není, není v tom") through m. 639, beat one, switch parts.
M. 647, beat three ("není, není v tom") through m. 665, switch parts.

Act III, sc. v:
M. 794 (Presto) through m. 808.
M. 843 (in the sextet, "Rozmysli si") through m. 887, the end of the sextet.[6]

Kecal has sometimes been played as a conniving swindler. Yet, he really is not this. Somehow, we hate to see him go at the end, this whirlwind figure who truly believes he has all the answers and abilities to provide for the well-being of his fellow villagers. He is perhaps likable because he is so transparent.

Kecal's name comes from the Czech verb *kecat*, "to chatter, to talk too much." It's actually the past participle, as in *kecal*, "he chattered." *Kecat* also translates as "to kid someone," as in *kecáš*, "you're kidding." Kecal can be compared to other East European marriage brokers, such as Fyokla Ivanovna in Nikolai Gogol's (1809–52) comedy *Zhenitba* [The marriage], written in 1842. It was made into an opera (unfinished) by Russian composer Modest Mussorgsky (1839–81) in 1868, and again by Czech composer Bohuslav Martinů (1890–1959) in 1952. Like Kecal, Ivanovna is an energetic chatterbox who has an answer for everything, and is never put off by any issue.[7] There is also Lyubov Grigoryevna in Chekhov's short story "A happy ending," from 1887. Here, however, roles are reversed as the marriage broker can hardly get a word in, and ends up being proposed to by her client.[8]

Kecal is very clear in the men's beer chorus that his formula for happiness is based on money and reason. He is absolutely sure of this and his abilities, and his arguments are delivered with such theatricality and rapidity that he demands the center of everyone's attention. The result is that most people actually listen and follow his advice because they don't have time to think, and Kecal has an answer for everything anyway. In many ways, he carries the show.

Critic Olin Downes (1886–1955), who witnessed the Met premiere of *Prodaná nevěsta* under Mahler, several Met productions after that, and one at the Prague National Theatre, described Kecal as:

> ". . . not a cheap, sly mountebank. He is on the contrary characterized by a certain peasant cunning, but also by a naïveté and sincere faith that his simple stratagems will prove his superior judgment and experience and make for the happiness of those whose lives he has momentarily in his officious care. He is funny, but he appeals to the understanding of the beholder."[9]

Kecal has:

". . . an essential simplicity. He plots for profit but has fellow-feelings for the fortunes of his own people. He is of them and fundamentally naïve—and . . . he is not trying to grab the show."[10]

There are several points that show Kecal is not malicious. The main one is the sextet in Act III, in which we see how Kecal really believes that his actions are for the good and well-being of all involved. In Act I, sc. iv, when Kecal says "Ah, jak svět je zvrácený!" [Ah, how the world is perverse!], after Mařenka refuses to give up Jeník and storms out, Kecal is reacting to a situation that for him goes against reason. Finally, the very end of the opera is telling. How does he take defeat? Kecal is completely dumbfounded that Jeník tricked him, and is at a complete loss about what to do. He is not vengeful, and we sense he may even be impressed with Jeník's cleverness. In any case, we know he will swallow his pride and be back someday, probably soon. He is really more mischievous and cunning than malicious, so that his defeat should still have an engaging energy.

Komedianti

The word *komedianti* is usually translated as "comedians," which is correct, but when it is nonspecific, it means "actors." So, not all *komedianti* are comedians. The *komedianti* in *Prodaná nevěsta* are all comedians to us, but except for any clowns that may be in the show, the characters take themselves as serious performers. This is part of what makes them so funny. These *komedianti* represent a low-budget, tatty, traveling circus that graced the villages of Eastern Europe in this time, and that could have also been seen in America and elsewhere into the twentieth century. If they are too polished and professional, then, the charm and humor are lost. They need to be good, and they need to have fun, colorful costumes, but they shouldn't be *too* good. That being said, one well-placed acrobatic number, or performing dogs, etc. is great, too.

[prɪntsɪpaːl kɔmɛdɪjantuː]

Principál komediantů [Principal comedian]   tenor

(optional)

The Principál is the ringmaster, or circus barker. Part used-car salesman, he can be high-strung, but only when the success of his show is in jeopardy. Profit is not his only motivation, as it shows that he really loves circus life.

[ɛsmɛralda]

Esmeralda, komediantka [comedienne]   soprán

This is the only soubrette part that Smetana ever wrote. Notice her name is *not* "Esmerelda," with an *e*. Looking at many productions at the Prague National Theatre, especially the early ones, she seems to have been modeled on the gypsy heroine Esméralda in *Notre Dame de Paris* [The hunchback of Notre Dame] by Victor Hugo (1802–85), published in 1831. Esmeralda was usually gypsy-like, then, and usually had a tambourine, or occasionally a small drum. She wore a short skirt, and had long, black hair. When Vašek says "That Indian girl has pretty legs!," he may be referring to Esmeralda or to another *komediantka*. Since Esmeralda walks on the high wire, other productions show her wearing more of a tutu. Smetana's character is charming and coquettish, and she sincerely likes Vašek.

[ɪndɪjaːn]

Indián, komediant [comedian]   bas

(optional)

The Principál describes the Indián as "a genuine Indian from the Tahitian islands." We then usually see a non-Indian man dressed in nonauthentic Sioux or Navajo clothing. Here lies the humor—what we are seeing is a nineteenth-century East European circus touring with their perception of an American Indian, who was often not Indian at all. Whether he comes from Tahiti, Oklahoma, or Wyoming does not matter, as all of these places are equally exotic and wild to the villagers.

American Indians appeared regularly in circuses, carnivals, plays, and medicine shows beginning in the 1840s, quickly moving from the United States to Europe. Some were actual Indians, while others were dressed like Indians. The villagers in *Prodaná nevěsta* would not have known the difference. By the time of the plethora of wild west shows from about 1900 to 1917, most notably the *Wild West* show of "Buffalo Bill" Cody (1846–1917), people were not fooled by bad imitation. Most, however, wanted to believe the romanticized stories that had poured into Europe from travelers, novels, and letters from immigrants.[11]

It is interesting to look at the photos of the Indián *komediant* at the Prague National Theatre. Looking at photos from 1909, the Indián could very well have been from some Polynesian island. It's really difficult to tell! Performances at the San Francisco Opera in 1964 and the Hawaii Opera Theatre in Honolulu in 1990 replaced the Indián with "Cannibal." Later photos at the National Theatre show the stereotypical American Indian of most productions.[12] This probably came about from Prague's increased exposure to American Indians through the wild west shows, and eventually through stereotypical portrayals in movies. Buffalo Bill and his group had even performed six times in August 1906 in neighboring Moravia—in Ostrava, Opava, Přerov, Brno, and Jihlava.[13]

Others

[zbɔr]

Sbor   Chorus   SATB

[vɛsɲɪt͡ski: lɪt]

Vesnický lid [village people]

The chorus conveys the communal, and in this setting, festive spirit of the village. Most of the villagers' days is spent with hard work, so they are thrilled to take a day off to celebrate. Within the tight-knit village community, they serve as witnesses to the contract, and openly give their approval or disapproval of all the various events in the opera.

Nonsinging roles are:

[kɔmɛdɪjant'ɪ]

Komedianti [Comedians]

See above for a description of the term komedianti—most were not "comedians."

[klut͡sɪ]

Kluci [boys]

Místo a čas děje: vesnice o posvícení, odpoledne a v podvečer.
Place and time of action: village fair, afternoon and early evening.

Notes

1. Antonín Dvořák, *Rusalka*, piano/vocal score (Kasel: Bärenreiter, 2006), 301.
2. Olin Downes, "*Bartered Bride* at Metropolitan," *New York Times*, 1 March 1941, 8.

3. Olin Downes, "*Bartered Bride* is well received," *New York Times*, 26 December 1936, 14.

4. John Tyrrell, *Czech opera* (Cambridge: Cambridge University Press, 1988), 180.

5. Max Ophül's 1932 movie of the opera did have Vašek running away with Esmeralda at the end. Some productions have done this, as well, such as Opera Boston's in 2009, directed by Daniel Pelzig.

6. Thanks to Jeremiah Butterfield for this, which worked very well in the 2007 University of Michigan production.

7. Nikolai Gogol, *Marriage*, trans. by Bella Costello (Manchester: Manchester University Press, 1969).

8. Anton Chekhov, "A happy ending," in *The horse-stealers and other stories*, vol. 10 of *The tales of Chekhov*, trans. by Constance Garnett (New York: The Macmillan Company, 1921), 141–47.

9. Olin Downes, "*Bartered Bride* is well received," *New York Times*, 26 December 1936, 14.

10. Olin Downes, "*Bartered Bride* at Metropolitan," *New York Times*, 1 March 1941, 8.

11. L.G. Moses, *Wild West shows and the images of American Indians 1883–1933* (Albuquerque: University of New Mexico Press, 1996), 19; and Carolyn Thomas Foreman, *Indians abroad 1493–1938* (Norman, Okla.: University of Oklahoma Press, 1943), 197.

12. See "*Prodaná nevěsta*," *Národní divadlo*, http://archiv.narodni-divadlo.cz/ (8 May 2009).

13. Email to the author from the Buffalo Bill Historical Center, 19 February 2009.

5

Czech Pronunciation and Inflection

For details, see the author's book *Singing in Czech: A Guide to Czech Lyric Diction and Vocal Repertoire*, with a foreword by Sir Charles Mackerras (Scarecrow Press, 2001). This book includes a CD where all the Czech sounds and IPA symbols are fully explained and demonstrated by native Czech opera singers, along with an overview of Czech vocal repertoire.

Czech Lyric Diction and the International Phonetic Alphabet (IPA)

In the following chart the IPA is in quasi-alphabetical order, since it is probably the IPA that the majority of readers will be referring to the most in this book.

IPA	Czech spelling	Nearest equivalent
[ʔ]		Glottal
[a]	a	Italian *fantasma*
[aː]	á	(The same, long)
[b]	b, p	Italian *bambino*
[d]	d, t	(Almost dental) Italian *dove*
[dʼ]	d, dʼ, dˇ, t, tʼ, tˇ	See (7) below; absolutely NOT [dj]
[d͡ʒ]	dž, č	Italian *giubilare*
[d͡z]	c	English *fads*, Italian *zero*
		(The letter *c* is only occasionally voiced, as in *leckdo* [many a person] [lɛd͡zgdɔ])
[ɛ]	e	Italian *celeste*
[ɛː]	é	(The same, long)
[f]	f, v	English *frank*
[g]	g, k	Spanish *gato*
[ɦ]	h, ch	Very close to the English exclamation *Heavens!*
[ɪ]	i, y	See (4) below. German *ich*
[iː]	í, ý	Italian *vino*
[j]	j (and sometimes with ě)	Like English *yes*, but clearer, more distinct
[ⁱ]	j	The same, but as a glide to a consonant or as an off-glide, as in the French *soleil* [sɔlɛⁱ]. See (5) below

[k]	k, g	Spanish *comer*
[l]	l	(Almost dental) Italian *liquido*—not like Russian!
[l̩]	l	The same, but vocalic (with no preceding *schwa*!)
[m]	m	English *music*
[n]	n	(Almost dental) Italian *naso*
[ɲ]	ň, n (mě)	(Never [nj]!) Italian *ogni*
[ŋ]	n	Further back than English *drink*, *sing*
[ɔ]	o	British *hot*
[ɔ:]	ó	(The same, long)
[p]	p, b	Italian *prego*
[r]	r	Italian *caro* or *carro*—roll depending on expression
[rr]	r	Italian *morrò*—if the author believes an *r* is particularly expressive, then he has marked it
[rr]		
[r̩]	r	Vocalic rolled *r*; unlike a vocalic *l*, it should begin with a *schwa* if the note is relatively long
[ř]	ř	See (8) below. No equivalents, voiced
[Ř]	ř	See (8) below. No equivalents, unvoiced
[s]	s, z	Italian *sono*
[ʃ]	š, ž	German *Schule*
[t]	t, d	(Almost dental) Italian *tenere*
[t']	t, t', ť, d, d', ď	See (7) below; absolutely NOT [tj]
[t͡s]	c	English *cats*, German *zu*
[t͡ʃ]	č	Brighter than English *cheek*
[u]	u	Similar to English *pool*
[u:]	ú, ů	(The same, long, and only slightly more closed)
[v]	v, f	Italian *vino*
[x]	ch, h	In between German *ich* and *ach*
[ɣ]	ch, h	Spanish *agua*. This is a voiced Czech [x]
[z]	z, s	Italian *casa*
[ʒ]	ž, š	French *je*

Vowels

(1) Glottals are really not very frequent, but in Czech they *must* be observed. The symbol is [ʔ].

(2) The Czech [a] and all other vowels are bright, like Italian. Czech is the brightest of all the Slavic languages and contrasts greatly with Russian in overall sound.

(3) There is no closed [e] sound in Czech, only its open [ɛ] counterpart. Be especially careful not to close final *e*'s, particularly in the word *se*.

(4) The open [ɪ] represents a sound that is a shade more open than the very closed Czech [iː]. It sits high and bright. The difference between [ɪ] and [iː] is similar to the distinction in German. Slovaks and Moravians tend to close even the short *i*, but formal Czech, particularly in Bohemia, opens the short *i*. This should be very apparent from listening to native Czech singers, where, for example, *byt* [apartment] and *být* [to be] sound very much like the English *bit* and *beat*, respectively. (Recorded examples can also be heard in *Singing in Czech*.) Czechs speak of *quantitative* (vowel length) differences in their vowels, not *qualitative* ones, but this distinction was made very clear to the author by the Czech conductor Bohumil Gregor, who explained the qualitative difference between these two vowels and insisted that they always be clear. Also, the author experienced a perfect lesson on these two vowels during rehearsals of the twenty-seventh production of *Prodaná nevěsta* at the Prague National Theatre. The opera was rehearsed with a triple cast of singers. Certain singers who were Slavic but not Czech sang every *i, y, í,* and *ý* with the same closed quality, [i], as if they were singing in Italian. The difference in their pronunciation and the native Czechs was obvious, and the non-Czechs were repeatedly corrected by the native Czech conductor and the native Czech diction coach to sing *i* and *y* open [ɪ].

(5) Words like *jsem* [ˈsɛm], *jdeme* [ˈdɛmɛ], etc., often omit the quick on-glide [ⁱ] in colloquial Czech, but they *must* be pronounced on the stage.

Consonants

(6) The Czech consonants are forward and unaspirated, very much like Italian.

(7) The sounds [n], [d], and [t] must be softened before the letter *i* or *í*. The following symbols for the three soft consonants are used:

[ɲ] [d'] [t']

The more precise IPA for these three sounds is:

[ɲ] [ɟ] [c]

As explained in *Singing in Czech*, this author has chosen to use [d'] and [t'] because they are the preferred symbols used by Czech linguists and are easier to equate with the sounds they represent. For those singers who have sung in Russian, note that these Czech *palatal* sounds are different from Russian *palatalized* consonants in sound and in formation—all three Czech sounds being formed with the tip of the tongue touching the bottom teeth. Czech has no palatalized consonants. To be especially avoided is the substitution of [nj], [dj], and [tj] for these sounds.

(8) The pronunciation of the Czech written *ř* is shown as follows:

[ř] represents the voiced sound
[Ř] represents the unvoiced sound

Remember that although [ř] is often described as the simultaneous pronunciation of rolled *r* and [ʒ] (and for the unvoiced [Ř] of an *un*voiced rolled *r* and [ʃ]), it is only *one* sound. For example, the word *moře* [sea] must *not* sound like *morže*. The position from which to learn this sound is a smile, not rounded lips. Both sounds are fully explained and demonstrated on a CD by native Czech singers in *Singing in Czech*, along with exercises.

(9) The Czech sound [ɦ], as opposed to the English [h], represents a voiced sound, one that *always* has a pitch. (It is not [x]!)

(10) The combination *mě*, by itself or anywhere in a word, must be pronounced as [mɲɛ], as if the spelling were *mně*. This is formal lyric pronunciation, required in opera. Thus, *měsíčku* is pronounced [mɲesiːt͡ʃku], not [mjɛsiːt͡ʃku].

(11) Double consonants, when performed similar to Italian, are shown with a colon in the IPA:

[sr̩t͡sɛm : miːm]
srdcem   mým

Otherwise, the sounds are rearticulated, or if there is no time, then pronounced as only one consonant. (See the chapter "Double Consonants" in *Singing in Czech*, where most of the double consonants in *Prodaná nevěsta* are used as examples.)

(12) The Czech [x] is not as far back as the German [x], nor as far forward as the German [ç]. Czech linguists use the symbol [x] to represent their sound that is in between the two German ones.

(13) Czech consonants work in voiced and unvoiced pairs, so that according to rules of assimilation a *b* could be pronounced [b] or [p], depending on context. This is why you will see, for example, the word *tak* [so] almost always pronounced [tak], but when Jeník sings very legato to Mařenka *tak zasmušilá* [so sullen] in Act I, sc. i, it is pronounced [tag] because of the voiced *z* after the *k*. There are clear-cut strict rules, and it often depends on whether the music is legato or not. (One rule is that nothing changes before a *v*: *svět* is pronounced [svjɛt], not [zvjɛt]. This is different from Italian, where *svago* is pronounced [zvago]. See "Assimilation" in *Singing in Czech*.)

(14) Consonants are pronounced as printed on the page—i.e., voiced consonants

must be sung on the correct pitches. So, for example, *na mne* must not be sung *nam ne*. The *m* must be sung on the same pitch as *–ne*, and not on the pitch of *na*. Every sound is pronounced as it looks on the page, lining up with the appropriate pitch.

(15) Despite the predominance of consonants, they are not used for expression in the same way as German or English. Emphasizing words comes mainly from the length of the vowels—the longer a long vowel is held, the stronger the word. Occasionally, normally short vowels are lengthened for expression. For consonants, the main exception is *r*, which can be flipped, slightly rolled, or rolled very strongly, all depending on the feelings of the speaker/singer. In this book, supercharged words with r's are marked in the IPA as:

[rr]

This indicates a long, expressive roll. Singers should feel free, however, to roll any r's in words that move them!

Two other consonants tend to be lengthened for expression. They are [s] and [ʃ]. In this book, the IPA is doubled for expressive words, as in the opening chorus, on the word:

[vɛssɛlɛ]
vesele [cheerful]

Czech choruses always double the *s* here (and make the preceding vowel very short). They even double the [ʃ] sound on their opening phrase, not because of the word itself, but because of the overall joyous feeling, on the word:

[ɡdɪʃʃ]
když [when]

Inflection

(1) Czech stress is always on the first syllable, except for prepositions and their objects. In those cases, the preposition takes over the initial stress, and the two words are pronounced as one. In the IPA, this is shown with a slur:

[na ‿ nɛbi]
na   nebi

The words *na nebi* [in heavens], then, are pronounced as if the two words were written *nanebi*, with the stress on *na*. The slur is shown in the IPA even if there is a glottal, as in:

[nat‿ ʔubɔɦiːm]
nad ubohým (over wretched)

Along with other languages that have fixed stress, such as French, Czech stress is gentle.

(2) Length in Czech is a separate issue from stress. Long vowels are clearly marked by the *čárka*—what looks like an accent mark—over the vowel, and are generally about twice as long as short vowels. The longer the long vowels are held, the stronger the word becomes. The letter *u* can have a *čárka* or a *kroužek* (little circle) over its long version, as in *Martinů*. The IPA used to indicate length is a special colon after the long sound:

[dvɔřaːk]
Dvořák

In Dvořák's name, the stress is on the short first syllable, followed by a long unstressed syllable, making for a syncopation:

Dvo - řák

In musical passages, composers usually account for short and long syllables. However, in recitative and free passages, singers often need to "bend" rhythms to obtain the right inflection. So, in the opening pages of "Och, jaký žal," which is an expressive recitative before Mařenka's second aria "Ten lásky sen," the singer should sing the word *jaký* not as two exact eighth notes, but more like a sixteenth followed by a dotted eighth—not precisely, but with this feeling. This bending of rhythms is not unlike Italian recitative, where a stream of equal eighth notes on the page translates to long and short note values when the inflection is delivered naturally. In Czech, mispronouncing a vowel long or short can completely alter the meaning of the word, change its grammatical function, or make the word unintelligible. The "short-long" rhythm, as in *jaký*, is very typical of Czech. Other words in Mařenka's recitative to be "bent" are *nevěřím, stojí, až s ním*, and *v nesnázi*.

Inflection in *Prodaná nevěsta*

Most of the Czech in *Prodaná nevěsta* is set idiomatically—that is, first-syllable stresses occur on downbeats, and long vowels are set longer than short vowels. The main exception to this is the typical Czech "short-long" rhythm, just noted. Even Janáček, who captured the inflection of the language so beautifully, sometimes notates this rhythm "perfectly," and sometimes marks it as two equal notes, leaving it up to the singer to inflect them. Notating this rhythm "incorrectly" as two equal notes is seen throughout Czech vocal literature—in art song, folk song, and in opera. Sometimes this is because it is impossible to notate the exact rhythm. In any case, Czechs naturally "bend" the rhythm unless the music is too rhythmic to allow it. These "short-long" rhythms, and others, too, occur so frequently throughout *Prodaná nevěsta*, that the author has not bothered to note them in Part II. After determining that the music allows for it, they should be marked to show that short vowels will be rushed so that long vowels can be held longer. One typical example is in the first recitative in Act I, mm. 505-506, where Jeník sings:

The word *smutné* should be sung more like:

Even in nonrecitative, musical passages, Czech singers will naturally bend some rhythms if the music allows for it. Thus, in Kecal's opening phrases, in Act I, sc. iii, although his music looks like this:

It is sung more like this, especially the word *pravím*:

Occasionally, the music must actually be rewritten. For example, at Jeník's first entrance in Act I, his music is written:

The stress is set wrong on *zasmušila*, but the tempo is slow and legato enough that *za-* can still be stressed. *Mařenko* is also set wrong, but it can be attributed to the rare cases when Czechs stress the wrong syllable for special expression, here to be especially affectionate and concerned. (Occasionally the name *Jeníč-ku* is also stressed wrong when Mařenka uses this endearing double-diminutive for her beloved.)[1] However, the vowel lengths in *drahá* are incorrect, and this is just too much with the other mis-stressed words in the phrase. So, Czech tenors sing this phrase as:

There are a few other places where this happens in the opera, and these are noted for the reader within Part II.

Remember that vowel length is a characteristic distinct from stress, which should come on the first syllables of words. Sometimes, however, Smetana does not write the first syllable on a strong beat, as just seen. Instead, he sets it as an upbeat, and puts the second syllable on a strong beat. When this happens in a recitative, often this is only visual. For example, in the very first recitative, Jeník sings in m. 3:

Since this is recitative, even though it is marked in common time, there is no real meter. There is no orchestral accompaniment here that sets up a meter, either. So, the singer can easily feel *Ma-* as the stress of the word. The fact that *-řen-* is set as a long vowel (relative to the other vowels in the word) means that Jeník is showing real concern for Mařenka—remember that Czechs sometimes lengthen normally short vowels in order to stress a word, and this is infinitely more common than stressing the wrong syllable.

Occasionally, the stresses are set wrong and there is no freedom possible to allow any "bending." Sometimes, these are, in fact, just plain wrong, and are discussed below. Other times they can be attributed to the extreme emotions of the character, as when Mařenka sings just before the Act I finale:

This is a climax that grew out of a free recitative, but here Mařenka's measures are accompanied by the orchestra with a strong, full chord on every main beat. The singer should bend the short-long rhythm of "Jeník," so that the two eighths are more like a sixteenth followed by a dotted eighth, but after that, she can only sing what is written. Smetana sets the long vowels of "nevíme" and "nepopustíme" correctly, but the stresses are on the wrong, second syllables instead of the first syllables for both of these words. Still, it works because Mařenka is so emotionally distraught at this point. She sings "I and Jeník don't know anything about that, and we won't give in!," stamps her feet, and storms out.

There are some other passages where emotions simply cannot account for Smetana's placing the stress on the wrong syllable. Some of them must stand as written. Others, especially in recitatives, can be rewritten slightly. Luckily, these are relatively few, but there are enough that in a recent Czech book on *Prodaná nevěsta* written for a general audience, a person asks the editor, Jiří Heřman:

"What is your opinion sir, on the declamation in *Prodaná nevěsta*?"[2]

The answer to that question lies in Czech history.

After the Czechs lost the Battle of White Mountain in 1621, they became a part of the Austro-Hungarian Empire under Hapsburg rule, which did not end until the outcome of World War I. Until reforms under Joseph II (1741–90), Czech culture—and language—had been relegated to activities in village life, and even with the reforms some cultural activities were still banned. In Smetana's youth, the Czech language was still prohibited from formal usage, including in schools. Even before 1621, Austrian and German influence had been strong. One can only imagine how strong that influence was in the nineteenth century, despite Czech nationalism, and especially in the arts and among the intellectual elite. In 1880, about 37 percent of Bohemia's population was German.[3] Well-to-do Czech families, such as Smetana's, were educated in German and spoke German as their first language. Poorer families, such as Dvořák's, grew up speaking Czech. In the early nineteenth century, as the Czech language began to be written again after almost two hundred years, Czech poets experimented with two different kinds of verse. One, *časomíra*, or "quantitative verse," was based on vowel length. The other, *přízvučný*, or "accentual verse," was based on first-syllable stress. Accentual verse followed the natural inflection of the language, with long vowels and the sole diphthong *ou* providing variety and melodiousness to the prevailing meter. On the other hand, quantitative verse often caused natural stresses to be misplaced.

In the case of *Prodaná nevěsta*, while Sabina did not overtly follow *časomíra* rules, there are some irregularities in his meter that may have tripped up Smetana here and there. In 1871, the Czech writer and poet Eliška Krásnohorská (1847–1926) cautioned composers to read librettists' Czech poetry as prose in order to avoid any traces of the unnatural stresses of *časomíra*. It was not only Smetana, but other composers who, as Krásnohorská complained, set Czech "with a foreign accent."[4] Having Czech be pronounced with German stresses may even have sounded more elevated to some. Eventually librettists and composers worked out the declamation problems, but for those few prob-lematical places in *Prodaná nevěsta* we can take them as a sign of the times.

Besides the struggles with Czech verse during the National Revival period, there was another, related issue underlying Smetana's occasional incorrect stresses. German was his first language, and while he did attain beautiful and natural Czech inflection in his operas and songs, it did not come without much conscious work and steady development. In 1860, Smetana wrote to his former student, music critic Ludevít Procházka (1837–88):

> "First of all I would ask you to excuse all my mistakes, both in spelling and grammar of which you will certainly find plenty in my letter, for up to the pre-sent day I have not had the good fortune to be able to perfect myself in our mother tongue. Educated from my youth in German, both at school and in so-ciety, I took no care, while still a student, to learn anything but what I was forced to, and . . . I must now confess that I cannot express myself adequately or write correctly in Czech. But this reproach falls not only on me, but also on our schools! However, I need hardly repeat that I am Czech, body and soul, and that it is my pride to be the heir to our glory."[5]

Through Krásnohorská's landmark three-part article called "On Czech musical declamation" in the newspaper *Hudební listy* in 1871, the declamation problems of the day were addressed. Among quite a few examples, she even cited two phrases from *Prodaná nevěsta* as sounding foreign.[6] Krásnohorská went on to become the librettist for Smetana's last three operas. Even more in-fluential for Czech musical declamation were the writings of Otakar Hostinský (1847–1910). In his 1886 essay "On Czech musical declamation," he praised Krásnohorská's earlier article, and gave suggestions on how to perform incor-rectly set words. For example, if the word *drahá* [dear] is set to two equal half notes in a sustained passage, the singer should sing a diminuendo or a *fp* on the first note to help offset its inappropriate length. Similarly, if *dráha* [railroad] is set the same way, he recommends a diminuendo to the second note. Hostinský also explained how lengthening normally short vowels stresses a word, and how the longer a vowel is lengthened, the more it is emphasized, as discussed above.[7]

A final factor in explaining some of the mis-stresses in Smetana's early opera may lie with his method of composition. In looking at his sketches and revisions, it seems that Smetana was more likely to alter a melodic line than a rhythm as he reworked passages. This especially brought about problems in word-setting in the three numbers that Smetana composed before he saw any of Sabina's libretto—the opening chorus, the Mařenka/Jeník love duet theme, and the Esmeralda/Principál duet (see chapter 1). For his later operas, if Smetana utilized preconceived themes from his "Notebook," he would have the orchestra play them while the voice sang a different line.[8]

For more details, the reader is referred to the author's chapter "Stress and Length" in *Singing in Czech*, along with its accompanying CD, in which native Czech singers demonstrate bending rhythms in recitatives in *Prodaná nevěsta*.[9] John Tyrrell also looks closely at Czech declamation in his book *Czech Opera*.[10]

In his book on *Prodaná nevěsta*, Heřman answered the question about declamation with:

"Luckily, the vernacular speech of the libretto led to a majority of accentual declamation. . . . As to the rest . . . today's artists know how to deal with the text expertly, so that the sound of the opera is not distorted too much by the audible stresses on weak syllables. The resulting experience of the musical speech in *Prodaná nevěsta* is alive and natural."[11]

"Today's artists" include not only Czechs, but non-Czechs who, once they get a feel for downbeat stresses and long and short vowels, easily bend rhythms when necessary and inflect in Czech as well as they do in Italian or any other language.

Note on Translations

The English translations of the libretto in Part II serve a two-fold purpose. First, there is a word-for-word translation, important for the performers and stage director, as well as interested listeners, for their understanding of what every word means. Also, for those wishing to make their own singing translation, this should prove essential. Second, there is an idiomatic English translation, often necessary to make sense of the very free Czech word order. Whenever possible, though, this translation follows the word order of the Czech, so that, for example, if the Czech sentence ends with the word *láska* [love], and the English translation works fine also ending with the word *love*, this word order is retained so that both the singer and audience will better understand the original. It is not meant to be "poetic," then, but to rather walk the line between a literal and an idiomatic English translation that reflects the original as much as possible. It is also available from the author as surtitles in an altered form.

Occasionally, the reflexive *si* or *se* cannot be translated by itself and is just translated with a dash:

že	se	s	ní	ožení.
that	-	with	her	he'll marry.

that he'll marry her.

Also, if a compound verb is separated by other words, then an ellipsis is used to show that the verb continues. An example is *jste vyřkl* [you have spoken]:

a	když	jste	to	slovo	vyřkl,	všecko	je	hotovo.
and	when	you have...	that	word	spoken,	everything	is	ready.

and when you've spoken it, everything is ready.

Translations of the Czech stage directions and expression marks are also provided. Finally, unless an entire section is repeated, word repetitions are given, since it is important for singers to work with them and motivate them.

Pronunciation Checklist

The following is a final Check/Czech list to guard against common Anglicisms in Czech lyric pronunciation.

(1) Are the [a] and other vowels bright, like Italian, along with Italianate unaspirated, forward consonants? They should be!

(2) Are all *e*'s—*é, e, ě*—open [ɛ]? Make sure, especially, that all final *e*'s are open, such as the word *se*.

(3) Make sure that every *mě* is pronounced [mɲɛ]. This is one of the few non-phonetic issues in Czech, and it is very important.

(4) Is every *d, n*, and *t* softened when it occurs before an *i/í* (except for foreign-derived words)? Remember "I Did, Didn't I?" in chapter 2 of *Singing in Czech* (Cheek 2001, 44–45)!

(5) Are all vocalic *r*'s rolled long enough?

(6) Is every [ɦ] voiced? In consonant clusters, approach them as grace notes. Also, make sure [ɦ] and [x] are two very different sounds!

(7) Remember that final *h* is pronounced [x].

(8) Make sure that *s* between vowels is pronounced [s], and *not* [z]. Do not confuse this with Italian and French pronunciation.

(9) Make sure not to carry over German rules into Czech: e.g., initial *sl* is sung [sl], and not [ʃl]. Czech [x] is more forward than German.

 (10) Look carefully at the rhythm and stress to make sure that words begin as notated on a strong beat, especially in recitative (unless they're set wrong and cannot be stressed correctly).

(11) Where the music allows for it, *bend* rhythms to accommodate long vowels. This is an important part of Czech inflection, and the music often allows for it.

(12) Make sure that the Czech diphthong *ou* is *not* pronounced as in the English word *ouch*.

(13) Are you observing the glottals? These come naturally to Czech singers, and they must be observed.

(14) Do not confuse the *čárka* sign with the *háček*: the words *mé, mne,* and *mě* are all pronounced differently: [mɛː], [mnɛ], and [mɲɛ].

Notes

1. Stressing the wrong syllable is extremely rare, and it usually happens in exclamations. Still, it sometimes occurs with names to show affection. See Timothy Cheek, *Singing in Czech: A guide to Czech lyric diction and vocal repertoire* (Lanham, Md.: Scarecrow Press, 2001), 113.
2. Jiří Heřman, ed., *Prodaná nevěsta,* (Prague: Petrklíč, 2001), 30.
3. Petr Čornej, *Dějiny českých zemí,* 3d ed. (Havlíčkův Brod: Fragment, 2003), 107. Parts of this section are taken from the author's article: Timothy Cheek, "Inflection and word setting in Czech vocal music," *Journal of Singing* 62, no. 3 (January/February 2006): 299–313.
4. Eliška Krásnohorská, "O české deklamaci hudební" [On Czech musical declamation], in *Hudební listy* [Music paper] II, 1–3, Ludevít Procházka, ed. (Prague: Emanuel J. Kittl, 1871), 1, 17. The entire article is on pages 1–4, 9–13, 17–19.
5. František Bartoš, *Bedřich Smetana: Letters and reminiscences,* trans. from the Czech by Daphne Rusbridge (Prague: Artia, 1955), 59–60.
6. Krásnohorská, "O české deklamaci hudební," 18.
7. Otakar Hostinský, "O české deklamaci hudební," in *O hudbě,* Miloslav Nedbal, ed. (Prague: Státní hudební vydavatelství, 1961, reprinted from 1886), 259–97.
8. Gerald Abraham, "The genesis of *The Bartered bride,*" in *Slavonic and Romantic music: Essays and studies* (New York: St. Martin's Press, 1968), 38; and John Tyrrell, *Czech opera* (Cambridge: Cambridge University Press, 1988), 263.
9. Cheek, *Singing in Czech,* 103–120.
10. Tyrrell, *Czech opera,* 253–64.
11. Heřman, ed., *Prodaná nevěsta,* 30.

Composer Bedřich Smetana (1824–84). Courtesy
of the Prague National Theatre Archives

Librettist Karel Sabina (1813–77). Courtesy
of the Prague National Theatre Archives

Ema Destinnová (1878–1930) as Mařenka, Adolf Krössing (1848–1933) as Vašek, Prague National Theatre, 1909. Courtesy of the Prague National Theatre Archives

Choreographer Otakar Bartík (1868–1936) and dancer Gina Torriani, New York Metropolitan Opera, 1909. Courtesy of the Metropolitan Opera Archives

Jarmila Novotná (1907–94) as Mařenka, New York Metropolitan Opera, 1941. Courtesy of the Metropolitan Opera Archives

Marilyn Horne (b. 1934), professional debut, as Háta, Los Angeles Guild Opera, 1954. Photo by Albert Duval from Marilyn Horne, with Jane Scovell, Marilyn Horne: My Life *(New York: Atheneum, 1983)*

Teresa Stratas (b. 1938) as Mařenka, Nicolai Gedda (b. 1925) as Jeník, New York Metropolitan Opera, 1978. Courtesy of the Metropolitan Opera Archives

Ara Berberian (1930–2005) as Kecal, New York Metropolitan Opera on tour at the Detroit Opera House, 1979. Courtesy of Ginny Berberian

Dancer Bohuslava Jelínková, Act III, Prague National Theatre, 1992. Courtesy of photographer Oldřich Pernica, Kladno

Bohuslava Jelínková with husband, author Timothy Cheek, Prague National Theatre, 1999. Courtesy of photographer Marie Jelínková

Chorus, Act I; Amita Prakash as Mařenka, Bernard D. Holcomb as Jeník, University of Michigan, 2007. Courtesy of Peter Smith of Smith Photography, Ann Arbor

Simone Osborne as Mařenka, Eric Olsen as Jeník, Opera Nuova summer program, Edmonton, Alberta, 2007.
Courtesy of Ed Ellis of Ellis Brothers Photography, Edmonton

Part Two

IPA and English Translations

6

Act I

Jednání I
Náves, po straně hospoda—pout^v

Act I
Village green, along the side a pub—country fair

Výstup I
Mařenka, Jeník, selský lid
[Opona vzhůru]

Scene i
Mařenka, Jeník, peasants
[Curtain up]

Sbor:
Chorus:

[prɔt͡ʃ bɪxɔm sɛ nɛt'ɛʃɪlɪ   gdɪʃʃ naːm paːn buːɣ zdraviː daː]

Proč	**bychom**	**se**	**netěšili,**	**když**[1]	**nám**	**Pán**	**Bůh**	**zdraví**	**dá?**
Why	would	we	not take delight,	when	to us	Lord	God	health	gives?

Why shouldn't we have a great time, when the Lord God grants us health?

[gdɔʃ   z ‿ naːs viː   zda   pɔud' budɔut͡siː vɛssɛlɛ tak ʔuɦiliːdaː]

Kdož	**z**	**nás**	**ví,**	**zda**	**pout'**	**budoucí**	**vesele**	**tak**	**uhlídá?**
Who	from	us	knows,	whether	fair	future	cheerful	so	will look?

Who of us knows if the next fair will be so cheerful?

[ʔa   gdɔ ʒɛnat   ktɛraː vdanaː]

A	**kdo**	**ženat,**	**která**	**vdaná,**
And	who	married (man),	which	married (woman),

And whoever's married, man or woman,

[rɔzʒɛfinɛⁱ sɛ   s ‿ radɔvaːŋkɪ]

rozžehnej se   s   radovánky!
switch off   with   revelry!

you'll have no more fun!

[ʒɛna   dɔma   ɦɔspɔdaři: muʃ   sɛ   ʔuklɪda: za ‿   d͡ʒbaːŋkɪ]

Žena   doma   hospodaří,   muž   se   uklidá   za   džbánky.
Woman   home   keeps house,   man   hides   behind   mugs.

Women keep house, men hide behind their drinks.

[ʔɔːuvɛⁱ ʔɔːuvɛⁱ   kɔnɛt͡s   radɔstiː]

Ouvej! Ouvej! Konec   radostí!
Alas!   Alas!   End   of joys!

Alas! Alas! The end of pleasure!

[ɦr̥nɔu sɛ   starɔst'ɪ   zlɔst'ɪ   mr̥zutɔst'ɪ   ʔɔːuvɛⁱ]

Hrnou se   starosti, zlosti, mrzutosti.   Ouvej!
They rush   worries,   spites,   ill humors.   Alas!

They rush in—worries, spite, and ill humor. Alas!

Proč bychom se netěšili, . . . když Pán Bůh zdraví dá?

[jɛnɔm tɛn   jɛ fpravd'ɛ   ʃt'astɛn   gdɔ   ʒɪvɔta   ʔuʒiːvaː]

Jenom ten   je vpravdě   šť asten,   kdo   života   užívá.
Only   that   is   really   happy,   who   life   will enjoy.

Only he is truly happy who enjoys life.

Jeník:

[prɔt͡ʃ ⁱsɪ   tag   zasmuʃɪlaː   maː   drafiaː   mařɛŋkɔ]

Proč jsi   tak   zasmušilá,   má   <u>drahá</u>[2]   Mařenko?
Why are you so   sullen,   my   dear   Mařenka?

Why are you so sullen, my dear Mařenka?

Mařenka:

[maːm   zlɛː   tuʃɛɲiː]

Mám   zlé   tušení—
I have evil   forebodings—

I feel something foreboding—

[mat'ɪt͡ʃka   mɲɛ   pravɪla]

matička   mně   pravila,
Mom   to me   said,

Mother told me

[ʒɛ   naːs   nafʃt'iːviː   ʔɔ ‿ pɔːut'ɪ   sɔuzɛniː   mɪ   ʒɛɲɪx   muːⁱ]

že   nás   navštíví   o   pouti   souzený   mi   ženich   můj—
that us   he will visit at   fair   predestined to me groom   my—

that my predestined bridegroom will visit us at the fair—

[bɔʒɛ   jak   tɔ   skɔnt͡ʃiː]

Bože,   jak   to   skončí?
God,   how   that   will end?

God, how will it end?

Jeník:

[dɔbře   ɲɪt͡s   sɛ nɛstraxuⁱ   ʔa   vɛ ‿ mnɛ   sɛ duːvjeřuⁱ]

Dobře!   Nic   se nestrachuj,   a   ve   mne   se důvěřuj!
Well!   Nothing don't worry about, and in   me   trust!

Well! Don't worry about anything, and trust in me!

[budɛ lɪ   jɛn   vuːle tvaː   pɛvnaː   ʔa   nɛʔuːstupnaː]

Bude-li   jen   vůle tvá   pevná   a   neústupná.
It will-if only will your steadfast and unyielding.

Just let your will be steadfast and unyielding.

Sbor:
Chorus:

[nɛxtɛ   vzdɛxuː   nɛxtɛ   lkaːɲiː]

Nechte   vzdechů,   nechte lkání,
Leave   of sighs,   leave   wailing,

Stop sighing, stop wailing,

[vaʃɛ   vjɛrnɛː   mɪlɔvaːɲiː   nɛmɪnɛ sɛ   pɔʒɛfinaːɲiː]

vaše   věrné   milování   nemine se   požehnání!
your   faithful beloved   will not pass by/miss blessed!

your faithful beloved will not miss being blessed!

Proč bychom se netěšili, ... když Pán Bůh zdraví dá?

Jenom ten je vpravdě šťasten, kdo život užívá!

[pɔjt'tɛ   s ‿ naːmɪ   k ‿ tant͡sɪ   k ‿ spjɛvu]

Pojd'te s   námi, k   tanci, k   zpěvu,
Come   with us,   to   dance, to   song,

Come with us to dance, to sing,

[vzɲɪknɔut   nɛdɔpŘɛⁱtɛ   ɦɲɛvu   pɔjt'tɛ]

vzniknout nedopřejte hněvu, pojd'te!
to arise   don't grant   anger, come!

don't let anger get the better of you, come!

[muzɪka zat͡ʃiːnaː   dɔ ‿ kɔla   dɔ ‿ kɔla]

Muzika začíná,   do   kola, do   kola!
Music   is beginning, to   round, to   round!

The music's beginning, let's dance, let's dance!

(Odejdou do hospody.) (They go to the pub.)

Výstup II   Scene ii
Mařenka, Jeník

Recitativ
Mařenka:

[tak tɛdɪ pŘɛt͡sɛ sɛ   tɔ staːt'ɪ   maː ʔɔː jaː nɛʃt'astnaː]

Tak tedy přece se   to   státi   má? Ó, já nešt'astná!
So   then   after all -   that to happen shall? Oh, I   unhappy!

So it will happen after all? Oh, I'm so unhappy!

Jeník:

[mařeŋkɔ t͡sɔ   t'ɛ tag zarmɔut'ɪlɔ   t͡sɔ   sɛ stalɔ]

Mařenko, co   tě   tak zarmoutilo? Co   se stalo?
Mařenka, what you so   grieved?   What happened?

Mařenka, what made you so unhappy? What happened?

Mařenka:

[nɛd'ɪf sɛ   jɛɲiːt͡ʃku]

Nediv se,   Jeníčku!
Don't wonder, Jeníček!

Don't wonder, Jeníček!

[dnɛs   maː pR̝ɪjiːt'ɪ sɛdlaːk miːxa sɛ ‿ sɪnɛm na ‿ naːmluvɪ k ‿naːm]

Dnes   má   přijíti³ sedlák Mícha se   synem na   námluvy k   nám.
Today should come   farmer Micha with son   to   courting to   us.

Today Mícha the farmer should be coming here with his son to court me.

[snat ʔuʃ   ⁱsɔu   vɛ ‿ fsɪ]

Snad   už   jsou   ve   vsi!
Maybe already they are in   village!

Maybe they're already in the village!

Jeník:

[ʔa   tɪ   t͡sɔ   jɪm   ʔɔtpɔviːʃ]

A   ty,   co   jim   odpovíš?
And you, what to them will you answer?

And you, what will you answer them?

Mařenka:

[t͡sɔ   jɪm   ʔɔtpɔviːm   na ‿ tɔ   sɛ   jɛʃt'ɛ   muːʒɛʃ   ptaːt'ɪ]

Co   jim   odpovím?   Na   to   se   ještě   můžeš   ptáti?
What to them will I answer? To that - still can you ask?

What will I answer them? How can you ask me that?

[mɔɦu   lɪ   pR̃ɪnaːlɛʃt'ɪ   jɪneːmu   nɛʃ   tɔbjɛ   jɛɲiːt͡ʃku]

Mohu-li   přináležti[4]   jinému,   než   tobě,   Jeníčku?
Can I-if belong   to other   than you,   Jeník?

Could I belong to someone other than you, Jeník?

[ʔalɛ   rɔd'ɪt͡ʃɛ   ʔɔtet͡s   muːⁱ   jɛst   vaːzaːn]

Ale   rodiče.   Otec   můj   jest   vázán.
But family.   Father my   has   promised.

But my family. My father has promised.

Jeník:

[tɔ   jɛ   ʔɔfʃɛm   smutnɛː]

To   je   ovšem   smutné!
That   is   indeed   sad!

That's sad, indeed!

Mařenka:

[tɪs   jaksɪ   nɛsmɲɛliː   jɛɲiːt͡ʃku   ʔa   ʔɔstiːxaviː]

Tys   jaksi   nesmělý,   Jeníčku,   a   ostýchavý,—
You are   a little   reticent,   Jeníček,   and   sheepish—

You're a little close-mouthed, Jeníček, and sheepish—

[jakɔ   bɪ sɛs   ɲɛt͡ʃɛɦɔ   baːl   t͡ʃɪ   snat   ɲɛkɔɦɔ]

jako by ses[5]   **něčeho**   **bál,   či   snad   někoho?**
as if   you were   of something   afraid, or   perhaps   of someone?

as if you were afraid of something, or maybe of someone?

[jɛɲiːt͡ʃku pR̝iːsaɦɛⁱ   mɪ   ʒɛ   nɛmaːʃ   jɪnɛː   laːskɪ]

Jeníčku,   přísahej   mi,   že   nemáš   jiné   lásky,
Jeníček,   swear   to me   that   you don't have   other   loves,

Jeníček, swear to me that you don't have another love,

[jɪnɛːɦɔ   zaːvasku]

jiného   závazku.[6]
of another   commitment.

another commitment.

[vjeŘ   ʒɛ   mɪ   ʔuʃ   nɛjɛdnɔu   napadlɔ]

Věr, že mi už nejednou[7] **napadlo,**
Believe that to me already many a time it occurred

Believe me, it's occurred to me many times

[ʒɛ truxliːʃ   prɔ ‿ ɲɛjakɔu   mɪlɛŋku]

že truchlíš   pro nějakou milenku.
that you're grieving for some other lover.

that you're grieving for some other lover.

Jeník:

[ɲɪgdɪ ɲɪgdɪ]

Nikdy, nikdy!
Never, never!

Never, never!

Árie
Mařenka:

[gdɪbɪx   sɛ   t͡sɔ   takɔvɛːɦɔ   ʔɔ ‿ tɔbjɛ   dɔvjɛd'ɛla]

Kdybych se co takového[8] **o tobě dověděla,**
If I - anything like that about you learned,

If I learned anything like that about you,

[t͡sɔ   takɔvɛːɦɔ   dɔvjɛd'ɛla]

co   takového   dověděla,
anything   like that   learned,

learned anything like that,

[krutou   pɔmstɪxt'ɪvou   zlɔbou   na ‿ t'ɛ   bɪɣ   zanɛvr̝ɛla]

krutou   pomstychtivou   zlobou   na   tě   bych   zanevřela,
with cruel   revengeful   anger   on you   would I come to hate,

with cruel, spiteful anger I would come to hate you,

[na ‿ t'ɛ   bɪɣ   zanɛvr̝ɛla]

na   tě   bych   zanevřela,
on   you   would I   come to hate,

I would come to hate you,

[krutou   pɔmstɪxt'ɪvou   zlɔbou   na ‿ t'ɛ   bɪɣ   zanɛvr̝ɛla]

krutou   pomstychtivou   zlobou   na   tě   bych   zanevřela,
with cruel   revengeful   anger   on   you   would I come to hate,

with cruel, spiteful anger I would come to hate you,

[na‿ t'ɛ   bɪɣ   zanɛvr̝ɛla   na‿ t'ɛ   bɪɣ   zanɛvr̝ɛla]

na   tě   bych   zanevřela,   na   tě   bych   zanevřela.
on   you   would I   come to hate,   on   you   would I come to hate.

I would come to hate you, I would come to hate you.

[tɛdɪ   pɔvjɛs   mɪ   jɛɲiːt͡ʃku   prɔt͡ʃ ⁱsɪ sɛ tak   rɔʒɦɲɛval]

Tedy   pověz   mi,   Jeníčku,   proč jsi se tak   rozhněval,
Then   tell   me,   Jeníček,   why   you -   so   were angry,

Then tell me, Jeníček, why were you so angry,

[ʒɛ   ⁱsɪ   dɔmɔf svuːⁱ   ʔɔpustʼɪl   ʔa   mɪlɛnt͡se   viːɦɔst   dal]

že   jsi   domov svůj   opustil   a   milence   výhost   dal,
that   you did home   your   abandon and beloved   banishment gave,

that you abandoned your home and banished your sweetheart,

[ʔa   mɪlɛnt͡se   viːɦɔst   dal]

a   milence   výhost   dal?
and   beloved   banishment   gave?

and banished your sweetheart?

[pɔvjɛs mɪ   pɔvjɛs mɪ   pɔvjɛs mɪ   pɔvjɛs mɪ   jɛɲiːt͡ʃku]

Pověz mi,   pověz mi,   pověz mi, pověz mi,   Jeníčku,
Tell   me,   tell   me,   tell   me,   tell me,   Jeníček,

Tell me, tell me, tell me, tell me, Jeníček,

[prɔt͡ʃ   ⁱsɪ   sɛ   tak   rɔʒɦɲɛval]

proč   jsi   se   tak   rozhněval?
why   did you   -   so   get angry?

why did you get so angry?

Kdybych se co takového o tobě dověděla...

Recitativ

[kɔnɛtʃɲɛ jɛ t͡sɛlaː mɪnulɔst | tvaː v‿jakɛːsɪ tajɛmstviː zafialɛna]

Konečně je celá minulost tvá v jakési tajemství zahalena
Finally is whole past your in a certain mystery secret

Your entire past is a secret mystery,

[ʔa ʔuʃ ʔɪ ʔɔtɛt͡s muːⁱ sɛ ɲɛkɔlɪkraːtɛ ʔɔ‿tɔm zmiːɲɪl]

a už i otec můj se několikráte o tom zmínil.
and already even father my - several times about that mentioned.

and even my father has already mentioned it several times.

Jeník:

[maː mɪnulɔst bɪla ʔɔvʃɛm vɛlmɪ trudnaː]

Má minulost byla ovšem velmi trudná!
My past was indeed very grievous!

My past was indeed very sad!

[ⁱsɛm sɪn dɔstʼɪ zaːmɔʒnɛːfiɔ ʔɔt͡sɛ ʔalɛ matka mɪ zaːfiɪ zɛmr̝ɛla]

Jsem syn dosti zámožného otce, ale matka mi záhy zemřela.
I am son rather of well-to-do father, but mother to me soon died.

I was the son of a fairly wealthy father, but before long my mother died.

[na‿nɛʃtʼɛstʼiː sɛ ʔɔtɛt͡s pɔ‿drufiɛː ʔɔʒɛɲɪl]

Na neštěstí se otec po druhé oženil
To misfortune - father after another married,

To my misfortune, Father took another wife,

[ʔa   maˈt͡sɛxa   mnɛ   br̥zɔ   vɪpud'ɪla   z ‿ dɔmu]

a   macecha   mne   brzo   vypudila   z   domu.
and   stepmother   me   quickly   drove out   from   home.

and my stepmother soon drove me out of the house.

[ʔɔdɛbral ⁱsɛm   sɛ   dɔ ‿ svjɛta]

Odebral jsem se   do   svĕta
I withdrew   myself   to   world

I went out into the world

[ʔa   nastɔupɪl ⁱsɛm   f ‿ slu3bɪ   ʔu ‿ t͡sɪziːx   lɪd'iː]

a   nastoupil jsem   v   služby   u   cizích   lidí.
and   I took up   in   employment   at   foreign   people.

and worked for strangers.

Duetto
Jeník, Mařenka:

[jakɔ matka   pɔ3ɛfinaːɲiːm   takʃ   klɛdbɔːu   maˈt͡sɛxa   zlaː]

Jako matka   požehnáním,   takž   kletbou   macecha   zlá,
As   mother   with goodwill,   so   with curse   stepmother   evil,

While a mother is a blessing, an evil stepmother is a curse

[gdɪ3   zanɛvřɛ   na ‿ sɪrɔtka   slɔva   laːskɪ   prɔɲ   nɛmaː]

když   zanevře   na   sirotka, slova   lásky   proň   nemá.
when   she comes to hate   orphan,   word   of love   for him   she doesn't have.

when she comes to hate her orphan, having not a word of love for him.

Recitative
Jeník:

[nɛx sɛ   jak   xt͡sɛ   d'ɛjɛ]

Nech se jak   chce   děje,
Let   -   how   it wants   it happens,

Let it happen how it will,

[vjɛrnɛː   mɪlɔvaːɲiː   nɛpр̌ɛruʃiː   ʒaːdnɛː   zlɔbɪ   nalɛːɦaːɲiː]

věrné   milování   nepřeruší   žádné   zloby   naléhání!
faithful   loving   will not stop   no   of anger   pressing!

faithful love cannot be stopped by any spiteful pressure!

Jeník, Mařenka:

[vjɛrnɛː   mɪlɔvaːɲiː   nɛpр̌ɛruʃiː   ʒaːdnɛː   zlɔbɪ   nalɛːɦaːɲiː]

Věrné   milování   nepřeruší   žádné   zloby   naléhání!
Faithful   loving   will not stop   no   of anger   pressing!

Faithful love cannot be stopped by any spiteful pressure!

[laːsku   ⁱsmɛ   sɪ   pр̌iːsaɦalɪ   slɔvɔ   ⁱsmɛ   sɛ   na ‿ vʒdɪ   dalɪ]

Lásku   jsme si přísahali,   slovo   jsme   se   na   vždy   dali,
Love   we swore to one another,   word   we...   one another   for   ever   gave,

Love we have sworn to one another, our word we have given each other forever,

[f ‿ kaʒdɛː   dɔbjɛ   vjɛrɲɪ   zuːstanɛmɛ   sɔbjɛ]

v   každé   době   věrni   zůstaneme   sobě!
in   every   time   faithful   we will remain   to one another!

always faithful we will remain to one another!

Mařenka:

[filɛ zdɛ   ⁱsɔu]

Hle, zde   jsou!
Hey, here   they are!

Hey, here they are!

[ʔɔtɛt͡s s ‿ ɲımı   př̝ıxaːziː filɛdajiː   mnɛ]

Otec   s   nimi   přichází,   hledají   mne!
Father with them   is coming, they're looking for me!

Father's coming with them, they're looking for me!

Jeník:

[nɛxt͡sı   bı   mnɛ   vıd'ɛlı]

Nechci,   by   mne   viděli!
I don't want   they would   me   see!

I don't want them to see me!

[zbɔɦɛm   zbɔɦɛm   d'iːfkɔ   mılɛnaː]

Sbohem, sbohem,   dívko   milená!
Farewell, farewell, girl   beloved!

Farewell, farewell, beloved girl!

[nɛzapɔmɛɲ na ‿ mnɛ zbɔɦɛm]

Nezapomeň na   mne, sbohem!
Don't forget   me,   farewell!

Don't forget me, farewell!

Mařenka:

[zbɔɦɛm zbɔɦɛm]

Sbohem, sbohem!
Farewell, farewell!

Farewell, farewell!

(Odejdou, každý jinou stranou.) (They leave, each by a different side.)

Výstup III   Scene iii
Ludmila, Krušina, Kecal

Kecal:

[jak vaːm praviːm panɛ kmɔtŘɛ vɪ vɪ ⁱstɛ dal   svɛː slɔvɔ]

Jak vám pravím,[9] **pane kmotře, vy, vy   jste dal   své   slovo,**
As   to you I say,   Mr. neighbor, you, you have given your word,

As I'm telling you, dear neighbor, you, you have given your word,

[ʔa gdɪʃ ⁱstɛ   tɔ slɔvɔ vɪŘkl̩ fʃɛt͡skɔ jɛ ɦɔtɔvɔ]

a   když jste   to   slovo vyřkl, všecko je hotovo.
and when you have… that word spoken, everything is   ready.

and when you've spoken it, everything is ready.

[jɛn jɛn sɛ vɛ ‿ mnɛ duːvjɛřuⁱtɛ maːm rɔzumu tɔlɪk]

Jen, jen se ve   mne důvěřujte, mám   rozumu tolik,
Only, only -   in   me   trust,   I have of reason so much,

Only, only trust in me, I have so much intelligence

[ʒɛ   nɛʔuⁱdɛ   bɪstrɔfilɛdu   mɛːmu   na ‿ zdʼɪ   kɔliːk]

že   neujde   bystrohledu   mému   na   zdi   kolík.
that   it's not passing   to shrewd look   to my   on   wall   pin.

that a pin on the wall wouldn't pass by my astute gaze.

[ʔa   jɛstlɪ   sɛ   t͡sɛra   vaʃɛ   budɛ   spjɛt͡ʃɔvatʼɪ]

A   jestli   se   dcera   vaše   bude   zpěčovati,
And   if   -   daughter   your   will   balk,

And if your daughter makes a fuss,

[ʔuzřiːtɛ   jak   jɪ   naʔut͡ʃiːm   pjɛkɲɛ   pɔslɔuxatʼɪ]

uzříte,   jak   ji   naučím   pěkně   poslouchati.
you will behold   how   her   I will teach   nicely   to listen.

you will behold how I'll teach her to politely listen.

[jak   vaːm   praviːm   panɛ   kmɔtŘɛ   vɪ   ⁱstɛ dal   svɛː   slɔvɔ]

Jak   vám   pravím,   pane   kmotře,   vy   jste dal   své   slovo,
As   to you   I say,   Mr.   neighbor,   you   have given   your   word,

As I'm telling you, dear neighbor, you have given your word,

[ʔa   gdɪʃ   ⁱstɛ   tɔ   slɔvɔ   vɪŘkl̩   fʃɛt͡skɔ   jɛ   fiɔtɔvɔ]

a   když   jste   to   slovo   vyřkl,   všecko   je   hotovo.
and   when   you have...   that   word   spoken,   everything   is   ready.

and when you've spoken it, everything is ready.

[jɛn sɛ vɛ ‿ mnɛ duːvjɛřuⁱtɛ]

Jen se ve mne, důvěřujte.
Only - in me, trust.

Just trust in me.

Křušina:

[nɔ nɔ t͡sɔ řiːkaːʃ matkɔ jaː jaː ⁱsɛm spɔkɔjɛn]

No, no, co říkáš, matko? Já, já jsem spokojen.
Well, well, what do you say, mother? I, I am satisfied.

Well, well, what do you say, dear? I, I'm satisfied.

Ludmila:

[tɔ sɛ nɛdaː prɔvɛːst za ‿ jɛd'ɪŋkiː dɛn]

To se nedá provést za jedinký den.
That it's not possible to carry out after sole day.

It can't be done in just one day.

[pɔtŘɛba tu pŘɛmiːʃlɛt'ɪ ʔa pɔptat sɛ nɛvjɛstɪ]

Potřeba tu přemýšleti a poptat se nevěsty,
Need at this point to reflect and to inquire of bride,

It's necessary at this point to reflect and inquire of the bride

[jɛstlɪ ɲɛjaka: pŘɛka:ʃka nɛvlɔʒi: sɛ dɔ ‿ t͡sɛstɪ]

jestli nějaká překážka nevloží se do cesty.
if any hurdle won't intervene to path.

whether any obstacle won't hinder the way.

Kecal:

[t͡sɔ   pЯɛkaːʃka   t͡sɔ   pЯɛkaːʃka   t͡sɔ   pЯɛkaːʃka]

Co   překážka,   co   překážka,   co   překážka?
What   obstacle,   what   obstacle,   what   obstacle?

What obstacle, what obstacle, what obstacle?

[vaʃɛ   vuːlɛ   ʔa   maː   xɪtrɔst   zviːtʼɛziː   nadɛ   fʃiːm]

Vaše   vůle   a   má   chytrost   zvítězí   nade   vším,
Your   will   and   my   brilliance   will prevail   over   everything

Your will and my brilliance will prevail over everything

[t͡sɔ   pЯɛkaːʃkɔu   sɛ   sɲatku   naːm   gdɛ   ʔɔbjɛviː]

co   překážkou   se   sňatku   nám   kde   objeví.
what   obstacle   -   of wedding   to us   where   it will arise.

where any obstacle to the wedding arises.

Ludmila:

[pЯɪⁱdɛ   na ‿ tɔ   jakiː   jɛ   ʒɛɲɪx   pЯɪⁱdɛ   na ‿ tɔ   jakiː   jɛ   ʒɛɲɪx]

Přijde na   to, jaký   je ženich, přijde na   to, jaký   je ženich!
Arrive to   that, what kind   is groom, arrive   to   that, what kind   is   groom!

Come to it, what's the groom like; come to it, what's the groom like!

Kecal:

[jakiː   ʒɛɲɪx   jakiː   ʒɛɲɪx   jakiː   ʒɛɲɪx]

Jaký   ženich,   jaký   ženich,   jaký   ženich?
What kind   groom,   what kind   groom,   what kind   groom?

What's the groom like, what's the groom like, what's the groom like?

[marnaːt'   vjɛru   ʔotaːska]

Marnát'   věru   otázka!
In vain   indeed   question!

A question truly asked in vain!

[ʒɛ   jɛ   dɔbriː   pɔxɔpiːtɛ   gdɪʒ   za ‿ ɲɛɦɔ   rutʃiːm   jaː   jaː   jaː]

Že   je   dobrý   pochopíte,   když   za   něho   ručím   já,   já,   já!
That   he is   good   you'll understand,   when   for   him   warrant   I,   I,   I!

You understand that he's good, when it's I who guarantees him—I, I, I!

[tɔbɪjaːʃɛ miːxu   znaːtɛ   tɔbɪjaːʃɛ miːxu   znaːtɛ]

Tobiáše   Míchu   znáte,   Tobiáše   Míchu   znáte!
Tobiáš   Mícha   you know,   Tobiáš   Mícha   you know!

Tobiáš Mícha you know, Tobiáš Mícha you know!

[nɛznaːtɛ lɪ   nɛznaːtɛ lɪ   praviːm vaːm]

Neznáte-li,   neznáte-li,   pravím   vám,
You don't know-if,   you don't know-if,   I'll say   to you,

If you don't know, if you don't know, I'll tell you,

[ʒɛ   za ‿ jɛɦɔ   kraːsniː   statɛk   ɦnɛt   tʃɪřɪtsɛt t'ɪsiːdz   daːm]

že   za   jeho   krásný   statek   hned   čtyřicet   tisíc   dám.
that   for   his   beautiful   farm   right away   forty   thousand   I'll give.

that for his beautiful farm I'll give forty-thousand gulden right away.

[jak vaːm praviːm panɛ kmɔtŘɛ vɪ vɪ ⁱstɛ dal svɛː slɔvɔ]

Jak vám pravím, pane kmotře, vy, vy jste dal své slovo,
As to you I say, Mr. neighbor, you, you have given your word,

As I'm telling you, dear neighbor, you, you have given your word,

[ʔa gdɪʃ ⁱstɛ   tɔ slɔvɔ vɪŘkl̩   fʃɛt͡skɔ jɛ fiɔtɔvɔ]

a když jste   to slovo vyřkl, všecko je hotovo.
and when you have... that word spoken, everything is ready.

and when you've spoken it, everything is ready.

Ludmila:

[tɔ sɛ nɛdaː   prɔvɛːst za ‿ jɛd'ɪŋkiː dɛn]

To se nedá   provést za jedinký den.
That it's not possible to carry out after sole day.

It can't be done in just one day.

Krušina:

[jaː ⁱsɛm spɔkɔjɛn]

Já jsem spokojen.
I am satisfied.

I'm satisfied.

Kecal:

[jɛn jɛn sɛ vɛ ‿ mnɛ duːvjɛřuⁱtɛ maːm rɔzumu tɔlɪk]

Jen, jen se ve mne důvěřujte, mám rozumu tolik,
Only, only - in me trust, I have of reason so much,

Only, only trust in me, I have so much intelligence

[ʒɛ   nɛʔuⁱdɛ   bɪstrɔfilɛdu   mɛːmu   na ‿ zd'ɪ   kɔliːk]

že	neujde	bystrohledu	mému	na	zdi	kolík.
that	it's not passing	to shrewd look	to my	on	wall	pin.

that a pin on the wall wouldn't pass by my astute gaze.

Recitativ
Krušina:

[ʔɔfʃɛm   tɔbɪjaːʃɛ miːxu   znaːm   ʔuʃ   ʔɔd ‿ d'ɛtstviː]

Ovšem,	Tobiáše	Míchu	znám	už	od	dětství.
Of course,	Tobiáš	Mícha	I know	as early as	from	childhood.

Of course, I know Tobiáš Mícha from childhood.

[maː   dva sɪnɪ   jɛɲiːka   s ‿ pr̩vɲiː   manʒɛlkɪ   ʔa   vaʃka   z ‿druɦɛː]

Má	dva	syny:	Jeníka	z	první	manželky	a	Vaška	z	druhé.
He has	two	sons:	Jeník	from	first	wife	and	Vašek	from	second.

He has two sons: Jeník from his first wife, and Vašek from his second.

[s ‿ t'ɛx   nɛznaːm   ʔaɲɪ   jɛdnɔɦɔ   ʔaɲɪ   druɦɛːɦɔ]

Z	těch	neznám	ani	jednoho	ani	druhého.
From these	I don't know	either	one	nor	other.

Of these I don't know either one or the other.

Kecal:

[tɔ   jɛ pravda]

To	je pravda.
That	is right.

That's right.

[vɪ ˈstɛ   sɛ ʔalɛ pŘɛd ⌋ daːvniːmɪ   lɛtɪ]

Vy jste   se ale před dávnými[10] **lety**
You have...   -   but before long past years

But many years ago

[rukɔu daːɲiːm pŘɛt ‿ svjɛtkɪ   zavaːzal]

rukou dáním   před svědky   zavázal,
hand giving before witnesses pledged,

you swore an oath before witnesses

[ʒɛ   daːtɛ   t͡sɛru   svɔu jɛɦɔ sɪnɔvɪ]

že   dáte   dceru   svou jeho synovi.
that you will give daughter your to his son.

that you will give your daughter to his son.

Ludmila:

[ʔa   za ‿ ktɛrɛːɦɔ tɔ sɪna vlastɲɛ   mluviːtɛ]

A   za   kterého to syna vlastně   mluvíte?[11]
And about which   that son actually are you speaking?

And about which son are you actually speaking?

Kecal:

[za ‿ ktɛrɛːɦɔ   vʒdɪtʼ   nɛmaː   nɛʃ jɛdnɔɦɔ vaʃka]

Za   kterého? Vždyť'   nemá   než jednoho—Vaška.
About which?   To be sure he doesn't have else   one—Vašek.

About which? Well, he only has one—Vašek.

[druɦiː   sɪn   s ‿ pr̩vɲiː   ʒɛnɪ   jɛ tulaːk   ʔa   nɛzbɛda]

Druhý   syn   z   první   zeny   je   tulák   a   nezbeda.
Other   son   from   first   wife   is   bum   and   misfit.

The other son from his first wife is a bum and a misfit.

[ɲɪgdɔ   ʔɔ ‿ ɲɛm   nɛviː]

Nikdo   o   něm   neví!
No one   about him   doesn't know!

No one knows anything about him!

Krušina:

[nu   ʔa   jakiː   pak   jɛ   tɛn   vaʃɛk]

Nu,   a   jaký   pak   je   ten   Vašek?
Well,   and   what kind   then   is   that   Vašek?

Well, and what kind of boy is this Vašek?

[prɔtʃ   ⁱstɛ   ɦɔ   nɛpR̝ɪvɛdl̩   ɦnɛt   s ‿ sɛbɔu]

Proč   jste   ho   nepřivedl   hned   s   sebou?
Why   have you…   him   not fetched   right away   with   you?

Why didn't you just bring him along with you?

Terzetto
Kecal:

[mlad'iːk   sluʃniː   ʔa   mravuː   viːt͡s   t'ɪxiːx]

Mladík   slušný   a   mravů   víc   tichých,
Youth   respectable   and   of manners   more   gentle,

The youth is respectable, with the most gentle manners,

[nɛvaːʒiː   nɛvaːʒiː sɪ   ʒɛrtuː ʔa   slɔf   lɪxiːx]

neváží,   neváží si   žertů   a   slov   lichých,
he doesn't value, he doesn't value jokes and words false,

he doesn't value, he doesn't value jokes and hollow words,

[praviː bɛraːnɛk praviː bɛraːnɛk tɔ   pɔvafiɔu]

pravý beránek, pravý beránek to   povahou.
true   lamb,   true   lamb   that disposition.

a true lamb, like a true lamb is his character.

[nɛɲiː   na ‿ ɲɛm vadɪ ʔaɲɪ vɪnɪ]

Není   na něm vady ani viny,
It's not on him   faults nor blames,

He has neither faults nor guilt;

[fʃɛt͡skɪ matkɪ   bɪ   sɪ pR̝aːlɪ sɪnɪ   z ‿ duʃiː jak vaʃkɔva pR̝ɛmɪlɔːu]

všecky matky by   si přály syny s   duší, jak Vaškova, přemilou.
all   mothers would enjoy   sons with souls like Vašek,   tender.

every mother would be glad to have sons with a soul like Vašek's—tender.

Mladík slušný. . . to povahou.

[nɛɲiː   vɛlkiː ʔaɲɪ maliː   nɛɲiː tut͡ʃniː ʔaɲɪ suxiː]

Není   velký ani malý, není   tučný ani suchý,
He's not large nor small, he's not fat   nor bony,

He's neither large nor small, neither fat nor bony,

[nɛɲiː   xrɔmiː   ʔaɲɪ filuxiː]

není   chromý ani hluchý,
he's not lame   nor deaf,

neither crippled nor deaf,

[nɛɲiː   furɪjant ʔaɲɪ filɔupiː nɛɲiː   vɛlkiː ʔaɲɪ maliː]

není   furiant ani hloupý, není   velký ani malý...
he's not boastful nor stupid, he's not large   nor small...

neither conceited nor stupid, neither large nor small. . .

[marnɔtratɲiːk ʔaɲɪ skɔupiː]

marnotratník ani   skoupý.
extravagant   nor stingy.

neither extravagant nor stingy.

[slɔvɛm   ffɛt͡skɔ   v ‿ miːr̝ɛ   pravɛː]

Slovem,   všecko   v   míře   pravé,
By word, everything in measure real,

In a word, everything is truly measured by him,

[t'ɛlɔ jakɔ liːpa   zdravɛː statɛk za ‿ tr̝ɪt͡sɛt t'ɪsiːt͡s]

tělo   jako lípa   zdravé, statek za   třicet tisíc!
body like lime tree healthy, farm at   thirty thousand!

a body as healthy as a horse, a farm worth thirty thousand!

[nuʒɛ   nuʒɛ   nuʒɛ   gdɔʃ   gdɔʃ   sɪ pR̆ɛjɛ   viːt͡s]

Nuže,   nuže,   nuže,   kdož,   kdož   si přeje   víc?
Well,   well,   well,   who,   who   wishes   more?

Well, well, well, who, who could wish for more?

[mlad'iːk   sluʃniː   ʔa   mravuː   viːt͡s   t'ɪxiːx]

Mladík   slušný   a   mravů   víc   tichých,
Youth   respectable   and   of manners   more   gentle,

The youth is respectable, with the most gentle manners,

[ʒertuː   ʔa   slɔf   lɪxiːx   sɪ nɛvaːʒiː]

žertů   a   slov   lichých   si neváží,
jokes   and   words   false   he doesn't value,

he doesn't value, he doesn't value jokes and hollow words,

[praviː   bɛraːnɛk   praviː   bɛraːnɛk   tɔ   pɔvaɦɔu]

pravý   beránek,   pravý beránek   to   povahou.
true   lamb,   true   lamb   that   disposition.

a true lamb, like a true lamb is his character.

Ludmila, Krušina:

[vaʃɛ   xvaːla   mnɔɦɔ platʼiː   vaʃɪm   slɔvuːm vjɛři:mɛ]

Vaše   chvála   mnoho platí,   vašim   slovům   věříme.[12]
Your   praise   much   is worth,   in your   words   we trust.

Your praise is worth much, we trust in your words.

Kecal:

[nɛɲiː   vɛlkiː ʔaɲɪ maliː   gdɔʃ sɪ pR̆ɛjɛ viːts]

Není   velký ani malý. . . kdož si přeje víc?
He's neither large nor small. . . who wishes more?

He's neither large nor small . . . who could wish for more?

Výstup IV   Scene iv
Mařenka, předešlí   Mařenka, previous

Quartetto
Kecal, Ludmila, Krušina:

[tu   jɪ   maːmɛ   tu   jɪ   maːmɛ rɔzumɲɛ   s ‿ ɲiː pɔjednaːmɛ]

Tu   ji   máme,   tu   ji   máme! Rozumně   s   ní   pojednáme.
Here her we have, here her we have! Reasonably with her let's discuss.

Here she is, here she is! Let's discuss it with her reasonably.

Mařenka:

[ʔaⁱ tatʼiːŋku ʔaⁱ mamɪŋkɔ prɔt͡ʃpak mnɛ   ɦlɛdaːtɛ]

Aj, tatínku, aj, maminko, pročpak mne   hledáte?
Ah, Dad,   ah, Mom,   why ever me   you're looking for?

Ah, Father, ah, Mother, why ever are you looking for me?

Kecal:

[ptal ⁱsɛm sɛ   jɪx   kɔɦɔ raːda maːtɛ]

Ptal jsem se jich, koho ráda máte?
 I asked   them, whom love you have?

I was asking them, are you in love with someone?

[nɛmaːtɛ lɪ   ʒaːdnɛːfɔ   sr̩tsɪ   svɛːmu   mɪlɛːfɔ]

Nemáte-li   **žádného**   **srdci**   **svému**   **milého,**
You don't have-if   no   to heart   your   dear,

If you have no one dear to your heart,

(vážně) (seriously)

[pr̝ɪvɛdu vaːm | mlad'iːka   vaːʒnɛːfɔ   ʔa   vzaːt͡snɛːfɔ]

přivedu   **vám**   **mladíka**   **vážného**   **a**   **vzácného.**
I'll fetch   to you   young man   earnest   and   rare.

I'll fetch you a young man who's earnest and rare.

Mařenka:

[vaːʒnɛːfɔ   ʔa   vzaːt͡snɛːfɔ]

Vážného   **a**   **vzácného?**
Earnest   and   rare?

"Earnest and rare?"

Krušina:

[vʒdɪd'   fɔ   ʔufiliːdaːʃ   sama   fɔ   pɔznaːʃ]

Vždyť'   **ho**   **uhlídáš,**   **sama**   **ho**   **poznáš!**
To be sure   him   you will set eyes on,   yourself   him   you will meet!

Of course you'll see him, you'll meet him yourself!

Ludmila:

[nɛbudɛ lɪ   sɛ   t'ɪ   liːbɪt]

Nebude-li   se   ti   líbit,
He won't-if   -   to you   is pleasing,

If you won't like him,

[kɔʃiːt͡ʃɛk   mu   daːʃ]

košíček   mu   dáš!
little basket   to him   you'll give (thrown on his head)!

you'll kick him out!

Mařenka:

[vʒdɪd'   ɦɔ   ʔufiliːdaːm   sama   ɦɔ   pɔznaːm]

Vždyť'   ho   uhlídám,   sama   ho   poznám,
To be sure   him   I will set eyes on,   myself   him   I will meet,

Of course I'll see him, I'll meet him myself,

[nɛbudɛ lɪ   sɛ   mɪ   liːbɪt]

nebude-li   se   mi   líbit,
he won't-if   -   to me   is pleasing,

if I won't like him,

[kɔʃiːt͡ʃɛk   mu   daːm]

košíček   mu   dám!
little basket   to him   I'll give (thrown on his head)!

I'll send him on his way!

Ludmila, Krušina:

[vʒdɪd'   fiɔ   ʔufiliːdaːʃ   sama   fiɔ   pɔznaːʃ]

Vždyť'   ho   uhlídás,   sama   ho   poznáš,
To be sure   him   you will set eyes on, yourself him   you will meet,

Of course you'll see him, you'll meet him yourself,

[nɛbudɛ lɪ   sɛ   t'ɪ   liːbɪt]

nebude-li   se   ti   líbit,
he won't-if   -   to you   is pleasing,

if you won't like him,

[kɔʃiːt͡ʃɛk   mu   daːʃ]

košíček   mu   dáš!
little basket   to him you'll give (thrown on his head)!

you'll send him on his way!

Kecal:

[vʒdɪd'   fiɔ   ʔufiliːdaː   sama   fiɔ   pɔznaː]

Vždyť'   ho   uhlídá,   sama   ho   pozná,
To be sure   him   she will set eyes on, herself him   she will meet,

Of course she'll see him, she'll meet him herself,

[nɛbudɛ lɪ   sɛ   jɪ   liːbɪt]

nebude-li   se   ji   líbit,
she won't-if   -   to her   is pleasing,

if she won't like him,

[kɔʃiːtʃɛk   mu   daː]

košíček   mu   dá!
little basket to him she'll give (thrown on his head)!

she'll send him on his way!

[tak   tɛdɪ   skɔntʃiːmɛ smlɔuvu   ʔutʃɪɲiːmɛ   mařɛŋka ʔatˀ řɛknɛ ʔanɔ]

Tak tedy skončíme, smlouvu   učiníme.   Mařenka at' řekne: ano,
So   then let's finish, contract let's administer. Mařenka let says: yes,

So, then, let's finish, let's fulfill the contract. Mařenka shall say "yes,"

[ʔa   budɛ   fʃɛ   ʔa   budɛ   fʃɛ   vɪkɔnaːnɔ]

a   bude   vše,   a   bude   vše   vykonáno!
and it will everything, and it will everything accomplished!

and everything, and everything will be settled!

Mařenka:

[tɔ   nɛⁱdɛ   tak rɪxlɛ   jak sɪ mɪsliːtɛ]

To   nejde   tak rychle, jak si myslíte,
That doesn't go so   quickly as   you think,

It doesn't work as quickly as you think,

[tɔ   nɛⁱdɛ   tɔ   nɛⁱdɛ   tɔ   nɛⁱdɛ]

to   nejde,   to   nejde,   to   nejde!
that doesn't go, that doesn't go, that doesn't go!

it doesn't work, it doesn't work, it doesn't work!

[jakiː   f ‿ tɔm   jɛ   ɦaːt͡ʃɛk   ʔaɲɪ   nɛviːtɛ]

Jaký   v   tom   je   háček,   ani   nevíte!
What kind of   in   that is   little hook, not even you don't know!

What snag there is, you don't even know!

Kecal:

[ɦaːt͡ʃɛk   sɛm   ɦaːt͡ʃɛk   tam   pR̝ɛkaːʃkɪ   pR̝ɛkaːʃkɪ   nɛznaːmɛ]

Háček   sem,   háček   tam,   překážky,   překážky   neznáme!
Little hook   here,   little hook there, hurdles,   hurdles   we don't know!

A snag here, a snag there, obstacles, obstacles we don't know!

[k ‿ t͡ʃɛmu jaː svuːⁱ rɔzum   daːm   fʃɛt͡skɔ   fʃɛt͡skɔ   pR̝ɛkɔnaːmɛ]

K   čemu já svůj rozum   dám,   všecko,   všecko   překonáme!
To   what I   my   intellect give, everything, everything we will surmount!

Whatever I put my mind to, everything, everything we'll overcome!

Mařenka:

[maːm ʔuʃ   jɪnɛːɦɔ]

Mám   už   jiného!
I have already another!

I already have another!

Ludmila, Krušina:

[maː   ʔuʃ   jɪnɛːɦɔ jiː   pR̝ɛmɪlɛːɦɔ]

Má   už   jiného, jí   přemilého!
She has already another, to her very dear!

She already has another very dear to her!

Mařenka:

[mɲɛ   pR̝ɛmɪlɛːɦɔ]

Mně   přemilého!
To me   very dear!

To me very dear!

Kecal:

[tɔmu   jɛʃtʲɛ   dnɛs   daː   kvɪndɛ]

Tomu   ještě   dnes   dá   kvinde,
To that   still   today   she will give   done with,

Still, today she'll break up with him,

[ʔatʲ   sɪ   fɪlɛdaː   ʃtʲɛstʲiː   jɪndɛ]

atʼ   si   hledá   štěstí   jinde!
let   himself   he'll search for   happiness   elsewhere!

he'll have to look for his happiness elsewhere!

Mařenka:

[slɔvɔ   svɛː   ⁱsɛm | mu   ʔuʒ   dala]

Slovo   své   jsem   mu   už   dala.
Word   my   I have…   to him already given.

I've already given him my word.

Kecal:

[na ‿ slɔvɔ mɪ ɲɪt͡s nɛdaːmɛ na ‿ slɔvɔ mɪ ɲɪt͡s nɛdaːmɛ]

Na slovo my nic nedáme, na slovo my nic nedáme.
On   word we nothing will give, on   word we nothing will give.

That word means nothing to us, that word means nothing to us.

Mařenka:

[smlɔːuvu ⁱsɛm ʔuʃ pɔdɛpsala]

Smlouvu jsem už podepsala!
Contract   I have… already signed!

I've already signed a contract!

Kecal:

[mɪ tu smlɔuvu rɔstr̩fiaːmɛ mɪ tu smlɔuvu rɔstr̩fiaːmɛ]

My tu smlouvu roztrháme, my tu smlouvu roztrháme.
We   that contract we'll tear up, we that contract we'll tear up.

We'll tear up that contract.

Mařenka:

[skustɛ tɔ skustɛ tɔ skustɛ tɔ skustɛ tɔ]

Zkuste to, zkuste to, zkuste to, zkuste to!
Try   that,   try   that, try   that, try   that!

Try it, try it, try it, try it!

Kecal:

[vjeřtɛ jɛnɔm v ‿ rɔzum : muːⁱ ʔa ʃʃɛ   puːⁱdɛ stuːⁱ t͡sɔ stuːⁱ]

Věřte jenom v rozum můj a vše   půjde stůj co stůj;
Trust just   in intellect my, and everything will go cost what cost;

Just trust in my intellect, and everything will go ahead at any cost;

[ʔɔstraː mɪsḷ   maː   ʔɔstraː mɪsḷ   maː]

ostrá   mysl   má,   ostrá   mysl   má,
keen   mind   I have, keen   mind   I have,

I have a sharp mind, I have a sharp mind,

[muːⁱ fɪlɛt muːⁱ fɪlɛt tɛn prɔɲɪknɛ tɛn prɔɲɪknɛ]

můj hled, můj hled, ten pronikne, ten pronikne,
my   gaze, my   gaze, that penetrates, that penetrates,

my gaze, my gaze, it penetrates, it penetrates,

[tɛn   prɔɲɪknɛ   t͡sɛliː svjɛt]

ten   pronikne   celý   svět!
that   penetrates   whole   world!

it penetrates the whole world!

[t͡sɔ ɲɪgdɔ nɛvɪpřɛdɛ   tɔ muːⁱ rɔzum dɔvɛdɛ tɔ muːⁱ rɔzum dɔvɛdɛ]

Co nikdo nevypřede,   to můj rozum dovede, to můj rozum dovede.
What no one doesn't manage, that my intellect is able, that my intellect is able.

What no one else can pull off, my intellect can do it, my intellect can do it.

Mařenka, Ludmila, Krušina:

[t͡sɔ ɲɪgdɔ nɛvɪpŘɛdɛ   jɛɦɔ rɔzum dɔvɛdɛ jɛɦɔ rɔzum dɔvɛdɛ]

Co nikdo nevypřede,   jeho rozum dovede, jeho rozum dovede.
What no one doesn't manage, his   intellect is able, his   intellect is able.

What no one else can pull off, his intellect can do it, his intellect can do it.

Kecal:

[t͡sɔ   ɲɪgdɔ   nɛvɪpŘɛdɛ]

Co   nikdo   nevypřede,
What no one doesn't manage,

What no one else can pull off,

[tɔ   muːⁱ rɔzum dɔvɛdɛ tɔ   muːⁱ rɔzum   dɔvɛdɛ]

to   můj rozum dovede, to   můj rozum dovede.
that my   intellect is able, that my   intellect is able.

my intellect can do it, my intellect can do it.

Recitativ
Mařenka:

[jɛɲiːk nɛʔupust'iː   tɔ   viːm   ʔa   mɔɦu za ‿ tɔ fsad'ɪt svuːⁱ ʒɪvɔt]

Jeník neupustí,   to   vím,   a   mohu za   to vsadit   svůj   život.
Jeník won't give up, that I know, and I can   on   that bet   my   life.

Jeník won't give in, that I know, and I can bet my life on it.

Krušina:

[ʔupustʼiː   nɛbɔ   nɛʔupustʼiː   na ‿ tɔm | maːlɔ zaːlɛʒiː]

Upustí   **nebo**   **neupustí,**   **na**   **tom**   **málo** **záleží.**
He'll give up   or   he'll not give up,   on   that   little   depends.

Whether he gives in or doesn't give in matters little.

[zavaːzal ˡsɛm sɛ   tɔbɪjaːʃɪ   miːxɔvɪ   pŘɛt ‿ svjɛtkɪ]

Zavázal jsem se   **Tobiáši**   **Míchovi**   **před**   **svědky.**
I vowed   to Tobiáš   Mícha   before   witnesses.

I swore to Tobiáš Mícha before witnesses.

Ludmila:

[ʔalɛ   prɔsiːm   tʼɛ   muʒɪ   jakiː   tɔ   zaːvazɛk]

Ale   **prosím**   **tě,**   **muži,**   **jaký**   **to**   **závazek?**
But   I implore   you,   man,   what kind of   that   binding agreement?

But please, dear, what kind of binding agreement is it?

Kecal:

[zdɛ   ɦɔ   maːm]

Zde   **ho**   **mám.**
Here   it   I have.

I have it here.

(Vytahuje úpis z kapsy.)   (He pulls out the note from his pocket.)

[t͡ʃɛrnɛː na ‿ biːlɛːm pɔdɛpsaːɲɪ miːxa ʔɪ kruʃɪna ʔɪ svjɛtkɔvɛː]

Černé na bílém! Podepsáni Mícha i Krušina i svědkové.
Black on white! Signed Mícha and Krušina and witnesses.

Black on white! Signed by Mícha, Krušina, and witnesses.

Mařenka:

[t͡sɔ jɛ dɔ ‿ tɔɦɔ tɔ ɲɪt͡s nɛplatʼiː]

Co je do toho! To nic neplatí.
What is to that! That nothing isn't valid.

What of it! None of it's valid.

[jaː ʔa jɛɲiːk ʔɔ ‿ tɔm ɲɪt͡s nɛviːmɛ ʔa nɛpɔpustʼiːmɛ]

Já a Jeník o tom nic nevíme a nepopustíme!
I and Jeník about that nothing we don't know and we won't give in!

I and Jeník don't know anything about that, and we won't give in!

(Dupne a odběhne.) (She stamps her foot and runs away.)

Kecal:

[ʔax jak svjɛt jɛ zvraːt͡sɛniː]

Ah, jak svět je zvrácený!
Ah, how world is perverted!

Ah, how the world is upside-down!

Krušina:

[gdɛpak   ⁱstɛ   ʔalɛ nɛxal   miːxu   ʔa   sɪna   jɛɦɔ]

Kdepak   jste[13]   **ale nechal   Míchu   a   syna   jeho,**
Wherever have you... but   left   Mícha   and son   his,

Where did you leave Mícha and his son,

[tɔɦɔ vaːʒnɛːɦɔ ʔa   vzaːt͡snɛːɦɔ ʒɛɲɪxa]

toho vážného   a   vzácného   ženicha?
that   earnest   and rare   bridegroom?

that earnest and rare bridegroom?

[bɪlɔ bɪ   sluʃnɔ ʔabɪ   ʔɔn prɔmluvɪl   s ‿ mařɛnkɔu]

Bylo by   slušno, aby   on   promluvil   s   Mařenkou.
It would be   proper if he were to he   speak   with Mařenka.

It would be proper if he were to speak with Mařenka.

Kecal:

[ʔɪnu ʔɔfʃɛm   ʔalɛ ʔɔn | nɛɲiː zvɪkliː   mluvɪt'ɪ sɛ ‿ ʒɛnskiːmɪ]

Inu,   ovšem!   Ale on   není   zvyklý   mluviti   se   ženskými.
Well, of course! But he   isn't used to speaking with women.

Well, of course! But he isn't used to speaking with women.

[jɛ   ʔɔstiːxaviː jakɔ panɛŋka]

Je   ostýchavý jako panenka!
He's bashful   like young girl!

He's bashful like a young girl!

Krušina:

[tɔ   budɛ   t'ɛʃkɛː   namlɔuvaːɲiː]

To   bude   těžké   namlouvání!
That   will be   difficult   winning over!

That'll make it difficult for courting!

Kecal:

[tɛt'   ʔalɛ   kmɔtŘɛ   bɪlɔ bɪ   nɛⁱliːp   gdɪbɪstɛ   jakɔ   naːfiɔdɔu]

Ted'   ale,   kmotře,   bylo by   nejlíp, kdybyste   jako   náhodou
Now   but,   neighbor,   it would be   best   if you would   as   chance

But, now, neighbor, it would be best if you would, as if by accident,

[sɛʃɛl sɛ   s‿ miːxɔu   v‿ drufiɛː   fiɔspɔd'ɛ]

sešel se   s   Míchou   v   druhé   hospodě!
meet   with   Mícha   in   other   pub!

meet Mícha in the other pub!

[tadɪ   budɛ   filutʃnɔ   xɪstajiː   sɛ   k ‿ tantsɪ]

Tady   bude   hlučno, chystají se   k   tanci!
Here   will be   noise,   they're preparing   to   dance!

Here it'll be noisy, they're getting ready for the dance!

(vážně) (seriously)

[jaː zatʼiːm   vɪfiledaːm   jɛɲiːka ʔa prɔmluviːm   s ‿ ɲiːm]

Já   zatím   vyhledám   Jeníka a   promluvím   s ním!
I   meanwhile will drop in on Jeník and I'll speak   with him!

In the meantime, I'll drop in on Jeník and speak with him!

(Odejdou.) (They leave.)

Výstup V   Scene v

Lid před hospodou. Staří za stoly.
People in front of the pub. The elderly at tables.

Mládež přistupuje k tanci.
Young people step up to dance.

Později sbor.
Later the chorus.   *Polka*

Sbor:
Chorus:

[pɔⁱtʼ   sɛm fiɔlka tɔt͡ʃ sɛ fiɔlka pɔkut   vaːbiː   skɔt͡ʃnaː pɔlka]

Pojď sem, holka, toč se, holka, pokud   vábí   skočná polka!
Come here, girl,   turn, girl, as long as it entices jumping polka!

Come here, girl, twirl, girl, for as long as the polka entices!

[ruka v ‿ rut͡se filedɪ   v ‿ filɛt s ‿ naːmɪ tɔt͡ʃ sɛ t͡sɛliː svjɛt]

Ruka v   ruce, hledy v   hled, s námi toč se   celý svět!
Hand in hand, gazes in gaze, with us   turns whole world!

Hand in hand, eye to eye, with us turns the whole world!

[basa brutʃiː t͡sɪmbaːl t͡sɪŋkaː kɔlɛm ʔuʃiː jɛn tɔ br̝ɪŋkaː]

Basa bručí, cimbál cinká, kolem uší jen to břinká;
Bass drones,   cimbál tinkles, around ears only that strums;

The bass is droning, the dulcimer is tinkling, around our ears we hear only
strumming;

[pɔd ‿ nɔɦamɪ skaːt͡ʃɛ zɛm vjɛru pɔstaːt nɛmuːʒɛm]

pod   nohami skáče   zem, věru postát nemůžem!
under feet   jumps   earth, really to stand we cannot!

under our feet the earth is jumping, we can't stand in one spot!

Opona spadne.   Curtain falls.

Konec prvního jednání.   End of the first act.

Notes

1. The Prague National Theatre chorus always sings a short vowel and a long [ʃʃ] on *když*. The same thing happens on the word *vesele* [ss] on the next line. The feeling is like a joyous cymbal crash on these words. See chapter 5.

2. Change the rhythm to ♪ ♩ on the word *drahá*.

3. Change the rhythm to thirty-second, dotted sixteenth, thirty-second on the word *přijíti*.

4. The conductor can place the chord one sixteenth earlier to line up with the stress on *při-*.

5. Not *jako bys se*.

6. Besides loosening up the short-long rhythms on *nemáš jiné*, change the rhythms on *jiného závazku*: sixteenth, dotted eighth, sixteenth, eighth, and two sixteenths.

7. Feel *že mi už* and *nejednou* as triplets.

8. Hold the –*vé* of *takového* slightly. This is a long vowel, and works hand-in-hand with the rubato.

9. Remember to loosen up the short-long rhythm on *pravím* every time. Czech singers do this naturally, even within the musical context. The same is true for *dal své*, a few words later.

10. Repeat the two *d*s so that *před* does not sound like *pře*.

11. Change the rhythm on *mluvíte* to sixteenth, eighth, sixteenth.

12. Ludmila should sing -*ři*-, m. 1052, earlier, on the B-flat, at the same time as Krušina, because it's a long vowel.

13. Think of *Kdepak jste* as a triplet, with the stress on *Kde-*.

7

Act II

Jednání II
Síň v hospodě

Act II
Hall in the pub

Výstup I
Sbor chasníků, Jeník a Kecal

Scene i
Chorus of farmhands, Jeník, and Kecal

Jeník a selská chasa po jedné straně za stolky při pivě. Na druhé straně dohazo-vač, též za stolkem.

Jeník and peasant farmhands along one side at small tables drinking beer. On the other side the broker, also at a small table.

Opona   Curtain

Sbor chasníků:
Chorus of farmhands:

[tɔ   pɪvɛt͡ʃkɔ   tɔ   vjɛru   jɛ   nɛbɛskiː   dar]

To   pivečko,   to   věru   je   nebeský   dar,
That   dear little beer,   that   really   is   heavenly   gift,

Beer is truly a gift from heaven,

[fʃɛ   psɔtɪ   ʔa   trampɔtɪ   vɛdɛ   na ‿ zmar]

vše   psoty   a   trampoty   vede   na   zmar,
all   of difficulty   and   of trouble   leads   to   ruin,

it leads all problems and troubles to ruin,

141

[ʔa   siːliː   ʔa   daːvaː kuraːʒe   ʔɛⁱxuxu   ʔɛⁱxuxu]

a   sílí   a   dává   kuráže![1] **Ejchuchu! Ejchuchu!**
and strengthens and gives guts!   Hoorah!   Hoorah!

and gives you strength, and gives you guts! Hoorah! Hoorah!

[bɛs ‿ pɪva   bɪ   t͡ʃlɔvjɛk smutniː   bɪl   zdɛ   ɦɔst]

Bez   piva   by   člověk smutný byl   zde   host;
Without beer   would man   sad   be   here   guest;

Without beer here a man would be a sad guest;

[jɛt'   starɔst'iː na ‿ svjɛt'ɛ bɛstɔɦɔ   dɔst]

jet'   starostí na   světě   beztoho dost—
it is   of cares on   world   anyway enough—

anyway, there are enough cares in the world—

[ʔa   blaːzɛn   gdɔ   na ‿ ɲe   sɛ   vaːʒe   ʔɛⁱxuxu   ʔɛⁱxuxu]

a   blázen, kdo   na   ně   se   váže! Ejchuchu! Ejchuchu!
and   fool   who   to   it himself ties! Hoorah!   Hoorah!

and he's a fool who ties himself to them! Hoorah! Hoorah!

Jeník:
(Vstane.) (He stands up.)

[ʔaⁱ   ɦɔʃɪ   mɲe   vjɛři̊tɛ   praviːm na ‿ svɔu   t͡ʃɛst]

Aj, hoši, mně věřte,   pravím na   svou   čest,
Ah, lads, me believe, I say   on   my   honor

Hey, boys, believe me, I say on my honor

[ʒɛ laːska nad ‿ viːnɔ ʔɪ   nat ‿ pɪvɔ jɛst]

že   láska   nad   víno   i   nad   pivo   jest
that   love   above   wine   and even   above   beer   is

that love is above wine, and even above beer,

[ʔa jɛdʼɪnaː na ‿ svjɛtʼɛ radɔst   jɛʒ   blaɦɛm   napl̩ɲujɛ mladɔst]

a   jediná   na   světě   radost,   jež   blahem   naplňuje mladost.
and   alone   on   world   happiness which   with bliss   fills   youth.

and it alone in the world brings happiness that fills youth with bliss.

Sbor chasníků:
Chorus of farmhands:

[tɪs   jɛɲiːku pɔ ‿ ʔuʃɪ zamɪlɔvaːn]

Tys',   Jeníku,   po   uši   zamilován.
You are,   Jeník,   up to   ears   in love.

You are, Jeník, up to your ears in love.

[jɛn ʔatʼ tʼɪ   tɔ nɛskaliː   tamɦɪlɛtɛn   paːn]

Jen   at'   ti   to   nezkalí   tamhleten   pán.
Just   let   to you   that   not thwart   that one over there   gentleman.

Just don't let that gentleman over there thwart your plans.

Kecal:

[nɔ   ʔa stanɛ lɪ sɛ tak ʔa   stanɛ lɪ sɛ   tak nɛbudɛ   miːt s ‿ tɔɦɔ ʃkɔdɪ]

No   a   stane-li se tak, a   stane-li se tak, nebude   mít   z   toho škody.
Well and   it stands-if so, and   it stands-if so, he won't   have from that   harms.

Well, and if it's so, and if it's so, he won't be harmed by it.

[dɔbraː   rada   ʔa   pɛɲiːzɛ ˈsɔːu dvjɛ paːkɪ ʒɪvɔta]

Dobrá   rada   a   peníze jsou dvě páky života,
Good   counsel and   money are two levers of life,

Good counsel and money are the two levers of life,

[gdɔ   jɪx   rɔzumɲɛ   ʔuʒiːvaː]

kdo jich rozumně užívá,
who them intelligently uses,

he who uses them wisely,

[tɛn sɛ tɛn sɛ svjɛtɛm nɛmɔtaː   gdɔ jɪx rɔzumɲɛ ʔuʒiːvaː]

ten se, ten se světem   nemotá,   kdo jich rozumně užívá,
that -, that - by world won't get entangled, who them intelligently uses,

that one, that one won't be ensnared by the world, he who uses them wisely,

[tɛn sɛ tɛn sɛ svjɛtɛm   nɛmɔtaː]

ten se, ten se světem   nemotá,
that -, that - by world won't get entangled,

that one, that one won't be ensnared by the world,

[sɛ svjɛtɛm   nɛmɔtaː   nɛmɔtaː nɛmɔtaː]

se světem   nemotá,   nemotá, nemotá!
- by world won't get entangled, entangled, entangled!

he won't be ensnared, ensnared, ensnared!

Sbor chasníků:
Chorus of farmhands:

[tɔ   pɪvetʃkɔ   tɔ vjɛru jɛ nɛbɛskiː   dar]

To   pivečko,   to věru je nebeský dar,
That dear little beer, that really is heavenly gift,

Beer is truly a gift from heaven,

[fʃɛ   psɔtɪ   ʔa trampɔtɪ   vɛdɛ   na ‿ zmar]

vše   psoty   a   trampoty   vede   na   zmar,
all   of difficulty and of trouble leads to   ruin,

it leads all problems and troubles to ruin,

[ʔa   siːliː   ʔa   daːvaː kuraːʒɛ   ʔɛⁱxuxu   ʔɛⁱxuxu]

a   sílí   a   dává kuráže!   Ejchuchu! Ejchuchu!
and   strengthens and gives guts!   Hoorah!   Hoorah!

and gives you strength, and gives you guts! Hoorah! Hoorah!

Kecal: Jeník:

[ʔa   pɛɲiːzɛ]   [ʔa   laːska jɛdˈɪnaː rradɔst]

A   peníze!   **A   láska jediná   radost!**
And   money!   And   love alone   happiness!

And money!   *And love alone brings happiness!*

[furɪjant]
Furiant

Výstup II   Scene ii[2]
Vašek:
(jako ženich oblečen) (dressed like a bridegroom)

[maː ma ma mat'ɪt͡ʃka pɔ pɔ   pɔviːdala]

Má	ma-	ma-	matička	po-	po-	povídala,
My	mo-	mo-	momma	to-	to-	told,

My mo- mo- momma to- to- told me

[ʒɛ ʒɛ bɪ   raː ʔaːda ʔu   ʔu   ʔufiliːdala]

že	že	by	rá-áda	u-	u-	uhlídala,
that	that	she would be	ha-appy	to	to	to see,

that that she would be ha-appy to to see

[gdɪbɪx   gdɪbɪx   sɛ ʔɔ ʔɔʒɛɲɪl svad svad   svadbu vɪ vɪstrɔjɪl]

kdybych,	kdybych	se o-	oženil,	svat-	svat-	svatbu	vy-vystrojil;
were I,	were I	ma-	married,	wed-	wed-	wedding	pla-planned;

when I would, when I would get ma-married, a wed- wed- wedding pla-planned;

[jɛst   jɛstlɪ k(ə) ‿ tɔmu   nɛ   nɛ   nɛdɔspjɛjɛ]

jest-	jestli	k	tomu	ne-	ne-	nedospěje,
i-	if	to	that	it doesn't	it doesn't	it doesn't come to fruition,

i- if it doesn't doesn't doesn't come about,

[t͡sɛlaː vɛ vɛs   sɛ   mɪ   vɪ vɪ vɪsmɲɛjɛ]

celá[3]	ve-	ves	se	mi	vy-vy-vysměje.
whole	vi-	village	-	to me	will la-la-laugh at.

the whole vi- village will la-la-laugh at me.

(Mařenka zatím vystoupí v pozadí.) (Mařenka meanwhile comes out from behind.)

Výstup III   Scene iii
Mařenka, Vašek
(Oba do sebe vrazí a dají se do smíchu.) (They run into one another, and she bursts out laughing.)

Recitativ
Mařenka:

[vɪ ⁱstɛ zajɪstɛː ʒɛɲɪx   kruʃɪnɔvɪ   mařɛŋkɪ]

Vy   jste   zajisté[4] **ženich   Krušinovy   Mařenky?**
You   are   surely   bridegroom   of Krušinová   Mařenka?

You are surely the bridegroom of Mařenka Krušinová?

Vašek:

[ʔa ʔanɔ ja   ja   ja   jak   tɔ   tɔ   tɔ   tɔ   viːtɛ]

A-ano,   ja- ja- ja- jak   to   to   to   to[5] **víte?**
Ye- yes,   ho- ho- ho- how   that that that that do you know?

Ye-yes, ho- ho- ho- how do- do- do- do you know that?

Mařenka:

[t͡sɔʃ   tɔ   nɛɲiː   na ‿ vaːs   vɪd'ɛt'ɪ]

Což   to   není   na   vás   viděti?
No doubt that isn't on   you   to see?

Isn't that obvious by looking at you?

[ˈstɛ   tak   vɪstrɔjɛn]

Jste   tak   vystrojen!
You're   so   dressed up!

You're all dressed up!

[t͡sɛlaː   vɛs   ʔɔ ‿ vaːs   mluviː   ʔa   lɪtujɛ   vaːs]

Celá   ves   o   vás   mluví   a   lituje   vás.
Whole   village   about   you   speaks   and   is sorry for you.

The whole village is talking about you, and feels sorry for you.

Vašek:

[lɪ lɪ lɪtujɛ   ʔa   prɔt͡ʃ]

Li-li-lituje?   A   proč?
Fe-fe-feels sorry?   And   why?

Fe-fe-feels sorry? And why?

Mařenka:

[prɔtɔʒɛ   mařɛŋka   vaːz budɛ ʃɪdˈɪt   nɛbɔtʼ   maː   jɪnɛːɦɔ]

Protože   Mařenka   vás bude šidit;   nebot'   má   jiného!
Because   Mařenka   you will cheat;   because   she has another!

Because Mařenka will cheat on you; because she has someone else!

Vašek:

[ja jakpak   muːʒɛ   miːt   jɪnɛːɦɔ gdɪʃ   maːʔaː   mnɛ]

Ja- jakpak   může   mít   jiného, když   má-á   mne?
Ho-how   can she have   another, when she ha-has me?

Ho-how can she have another, when she ha-has me?

Mařenka:

[vaːs   t͡sɔpak   vaːz znaː   ʔa vɪ jɪ]

Vás? (ha ha ha) Copak   vás zná,   a vy ji?
You? (ha ha ha) I wonder what you does she know, and you her?

You? I wonder if she knows you, and you know her?

Vašek:

[nɛ nɛ nɛ nɛznaː]

Ne- ne- ne- nezná;
She doesn't kno-kno-kno-know;

She doesn't kno-kno-kno-know;

[ʔa ʔalɛ viː   ʒɛ   jaː ˡsɛm jɛ jɛ jɛjiː   ʒɛɲɪx]

a- ale   ví,   že já jsem je- je-její ženich!
bu-but she knows that I am   he-he-her bridegroom!

bu-but she knows that I'm he-he-her bridegroom!

Mařenka:

[ʔɔfʃɛm   ʒɛ viː   ʔa   prɔtɔ   sɛ tʼɛʃiː   na ‿ tɔ]

Ovšem   že ví,   a   proto   se těší   na to,
Of course that she knows, and that is why she looks forward to that,

Of course she knows that, and that's why she's looking forward

[jak   vaːz budɛ   ʃɪdʼɪt ʔa vaːs sɔuʒɪt ʔabɪstɛ   bᵣzɔ   ʔumr̝ɛl]

jak vás bude   šidit a   vás soužit, abyste   brzo   umřel.
how you she will cheat and you harass so that you quickly would die.

to cheating you and harassing you so you'll soon die.

Vašek:

[tɔ tɔ tɔ jɛ firuːza]

To- to- to je hrůza!
Tha-tha-that is horror!

Tha-tha-that's horrible!

[ʔa ʔa ʔa ʔalɛ ma ma ma ma mamɪŋka mɪ řɛkla]

A- a- a- ale ma- ma- ma- ma- maminka mi řekla,
Bu-bu-bu-but mom-mom-mom-mom-momma to me said

Bu-bu-bu-but Mom-Mom-Mom-Mom-Momma told me

[ʒɛ sɛ mu mu mu musiːm ʔɔʒɛɲɪt]

že se mu- mu- mu- musím oženit!
that -   I ha-ha-ha-have to   get married!

that I ha-ha-ha-have to get married!

Mařenka:

[ʔofʃɛm prɔt͡ʃ bɪ nɛ tak ʃvarniː fiɔx]

Ovšem, proč by ne, tak švarný hoch!
Of course, why would it not, so handsome lad!

Of course, why wouldn't you, such a handsome boy!

[tadɪ jɛ nɛvjɛst ʔaʃ nazbɪt jɛn gdɪbɪstɛ xtʼɛl]

Tady je nevěst až nazbyt, jen kdybyste chtěl!
Here is of brides up to excess, just if you would want!

Here they're overflowing in brides, if only you want!

Vašek:

[ja: x͡tsɪ]

Já chci!
I   want!

I want!

Duetto
Mařenka:

[zna:mt' ja: jɛdnu   d'i:ft͡ʃɪnu   ta   pɔ ‿ va:s jɛn   fiɔři:]

Známt' já   jednu   dívčinu,   ta   po   vás   jen   hoří,
I know   I   one   sweet girl, that one   for   you   just   burns,

I know of one sweet girl who's burning for you,

[dlɔufiɔ   dlɔufiɔ   sɛ   prɔ ‿ va:s   s̩r̥t͡sɛ   jɛji: mɔři:]

dlouho,   dlouho   se   pro   vás   srdce   její   moří,
a long time,   a long time   -   for   you   heart   her   consumes,

for a long time, for a long time her heart has pined for you,

[s̩r̥t͡sɛ   s̩r̥t͡sɛ   jɛji: mɔři:]

srdce, srdce její   moří.
heart,   heart   her   consumes.

her heart, her heart has pined.

Vašek:

[ʔɔ ʔɔ ʔɔx ʔɔɣ bɔʒiːtʃku jakɛː ʃtʼɛstʼiː]

O- o- och, och, božíčku, jaké štěstí,
Oh- oh oh oh, my goodness, what kind of good luck,

Oh- oh- oh, oh, my goodness, what good luck,

[gdɪ gdɪʒ dʼiːftʃɪna pɔ ‿ mɲɛ tř̌ɛʃtʼiː]

kdy- když dívčina po mně třeští.
whe- when sweet girl for me is delirious.

whe- when a sweet girl is crazy about me.

[ʔɔː jakɛː ʃtʼɛstʼiː ʔa ʔalɛ mařɛŋka t͡sɔ bɪ řekla]

Ó, jaké štěstí! A- ale Mařenka, co by řekla?
Oh, what kind of good luck! Bu- but Mařenka, what would she say?

Oh, what good luck! Bu- but Mařenka, what would she say?

Mařenka:

[ɲɪt͡s vʒdɪdʼ bɪ vaːm bɛstɔfɪɔ pɔ ‿ svadbjɛ ʔutɛkla]

Nic, vždyť by vám beztoho po svatbě utekla.
Nothing, yet she would to you anyhow after wedding run away.

Nothing, because she'd run away anyway after the wedding.

Vašek:

[ʔa   maː mamɪŋka   ta   bɪ   kr̝ɪt͡ʃɛla]

A   má maminka! ta   by   křičela!
And my   mom!   that she would scream!

And my mom! She would yell!

Mařenka: Vašek:

[pr̝ɛstala bɪ   nɛvjɛstu jag bɪ ʔuvɪd'ɛla]   [jɛ   jɛ lɪ   ɦɛzɔuŋkaː]

Přestala by, nevěstu jak by uviděla.   **Je-   je-li   hezounká?**
She would stop bride   as   she would see.   Is she is she-if pretty?

She would stop when she saw your bride.   *Is- is she maybe pretty?*

Mařenka: Vašek:

[zrɔvna jak   mar̝ɛŋka]   [jɛ   jɛ lɪ   mlad'ɔuŋkaː]

Zrovna jak Mařenka.   **Je   je-li   mlad'ounká?**
Just   like Mařenka.   Is she is she-if young?

Just like Mařenka.   *Is- is she maybe young?*

Mařenka:

[zrɔvna jak   mar̝ɛŋka zrɔvna   jak   mar̝ɛŋka]

Zrovna jak Mařenka, zrovna   jak Mařenka.
Just   like Mařenka, just   like Mařenka.

Just like Mařenka, just like Mařenka.

[znaːmt' jaː jɛdnu   d'iːftʃɪnu ta   pɔ ‿ vaːs jɛn fiɔři:]

Známt' já jednu dívčinu, ta   po   vás jen hoří,
I know   I   one   sweet girl, that one for you just burns,

I know one sweet girl who's burning for you,

[dlɔufiɔ   dlɔufiɔ   sɛ pro ‿vaːs sr̂tsɛ jɛjiː mɔři:]

dlouho,   dlouho,   se pro vás srdce její moří.
a long time, a long time, - for you heart her consumes.

for a long time, for a long time her heart has pined for you.

Vašek:

[ʔɔ bɔʒiːtʃku   jakɛː   ʃt'ɛst'iː]

Ó, božíčku,   jaké   štěstí!
Oh, my goodness, what kind of good luck!

Oh, my goodness, what good luck!

[ʔa   ta   ʒɛ   bɪ   mnɛ   fskutku   xt'ɛla]

A   ta   že   by   mne   vskutku   chtěla?
And that that she would me   truly   want?

And would she really want me?

Mařenka:

[ʔɔx gdɪbɪstɛ   vɪ   nɛxt'ɛl   ʒalɛm   bɪ ʔumřɛla]

Och, kdybyste vy   nechtěl,   žalem   by umřela.
Oh, if you were you not to want, by grief would she die.

Oh, if you didn't want her, she would die of grief.

[dɔ ‿ vɔdɪ bɪ skɔtʃɪla ʔufiliːm bɪ sɛ zdusɪla]

Do vody by skočila, uhlím by se zdusila,
To water she would jump, with coal she would choke herself,

She would jump in the water, she would take coal and choke herself,

[dnɛm nɔt͡siː bɪ plakala]

dnem nocí by plakala,
by day by night she would cry,

day and night she would cry,

[ʒɛ ʒɛ vaːs nɛdɔstala ʒɛ vaːs nɛdɔstala]

že— že vás nedostala, že vás nedostala!
that— that you she didn't get, that you she didn't get!

because— because she couldn't have you, because she couldn't have you!

Vašek:

[prɔtʃ prɔt͡ʃ plaː plaːt͡ʃɛtɛ]

Proč- proč, plá- plá-čete?
Why- why, are you cry- crying?

Why- why are you cry-crying?

Mařenka: Vašek:

[prɔtɔʒɛ jɪ nɛxt͡sɛtɛ] [jaː jaː bɪx jɪ xtʼɛl jɛn jɛn gdɪbɪx smɲɛl]

Protože ji nechcete! Já já bych ji chtěl, jen- jen kdybych směl!
Because her you don't want! I I would her want, only only were I allowed!

Because you don't want her! I- I would want her, only- only if I were allowed!

Mařenka:

[vɪ sɛ jɛn vɪmlɔuvaːtɛ]

Vy se jen vymlouváte
You - just are using it as an excuse

You're just using that for an excuse,

[ʔa tu   jɛʃ vaːs mɪlujɛ jɛʃ vaːs mɪlujɛ laːskɔu ʔumřiːt nɛxaːtɛ]

a tu, jež vás miluje, jež vás miluje, láskou umřít necháte.
and that one which you loves, which you loves, by love to die you'll let.

and the one who loves you, who loves you, you'll let die of love.

Vašek:

[nɛ nɛ nɛ nɛ nɛnɛxaːm   nɛ nɛ nɛ nɛ nɛnɛxaːm]

Ne- ne- ne- ne- nenechám,[6] **ne- ne- ne- ne- nenechám,**
I won't le- le- le- le- let,   I won't le- le- le- le- let,

I won't le- le- le- le- let her, I won't le- le- le- le- let her,

[nɛnɛxaːm nɛnɛxaːm nɛnɛxaːm   nɛnɛxaːm]

nenechám, nenechám, nenechám, nenechám!
I won't let, I won't let, I won't let, I won't let!

I won't let her, I won't let her, I won't let her, I won't let her!

(nesměle) (shyly)

[jɛ   jɛ lɪ   ja jakɔ vɪ   jɛ lɪ   ja jakɔ   vɪ]

Je- je-li ja- jako vy, je-li ja- jako vy,
She is- she is-if li- like you, she is-if li- like you,

If she's- if she's li- like you, if she's li- like you,

[ʔuʃ   ʔuʃ   raːt   jɪ   maːm]

už-   už   rád   ji   mám!
already- already love   her   I have!

I already- already love her!

Mařenka: **Vašek:**

[jaː bɪx   sɛ   vaːm   liːbɪla]   [liː   liː   liːbɪla]

Já bych se vám   líbila?   **Lí-   lí- líbila!**
I   would -   to you   be pleasing?   Would be plea- plea- pleasing!

Would you like me?   *Would li- li- like!*

Mařenka: **Vašek:**

[mnɛ bɪstɛ   sɪ fskutku   vzal]   [vza   vza vza vzal]

Mne byste   si vskutku   vzal?   **Vza-   vza- vza- vzal!**
Me   would you   -   really   marry?   Would ma- ma- ma- marry!

It's truly me you'd marry?   *Would ma- ma- ma- marry!*

Mařenka:

[jaː bɪx   vaːs mɪlɔvala jakɔ f ‿ plɛŋkaːx jakɔ f ‿ plɛŋkaːx‿xɔvala]

Já bych vás milovala, jako v   plenkách, jako v   plenkách chovala.
I   would you love   like in diapers, like in diapers   care for.

I would love you, caring for you as much as a little baby, a little baby.

Mařenka:

[jaː bɪx   sɛ vaːm liːbɪla]

Já bych se vám   líbila?
I   would -   to you be pleasing?

Would you like me?

Vašek:

[liː   liː   liːbɪla]

Lí-   lí-   líbila!
Would be plea- plea- pleasing!

Would li- li- like!

Mařenka:

[mnɛ bɪstɛ   sɪ fskutku vzal]

Mne byste   si   vskutku vzal?
Me   would you -   really   marry?

It's truly me you'd marry?

Vašek:

[vza   vza vza   vzal]

Vza-   vza- vza- vzal!
Would ma- ma- ma-   marry!

Would ma- ma- ma- marry!

Mařenka:

[tɛdɪ   ruku na ‿ tɔ   dɛⁱtɛ pŘi̓ːsafiɛⁱtɛ]

Tedy ruku na   to   dejte, přísahejte!
Then hand on   that give,   swear!

Then raise your hand, swear!

[pŘi̓ːsafiɛⁱtɛ ʒɛ mařɛŋka   nɛxt͡sɛtɛ]

Přísahejte, že Mařenka   nechcete,
Swear   that Mařenka   you don't want,

Swear that you don't want Mařenka,

[ʒɛ sɛ jiː na ‿ vjɛkɪ vjɛkuːf ʔɔd ‿ dnɛʃka ʔɔdřɛknɛtɛ   pŘi̓ːsafiɛⁱtɛ]

že se jí na   věky věkův od   dneška odřeknete!   Přísahejte!
that -   her for ages of ages from today you renounce! Swear!

that from today, for all time to come, you renounce her! Swear!

Vašek:
(Škrabe se za ušima.) (He scratches behind his ears.)

[pr̝iːsaɦatʼɪ maːm   tɔtɔ   nɛʔudʼɛlaːm]

Přísahati   mám?   toto   neudělám!
To swear   I have?   that   I won't do!

I have to swear? That I won't do!

Mařenka:

[maře̞ŋku   gdɔ   budɛ   xtʼiːt]

Mařenku   kdo   bude   chtít,
Mařenka   whoever   will   want,

Whoever wants Mařenka,

[zlɛ sɛ mu   zdɛ budɛ   dʼiːt   pɔmsta   ɦɔ   tu   nɛmɪnɛ]

zle se mu   zde bude   dít,   pomsta   ho   tu   nemine!
evil - to him   then   it will   happen,   vengeance   him   then   will not pass by!

bad things will happen to him then, vengeance will not pass him by!

[rɪxlɛ   sɛ rɔzfiɔdɲɛtɛ   pr̝iːsaɦu   ɦnɛt   vɪr̝kɲɛtɛ]

Rychle   se rozhodněte,   přísahu   hned   vyřkněte!
Quickly   make up your mind,   oath   right away   say!

Quickly make up your mind, say the oath right away!

Vašek:
(plačtivě) (tearfully)

[pŘi: pŘi: pŘi:safia:m]

Pří- pří- přísahám!
I swea- swea- swear!

I swea- swea- swear!

Mařenka:

[mařɛŋkɪ sɛ ʔɔdři:ka:m]

Mařenky se odříkám,
Mařenka I renounce,

Mařenka I renounce,

Vašek:

[ʔɔ ʔɔ ʔɔdři:ka:m]

o- o- odříkám,
I re- re- renounce,

I re- re- renounce,

Mařenka:

[nɛxt͡sɪ   jɪ   ɲɪ   vɪd'ɛt'ɪ]

nechci   ji   ni   viděti,
I don't want her   ever to see,

I don't want to ever see her,

Vašek:

[ɲɪ   vɪd'ɛt'ɪ]

-ni   viděti,
ever to see,

ever see her,

Mařenka:

[nɛxt͡sɪ   ʔɔ ⌣ ɲi: slɪʃɛt'ɪ]

nechci   o   ní   slyšeti,
I don't want about her to hear,

I don't want to hear about her,

Vašek:

[ɲɪ   slɪʃɛt'ɪ]

-ni   slyšeti,
ever to hear,

ever hear,

Mařenka:

[ɲɪ   vɪd'ɛt'ɪ]

ni   viděti,
ever to see,

ever see,

Mařenka:

[sɛ jiː na ‿ vjɛkɪ ʔɔdři̇ːkaːm]

se jí na věky odříkám!
- her for ages I renounce!

I renounce her forever!

Vašek:

[na ‿ vjɛkɪ ʔɔdři̇ːkaːm]

na věky odříkám!
for ages I renounce!

I renounce her forever!

Mařenka:

[znaːmt' jaː jɛdnu d'iːftʃɪnu ta   pɔ ‿ vaːs jɛn fiɔři̇ː]

Známt' já jednu dívčinu, ta   po vás jen hoří,
I know I one sweet girl, that one for you just burns,

I know one sweet girl who's burning for you,

[dlɔufiɔ   dlɔufiɔ   sɛ prɔ ‿vaːs sr̩t͡sɛ jɛjiː jɛjiː mɔři̇ː]

dlouho,   dlouho,   se pro vás srdce její, její moří!
a long time, a long time, - for you heart her, her consumes!

for a long time, for a long time her heart has pined for you!

Vašek:

[ʔɔ ʔɔ ʔɔ ʔɔɣ bɔʒiːt͡ʃku   jakɛː   ʃt'ɛst'iː   jakɛː   ʃt'ɛst'iː]

O- o- o- och, božíčku,   jaké   štěstí,   jaké   štěstí!
Oh- oh- oh- oh, my goodness, what kind of good luck, what kind of good luck!

Oh- oh- oh- oh, my goodness, what good luck, what good luck!

(Odejdou.) (They leave.)

Výstup IV   Scene iv
Jeník, Kecal

Recitativ
Kecal:

[jak praviːm ɦɛska: jɛ   ɦɔdna: bɔɦata: ʔa   ⁱmɛnujɛ sɛ bjɛla]

Jak pravím, hezká je,   hodná, bohatá, a   jmenuje se Běla.
As   I say,   pretty she is, nice, rich,   and she is named Běla.

As I was saying, she's pretty, nice, rich, and her name is "Běla."

Jeník:

[ʔɪnu ʔalɛ   gdɔʃ viː   budɛ lɪ   mnɛ   xt'iːt]

Inu,—ale   kdož ví,   bude-li   mne   chtít.
Well,—but who   knows   she will-if   me   want to have.

Well, but who knows if she'll have me.

Kecal:

[tɔ   jɛ maː starɔst   jɛn řɛkɲɪ ʒɛ   sɛ   mařɛŋkɪ   ʔɔdřiːkaːʃ]

To   je má starost! Jen řekni, že   se Mařenky   odříkáš.
That is my worry!   Just say   that -   Mařenka   renounce.

That's my worry! Just say that you renounce Mařenka.

Jeník:

[nɛ   tɔ   neⁱdɛ   sr̩tsɛ   bɪ   mɪ   pŘɪ ‿ tɔm   puklɔ]

Ne, to   nejde!   Srdce by   mi   při   tom   puklo.
No, that doesn't go! Heart would to me with   that burst.

No, no way! My heart would burst if I did that.

Kecal:

[blaːʒɪ bɪlɪ kɔrdɪ mɲɛlɪ filavɲiː vjet͡s ⁱsɔu tɛt' pɛɲiːzɛ]

Blázni   byli,   kordy   měli!   Hlavní   věc   jsou   ted'   peníze!
Fools   they were,   swords   they had!   Main   thing   are   now   money!

Fool, romantic hogwash! The main thing now is money!

Jeník:

[nɔ ʔa ta t͡sɔ mɪ dɔfiazujɛtɛ ta maː pɛɲiːzɛ]

No,   a   ta,   co   mi   dohazujete,   ta   má   peníze?
Well,   and   that one,   what   to me   you mediate,   that one   has   money?

Well, and the girl you're negotiating for me, she has money?

Kecal:

[ʔɔfʃɛm]

Ovšem!
Of course!

Of course!

Duetto

(vesele) (cheerfully)

[nuʒɛ mɪliː xasɲiːku dɔpŘɛⁱ pak slɔviːt͡ʃku]

Nuže,   milý   chasníku,   dopřej   pak   slovíčku!
Well, then,   dear   farm boy,   grant   then   little word!

Well, then, dear boy, grant me a word or two!

Jeník:

[rad'ɛjɪ bɪx pɔsɛd'ɛl tam pŘɪ ‿ svɛːm pɪviːt͡ʃku]

Raději bych poseděl tam při svém pivíčku.
Rather would I sit there with my little beer.

I'd rather sit over there with my beer.

Kecal:

[znaːʃlɪ pak mnɛ ʔɔsɔbɲɛ]

Znáš-li pak mne osobně?
Do you know-if then me personally?

Do you know me personally?

Jeník:

[nɛmaːm t͡ʃɛst panaːt͡ʃku nɛ ʔa vɪ tɛːʃ nɛznaːtɛ mnɛ]

Nemám čest, panáčku, ne! A vy též neznáte mne?
I don't have honor, dear sir, no! And you also don't know me?

I don't have the honor, dear sir, no! And you, too, don't know me?

Kecal:

[slɪʃɛl ⁱsɛm ʒɛs ɦɔdniː ɦɔx]

Slyšel jsem, že's hodný hoch,
I've heard that you're nice boy,

I've heard that you're a nice boy,

[slɪʃɛl ˡsɛm   ʒɛs   fiɔdniː fiɔx   xasɲiːk   pratˢɔvɪtiː]

slyšel jsem,   že's   hodný hoch, chasník   pracovitý;
I've heard   that you're nice   boy, village boy hard-working;

I've heard that you're a nice boy, a hard-working villager;

[ʔalɛ v‿laːsˢɛ v‿laːsˢɛ priːs   xlapiːk   ʃlakɔvɪtiː]

ale v lásce—v lásce prý's   chlapík   šlakovitý.
but in love—in love they say good fellow devilish.

but in love—in love they say you're a devilish fellow.

[maːʃlɪ   pak   tɛːʃ   pɛɲiːzɛ]

Máš-li   pak   té   peníze?
Have you-if   then also money?

Have you, then, also money?

Jeník:

[vʒdɪt'   sɛ   mnɔfiː ʔɔʒɛɲiː   bɛs ‿ krejˢsaru f ‿ kapsɛ]

Vždyť   se   mnohý ožení   bez   krejcaru v   kapse;
To be sure -   many   marry without coin   in pocket;

Surely many a man marries without a penny in his pocket;

[ʃvarnɛː   d'iːfkɪ filed'iː spiːʃ   na ‿ ʃvarnɛː   zas   xlapˢsɛ]

švarné   dívky   hledí   spíš   na   švarné   zas   chlapce.
beautiful girls   look   rather for handsome again boys.

rather, beautiful girls look for handsome boys.

Kecal:

[mɲɛ vjɛŘ jaː ˡsɛm rɔzumniː ʔa maːm skuʃɛnɔstˀɪ]

Mně věř, já jsem rozumný a mám zkušenosti:
Me believe, I am wise, and I have experience:

Believe me, I am wise and have experience:

[bɛs ‿ pɛɲɛs bɛs ‿ pɛɲɛs]

bez peněz, bez peněz,
without money, without money,

without money, without money,

[bɛs ‿ pɛɲɛs jɛ ʒɛɲɪdlɔ jɛnɔm fɲiːzdɔ zlɔstˀɪ]

bez peněz je ženidlo jenom hnízdo zlosti,
without money is marriage just nest of spite,

without money, marriage is just a nest of spite,

[jɛnɔm fɲiːzdɔ zlɔstˀɪ jɛnɔm fɲiːzdɔ zlɔstˀɪ]

jenom hnízdo zlosti, jenom hnízdo zlosti!
just nest of spite, just nest of spite!

just a nest of spite, just a nest of spite!

[ʔɔtkut ˡsɪ pɔvjɛs mɪ]

Odkud jsi, pověz mi!
From where are you, say to me!

Where are you from, tell me!

[da:m   t'ɪ   dɔbrɛ: radɪ   zna:m   sɛ   vɛ ‿ ʃʃɛm   ʃʃadɪ]

Dám   ti   dobré   rady,   znám   se   ve   všem   všady.
I'll give to you good   advice, I know -   in everything everywhere.

I'll give you good advice, I know everything you need to know.

Jeník:

[z ‿ dalɛka   panɛ   ⁱsɛm   z ‿ dalɛka]

Z   daleka, pane, jsem—z   daleka,
From far away, sir,   I am—from far away,

From far away, sir, I am—from far away,

[ʔaʒ   z ‿ mɔrafski:ɣ   firaɲits͡ ʔaʒ   z ‿ mɔrafski:ɣ   firaɲits͡]

až   z   moravských   hranic, až   z   moravských   hranic.
as far as from   Moravian   borders, as far as from   Moravian   borders.

all the way to the Moravian border, all the way to the Moravian border.

Kecal:

[tam   sɛ ʔɔʒɛɲ   tam   sɛ ʔɔʒɛɲ]

Tam   se ožeň,   tam   se ožeň,
There   marry,   there   marry,

Get married there, get married there,

[zdeⁱʃi: panɪ   zdeⁱʃi: panɪ   nɛstɔji: nɛstɔji: ʔuʒ za ‿ ɲits͡]

zdejší panny, zdejší panny   nestojí,   nestojí   už   za   nic.
local maidens, local   maidens aren't worth, aren't worth else for   nothing.

the local girls, the local girls aren't worth, aren't worth anything.

Jeník:

[mɔʒnaː   ʒɛ   tɪ   ʔɔstatɲiː   mɔʒnaː   ʒɛ   tɪ   ʔɔstatɲiː]

Možná,[7] **že** **ty** **ostatní, možná,** **že** **ty** **ostatní,**
It's possible that those others, it's possible that those others,

Maybe the others aren't, maybe the others aren't,

[ʔalɛ maː mařɛŋka   ta   jɛ prraviː dɪjamant nɛⁱkrrasʃiː   kraːsɛŋka]

ale **má** **Mařenka** **ta** **je** **pravý** **diamant,** **nejkrasší** **krásenka!**
but my Mařenka that is true diamond, most beautiful beauty!

but my Mařenka, she is a true diamond, the most beautiful of all beautiful girls!

Kecal:

[kaʒdiː jɛn   tu   svɔu   maː   za ‿ jɛd'ɪnɔu maː   za ‿ jɛd'ɪnɔu]

Každý **jen** **tu** **svou** **má** **za** **jedinou, má** **za** **jedinou,**
Each only that his has after only, has after only,

Every boy has a girl who's one-of-a-kind, who's one-of-a-kind,

[fʃɛt͡skɪ kraːsɪ   svjɛta fʃɛt͡skɪ kraːsɪ   svjɛta   v ‿ ɲiː   vɪd'iː]

všecky **krásy** **světa, všecky** **krásy** **světa** **v** **ní** **vidí,**
all beauties of world, all beauties of world in her he sees,

all the beautiful women in the world, all of them he sees in her,

[ʔaʃ přɪⁱdɔu   t͡ʃasɪ gdɛ ɦɔ ʔɔʃid'iː   gdɛ ɦɔ ʔɔʃɪd'iː]

až **přijdou** **časy, kde** **ho** **ošidí,** **kde** **ho** **ošidí.**
until they arrive times when him she will cheat, when him she will cheat.

until the time comes when she cheats on him, when she cheats on him.

[pɔtɔm   lɪtujɛ   gdɪʃ   ʔuʃ   pɔzd'ɛ   jɛ]

Potom   lituje,   když   už   pozdě   je,
Then   he's sorry   when   already too late it is,

Then he's sorry, but it's already too late,

[gdɪʃ ʔuʃ   pɔzd'ɛ   jɛ   bɪxa   fiɔɲɪt'ɪ]

když už   <u>pozdě</u>   je   <u>bycha honiti</u>.[8]
when already   too late   it is   "to have regrets over something you can't change."

but it's already too late to cry over spilled milk.

[pɔtɔm bjɛdujɛ pɔtɔm   bjɛdujɛ   gdɪʃ   ʔuʃ   sɛ nɛdaː t͡ʃɛfiɔ   mɲɛɲɪt'ɪ]

Potom běduje, potom   běduje,   když už   se nedá   čeho   měniti.
Then he laments, then   he laments, when already   there's no anything to change.

Then he laments, then he laments, when he can't change a thing.

[rɔzumniː   fʃak   muʃ   pɔvaːʒlɪviː]

Rozumný   však   muž,   povážlivý,
Intelligent   however   man,   serious,

An intelligent man, however, being serious,

[jɛʃt'ɛ   pR̝ɛt _ svadbɔu   vɪstR̝iːzlɪviː]

ještě   před   svatbou   vystřízliví.
still   before   wedding   he'll come to his senses.

will come to his senses before the wedding.

[pɔtʃiːtaː t͡sɔ mu tɔ pɔtʃiːtaː t͡sɔ mu tɔ vɪnɛssɛ]

Počítá,[9] **co** **mu** **to,** **počítá,** **co** **mu** **to** **vynese,**
He counts what to him that, he counts what to him that yields,

He figures out what there is for him, he figures out what's in it for him,

[ʔa gdɪʃ ɲit͡s ʔa gdɪʃ ɲit͡s]

a **když** **nic,** **a** **když** **nic,**
and when nothing, and when nothing,

and when there's nothing, and when there's nothing,

[pak xɪtŘɛ vɪfinɛ sɛ vɪfinɛ sɛ]

pak **chytře** **vyhne se,** **vyhne se!**
then cleverly he steers clear, he steers clear!

then he cleverly escapes, escapes!

Jeník:

[t͡sɔ tʼiːm ː miːɲiːtɛ ři͡ːt͡sɪ jaː vaːm nɛrɔzumiːm]

Co **tím** **míníte** **říci?** **Já** **vám** **nerozumím.**
What that do you mean to say? I you don't understand.

What do you mean to say? I don't understand you.

Kecal:

[ʒɛ ʔɔ ‿ lɛpʃiː nɛvjɛstʼɛ prɔ ‿ tɛbɛ ɦɔchu viːm]

Že **o** **lepší** **nevěstě** **pro** **tebe,** **hochu,** **vím.**
That about better bride for you, boy, I know.

That I know a better bride for you, boy.

[znaːm   jɛdnu   d'iːfku   ta   maː   dukaːtɪ   maː   dukaːtɪ]

Znám   jednu   dívku,   ta   má   dukáty,   má   dukáty,
I know   one   girl,   that one   has   ducats,   she has   ducats,

I know a girl, she has money, she has money,

Jeník:

[znaː   jɛdnu   d'iːfku   ta   maː   dukaːtɪ   maː   dukaːtɪ]

Zná   jednu   dívku,   ta   má   dukáty,   má   dukáty,
He knows   one   girl,   that one   has   ducats,   she has   ducats,

He knows a girl, she has money, she has money,

Kecal:

[ʔa   xalupu   ʔa   xalupu   dɔstanɛ   ʔɔt ‿ | taːtɪ]

a   chalupu,   a   chalupu   dostane   od   táty![10]
and   cottage,   and   cottage   she'll get   from   dad!

and a cottage, and a cottage she'll get from her father!

Jeník:

[ʔa   xalupu   ʔa   xalupu   dɔstanɛ   ʔɔt ‿ | taːtɪ]

a   chalupu,   a   chalupu   dostane   od   táty!
and   cottage,   and   cottage   she'll get   from   dad!

and a cottage, and a cottage she'll get from her father!

Kecal:

[znaːm   jɛdnu   d'iːfku   ta   maː   dukaːtɪ   maː   dukaːtɪ]

Znám   **jednu**   **dívku,**   **ta**   **má**   **dukáty,**   **má**   **dukáty,**
I know   one   girl,   that one   has   ducats,   she has   ducats,

I know a girl, she has money, she has money,

Jeník:

[znaː   jɛdnu   d'iːfku   ta   maː   dukaːtɪ   maː   dukaːtɪ]

Zná   **jednu**   **dívku,**   **ta**   **má**   **dukáty,**   **má**   **dukáty,**
He knows   one   girl,   that one   has   ducats,   she has   ducats,

He knows a girl, she has money, she has money,

Kecal:

[ʔa   xalupu   ʔa   xalupu   dɔstanɛ   ʔɔt ‿ | taːtɪ]

a   **chalupu,**   **a**   **chalupu**   **dostane**   **od**   **táty!**
and   cottage,   and   cottage   she'll get   from   dad!

and a cottage, and a cottage she'll get from her father!

Jeník:

[ʔa   xalupu   ʔa   xalupu   dɔstanɛ   ʔɔt ‿ | taːtɪ]

a   **chalupu,**   **a**   **chalupu**   **dostane**   **od**   **táty!**
and   cottage,   and   cottage   she'll get   from   dad!

and a cottage, and a cottage she'll get from her father!

Kecal:

[dvjɛ kraːvɪ maː ʔa fiɛsskɛː tɛlaːtkɔ fius kaxɛn dɔst ʔa ɲaːkɛː sɛlaːtkɔ]

Dvě krávy má   a hezké telátko,   hus, kachen dost   a ňáké selátko,
Two cows she has and lovely little calf, geese, ducks enough and some   pigs,

*She's got two cows, a lovely little calf, a fair amount of geese, ducks, and some
pigs,*

[kus   pɔlɛ   maː   ʔa   nɔvou   ʔalmaru   ʔa   nɔvou   nɔvou   ʔalmaru]

kus   pole   má   a   novou   almaru,   a   novou,   novou   almaru!
piece of field she has and new   cupboard, and new,   new   cupboard!

she's got a piece of land and a new cupboard, and a new, a new cupboard!

Jeník:

[dvjɛ kraːvɪ maː ʔa fiɛsskɛː tɛlaːtkɔ fius kaxɛn dɔst ʔa ɲaːkɛː sɛlaːtkɔ]

Dvě krávy má   a hezké telátko,   hus, kachen dost   a ňáké selátko,
Two cows she has and lovely little calf, geese, ducks enough and some   pigs,

*She's got two cows, a lovely little calf, a fair amount of geese, ducks, and some
pigs,*

[kus   pɔlɛ   maː   ʔa   nɔvou   ʔalmaru   ʔa   nɔvou   nɔvou   ʔalmaru]

kus   pole   má   a   novou   almaru,   a   novou,   novou   almaru!
piece of field she has and new   cupboard, and new,   new   cupboard!

she's got a piece of land and a new cupboard, and a new, a new cupboard!

Kecal:

[nɔ   tɔ   bɪ bɪlɔ   ɲɛt͡sɔ]

No,   to   by bylo   něco,
Well,   that   would be   something,

Well, that would be something,

[nɔ   tɔ   bɪ bɪlɔ   ɲɛt͡sɔ   ku ‿ zdaru]

no,   to   by bylo   něco   ku   zdaru.
well,   that   would be   something   toward prosperity.

well, that would be something toward your prosperity.

Jeník:

[nɔ   tɔ   bɪ bɪlɔ   ɲɛt͡sɔ]

No,   to   by bylo   něco,
Well,   that   would be   something,

Well, that would be something,

[nɔ   tɔ   bɪ bɪlɔ   ɲɛt͡sɔ   ku ‿ zdaru]

no,   to   by bylo   něco   ku   zdaru.
well,   that   would be   something   toward prosperity.

well, that would be something toward your prosperity.

Kecal:

[znaːm   jɛdnu   dʼiːfku   ta   maː   dukaːtɪ]

Znám   jednu   dívku,   ta   má   dukáty,
I know   one   girl,   that one   has   ducats,

I know a girl, she has money,

[tɔ   bɪ bɪlɔ   ɲɛt͡sɔ   ku ‿ zdaru]

to   by bylo   něco   ku   zdaru!
that would be something toward prosperity!

that would be something toward your prosperity!

Jeník:

[znaː   jɛdnu jɛdnu d'iːfku ta   maː dukaːtɪ ta   maː dukaːtɪ]

Zná   jednu, jednu dívku, ta   má dukáty, ta   má dukáty.
He knows one,   one   girl, that one has ducats, that one has ducats.

He knows a girl, she has money, she has money.

[tɔ   bɪ bɪlɔ   ɲɛt͡sɔ   ku ‿ zdaru]

To   by bylo   něco   ku   zdaru,
That would be something toward prosperity,

That would be something toward my prosperity,

[nɔ   tɔ bɪ bɪlɔ   ɲɛt͡sɔ   ku ‿ zdaru]

no,   to by bylo   něco   ku   zdaru!
well, that would be something toward prosperity!

well, that would be something toward my prosperity!

Recitativ
Kecal:

[ʔɔdr̝ɛknɛʃlɪ sɛ   mar̝ɛŋkɪ vɪplat'iːm   t'ɪ   takeː ɲɛt͡sɔ]

Odřekneš-li se   Mařenky, vyplatím   ti   také něco.
You renounce- if Mařenka, I will pay to you also something.

If you'll renounce Mařenka, I'll pay you something, too.

[ʔanɔ tu maː ruka na‿tɔ]

Ano, tu má ruka na to,
Yes, here my hand on it,

Yes, here's my hand on it,

(vážně) (seriously)

[stɔ   zlatiːx   tʼɪ   daːm   za ‿ ʔɔtstɔupɛɲiː]

sto   zlatých ti   dám   za   odstoupení.
one hundred gold ones to you I'll give for renouncement.

I'll give you one hundred gold coins for renouncing her.

Jeník:

[jɛnɔm stɔ   zlatiːx   tɔ   jɛ maːlɔ pɛɲɛz | za ‿ tak mnɔfiɔ laːskɪ]

Jenom sto   zlatých? To je <u>málo peněz</u>[11] za   tak mnoho lásky!
Only   one hundred gold ones? That is little   money   for   so   much   love!

Only one hundred gold coins? That's too little money for so much love!

[tak   lat͡sɪnɔ jɪ   nɛprɔdaːm]

Tak   lacino   ji   neprodám!
So   cheap   her   I won't sell!

For so cheap I won't sell her!

Kecal: ## Jeník:

[nuʒɛ tɛdɪ dvjɛ stʼɛ   daːm]   [tɔ jɛ fʃɛt͡skɔ maːlɔ]

Nuže, tedy dvě stě   dám!   **To je všecko   málo!**
Well, then two hundred I'll give!   That is everything little!

Well, then, I'll give you two hundred!   *That's way too little!*

Kecal:

[tɛdɪ   tři   sta]

Tedy   tři   sta!
Then   three   hundred!

Then three hundred!

[t͡ʃɪɲiːm   tɔ   jɛn   prɔtɔ   ʔabɪ bɪlɔ   bɛz ͜ dlɔuɦiːx   prɔt͡sɛsuː]

Činím   to   jen   proto,   aby bylo   bez   dlouhých   procesů.
I'll do   that   only   so that   it would be   without   long   processes.

I'll do it only so it won't be a lengthy process.

[nɛpɔdaːʃlɪ sɛ   nɪɲiː   tɛdɪ   nasad'iːmɛ   fʃɛt͡skɪ   ɦaːkɪ]

Nepodáš-li se   nyní,   tedy   nasadíme   všecky   háky
You won't give-if   at present time,   then   we will set   all   hooks

If you won't deal now, then we'll muster all our resources

[ʔa   fstaːɦinɛmɛ   t'ɛ   kɔnɛt͡ʃɲɛ   přɛt͡s   ʔɔt͡tut]

a   vztáhneme   tě   konečně   přec   odtud.[12]
and   we'll pull out   you   finally   after all   from here.

and we'll end up driving you out of here.

[nɛbudɛʃ   pak   miːt'ɪ   nɛvjɛstɪ   ʔaɲɪ   třiː   sɛd   zlatiːx]

Nebudeš   pak   míti   nevěsty   ani   tří   set   zlatých!
You won't   then   have   bride   nor   of three hundred   gold ones!

Then you'll have neither a bride nor three hundred gold coins!

Jeník:

[tak   tak   ʔalɛ   gdɔ   pak   tɪ   tr̝̊ɪ   sta   mɪ   vɪplat'iː]

Tak-   tak-   ale   kdo   pak   ty   tři   sta   mi   vyplatí?
So-   so-   but   who   then   those   three hundred   to me   will pay?

So—so—but who, then, will pay me the three hundred?

Kecal:

[jaː   saːm]

Já   sám!
I   myself!

I myself!

Jeník:

[vɪ   snat   nɛ   za ‿ sɛbɛ]

Vy?   snad   ne   za   sebe?
You?   maybe   not   for   yourself?

You? maybe you'll keep her for yourself?

[vaːm   svɔu   mar̝ɛŋku   nɛprɔdaːm   ʔaɲɪ   za ‿ mɪlɪjɔn]

Vám   svou   Mařenku   neprodám   ani   za   milion!
To you   my   Mařenka   I won't sell   even   for   million!

I won't sell you Mařenka for even a million!

Kecal:

[nɛbud' filoupiː pro ‿sɛbɛ jɪ nɛxt͡sɪ]

Nebud' hloupý! Pro sebe ji nechci.
Don't be stupid! For myself her I don't want.

Don't be stupid! I don't want her for myself.

[maːm jɛdnɛː ʒɛnɪ ʔuʃ ʔaʃ po‿kr̩k]

Mám jedné ženy už až po krk!
I have one woman already up to neck!

I already have a woman up to my ears!

[t͡soʃ nɛviːʃ]

Což nevíš,
No doubt you don't know

No doubt, you don't know

[ʒɛ vɪjɛdnaːvaːm za ‿ sɪna sousɛda tobɪjaːʃɛ miːxɪ]

že vyjednávám za syna souseda Tobiáše Míchy?
that I'm negotiating on behalf of son of neighbor Tobiáš Mícha?

that I'm negotiating on behalf of the son of our neighbor Tobiáš Mícha?

[jag budɛ vjɛt͡s potvr̩zɛna]

Jak bude věc potvrzena,
As it will be matter confirmed,

As soon as the matter is confirmed,

[dɔstanɛʃ   tŘɪ   sta   ʔalɛ pak   finɛd   fiaⁱdɪ   ʔɔt|tut]

dostaneš   tři   sta,   ale pak   hned   hajdy   odtud![12]
you'll receive   three hundred, but then   right away   away   from here!

you'll receive your three hundred, but then right away you're out of here!

Jeník:

[nuʒɛ   staɲɪʃ sɛ   tŘɪ   sta   ⁱsɔu   tŘɪ   sta]

Nuže,   staniž se! Tři   sta   jsou   tři   sta!
Well,   be it done! Three hundred are   three hundred!

Well, so be it! Three hundred is three hundred!

[pɛɲiːzɛ na ‿ dřɛvɔ ʔa   budɛ   kɔnɛt͡s]

Peníze[13] **na   dřevo a   bude   konec.**
Money   on   wood   and   it will be end.

Put your money on the table, and it'll be finished.

[ʔalɛ tɔ   vaːm praviːm ʒɛ   mařɛŋku   ɲɪgdɔ jɪniː   dɔstatʼɪ   nɛsmiː]

Ale to   vám pravím, že   Mařenku   nikdo jiný   dostati   nesmí,
But   that to you I say, that Mařenka   no one other to receive may not,

But I say this to you, that Mařenka may marry no one else

[nɛʒlɪ sɪn tɔbɪjaːʃɛ miːxɪ   sit͡sɛ z ‿ naʃiː smlɔuvɪ   nɛbudɛ   praɲit͡s]

nežli syn Tobiáše Míchy, sice   z   naší smlouvy nebude   pranic.
than son of Tobiáš Mícha, rather from our   contract it won't be nothing at all.

but the son of Tobiáš Mícha, or the contract is void.

Kecal:

[ʔɪ   zlatɔuʃku   ʔɪ   zlatɔuʃku   tɔt'   sɛ rɔzumiː]

I   zlatoušku, i   zlatoušku, tot'   se rozumí,
And   dear one,   and   dear one,   of course   it's understood

My dear young man, my dear young man, of course it's understood

[ʒɛ   jɪ   jɪniː   nɛdɔstanɛ   nɛʒlɪ   miːxuf   sɪn]

že   ji   jiný   nedostane,   nežli   Míchuv   syn!
that   her   other   doesn't receive than   Mícha's   son!

that no one else will marry her but Mícha's son!

Jeník:

[ʔa   jaː   jɪ   jɪnɛːmu   ɲɪkɔmu   nɛpŘɛnɛxaːvaːm   nɛʒlɪ   miːxɔvu sɪnɔvɪ]

A   já   ji   jinému   nikomu   nepřenechávám,   nežli   Míchovu synovi.
And   I   her   to other no one   I am not entrusting, than   Mícha's   son.

And I'm not entrusting her to anyone other than Mícha's son.

[vɪɦrad'iːm sɪ   tɔ   vɛ ‿ smlɔuvjɛ]

Vyhradím si   to   ve   smlouvě!
I will stipulate that in   contract!

I'm stipulating that in the contract!

Kecal:

[ʔutʃɪɲiːmɛ   smlɔuvu   finɛtkɪ   ʔa   pŘɪvɔlaːmɛ sɪ   svjɛtkɪ]

Učiníme   smlouvu   hnedky   a   přivoláme si   svědky.
We'll make   contract   right away and   we'll call in   witnesses.

We'll make the contract right away, and we'll call in witnesses.

Jeník: Kecal:

[jɛʃt'ɛ slɔviːt͡ʃkɔ]   [mluf]

Ještě slovíčko!   **Mluv!**
Still   little word!   Speak!

One more little word!   *Speak!*

Jeník:

[daːlɛ   tam   fpiːʃɛtɛ]

Dále   tam   vpíšete,
Further   there you will inscribe

You will inscribe there further

[ʒɛ   jakmɪlɛ   mařɛŋka   ʔa   miːxuf   sɪn   sɪ   rut͡sɛ   pɔdajiː]

že,   jakmile   Mařenka   a   Míchuv   syn   si   ruce   podají
that   as soon as Mařenka   and Mícha's son   one another hands   they'll give

that as soon as Mařenka and Mícha's son take one another's hands

[ʔa   f ‿ sɲatɛk   svɔliː]

a   v   sňatek   svolí,
and   in marriage   consent,

and consent to marriage,

[ʔustanɛ   ʔɔtɛt͡s   miːxa   ʔɔd ‿ nalɛːɦaɲiː   na‿mařɛnt͡sɪna   ʔɔt͡tsɛ]

ustane   otec   Mícha   od   naléhání   na Mařencina   otce
he will cease father   Mícha   from pressure   to Mařenka's   father

Mícha will stop all pressure on Mařenka's father

[stran   dluɦu]

stran   dluhu.
as regards   debt.

as regards to debts.

[ˈsɔu   dɔt͡ʃɪsta   vɪrɔvnaːɲɪ]

Jsou   dočista   vyrovnáni.
They are   completely   compensated.

They are completely paid off.

Kecal:

[ʔanɔ ʔanɔ ʔanɔ dɔ ‿ smlɔuvɪ   f͡ʃɛt͡skɔ   daːm]

Ano,   ano,   ano,   do   smlouvy   všecko   dám.[14]
Yes,   yes,   yes,   to   contract   everything I'll put.

Yes, yes, yes, I'll put it all in the contract.

(Odkvapí.) (They hurry off.)

Výstup V   Scene v
Jeník

[ʔaʃ   ʔuzr̝iːʃ   kɔmus   kɔupɪl   nɛvjɛstu]

Až   uzříž,   komus   koupil   nevěstu,
When   you will behold, for whom   you did buy   bride,

When you see the one you bought the bride for,

[smutɲɛ   nastɔupiːʃ   spaːtɛt͡ʃɲiː   t͡sɛstu]

smutně   nastoupíš   zpáteční   cestu.
sadly   you will embark   homeward   path.

you will sadly leave for home.

[jak   mɔʒnaː   vjɛři̇t   ʒɛ   bɪx   jaː   prɔdal   svɔjɪ   mařɛŋku]

Jak   možná   věřit,   že   bych[15] **já   prodal   svoji   Mařenku?**
How   possible   to believe,   that   would   I   sell   my   Mařenka?

How is it possible to believe that I would sell my Mařenka?

[jak   mɔʒnaː   vjɛři̇t   ʒɛ   bɪx   jaː   prɔdal   svɔjɪ   mařɛŋku]

Jak   možná   věřit,   že   bych já   prodal   svoji   Mařenku?
How   possible   to believe,   that   would I   sell   my   Mařenka?

How is it possible to believe that I would sell my Mařenka?

[drafiɔːu   mařɛŋku   ʔandʼiːlka   svɛːfiɔ]

Drahou   Mařenku,   andílka   svého,
Dear   Mařenka,   little angel   my,

Dear Mařenka, my angel,

[prɔ ‿ ɲɛⁱʃ   mɪ   nɛɲiː   ɲi͡ts   ʔɔptʼiːʒnɛːfiɔ]

pro   nějž   mi   není   nic   obtížného,
for   whom   to me   is not   nothing   burdensome,

for whom I would bear anything,

[prɔ ‿ ɲɛⁱʃ   mɪ   nɛɲiː   ɲi͡ts   ʔɔptʼiːʒnɛːfiɔ]

pro   nějž   mi   není   nic   obtížného,
for   whom   to me   is not   nothing   burdensome,

for whom I would bear anything,

[ɲɪ   za ‿ tʼɪsiːt͡sɛ   bɪx   nɛʔɔtstɔupɪl]

Ni   za   tisíce   bych   neodstoupil;
Not even   for   thousands   would I   renounce;

Not even for thousands would I forsake her;

[na ‿ t͡sɛlɛːm   svjɛtʼɛ   rɔvnɛː   jiː   nɛɲiː]

na   celém   světě   rovné   jí   není.
in   whole   world   equal   to her is not.

in the whole world there is no one like her.

[vʒdɪtʼ   jɛnɔm   laːska   laːsku   ʔot͡sɛɲiː]

Vždyť'   jenom   láska   lásku   ocení,
To be sure   only   love   love   values,

Only love can value love,

[vʒdɪtʼ   jɛnɔm   laːska   laːsku   ʔot͡sɛɲiː]

vždyť'   jenom   láska   lásku   ocení.
to be sure   only   love   love   values.

only love can value love.

(Odejde.) (He leaves.)

Výstup VI   Scene vi   *Finale*
Jeník, Kecal, Krušina, Lid [People]

Kecal:

[pɔⁱtʼtɛ lɪdʼɪt͡ʃkɪ   pɔⁱtʼtɛ   lɪdʼɪt͡ʃkɪ   pɔⁱtʼtɛ   pɔⁱtʼtɛ   pɔⁱtʼtɛ   lɪdʼɪt͡ʃkɪ]

Pojd'te lidičky,   pojd'te lidičky,   pojd'te, pojd'te, pojd'te lidičky,
Come   dear people, come   dear people, come,   come,   come   dear people,

Come, dear people, come, dear people, come, come, come, dear people,

[pɔzɔr dɛⁱtɛ pɔzɔr dɛⁱtɛ naʃiː smlɔuvjɛ svjɛdɛt͡stviː dɛⁱtɛ]

pozor dejte, pozor dejte, naší smlouvě svědectví dejte!
heed give, heed give, to our contract witness give!

pay heed, pay heed, witness our contract!

Sbor [Chorus]:

[pɔzɔr daːmɛ svjɛdɛt͡stviː daːmɛ]

Pozor dáme, svědectví dáme.
Heed we'll give, witness we'll give.

We'll give heed, we'll witness it.

Kecal:

[tu na ͜ papiːru zaznamɛnaː sɛ t͡sɔ vɪkɔnaː t͡sɔ vɪkɔnaː sɛ]

Tu na papíru, zaznamená se, <u>co   vykoná, co   vykoná</u>[16] se.
Here on paper, it'll be recorded, what will do, what will be done.

Here on paper we'll set down what we'll do, what we'll do.

Sbor [Chorus]:

[zaznamɛnaː sɛ zaznamɛnaː sɛ t͡sɔ vɪkɔnaː t͡sɔ vɪkɔnaː sɛ]

Zaznamená se, zaznamená se, <u>co   vykoná, co   vykoná</u>[16] se.
It'll be recorded, it'll be recorded, what will do, what will be done.

They'll set down what they'll do, what they'll do.

Kecal:

(Sedne ke stolu a píše.) (He sits at the table and writes.)

[t'iːmtɔ jaː sɛ zavazujɪ   ʒɛ   svɔu   mɪlɔːu ʔɔtstupujɪ]

Tímto   já se zavazuji,   že   svou   milou   odstupuji.
By that   I   vow   that   my   dear   I renounce.

"Hereby I vow that I do renounce my sweetheart."

Sbor [Chorus]:

[t'iːmtɔ ʔɔn sɛ zavazujɛ   ʒɛ   svɔu   mɪlɔːu ʔɔtstupujɛ]

Tímto   on se zavazuje,   že   svou   milou   <u>odstupuje</u>.[17]
By that   he   vows   that   his   dear   he renounces.

Hereby he vows that he renounces his sweetheart.

Jeník:

[ɲɪkɔmu   fʃak   jɪnɛːmu nɛʒlɪ   vɛlɛt͡st'ɛnɛːmu sɪnu   tɔbɪjaːʃɛ miːxɪ]

Nikomu   však   jinému, nežli   velectěnému   synu Tobiáše Míchy!
To no one however to other than   to honorable   son   of Tobiáš Mícha!

But to no one other than the honorable son of Tobiáš Mícha!

Kecal:

[sɪnu   tɔbɪjaːʃɛ miːxɪ]

Synu   Tobiáše Míchy.
To son   of Tobiáš Mícha!

To the son of Tobiáš Mícha!

Jeník:

[jɛstlɪʒɛ jɪ   mɪlujɛ sr̩t͡sɛ svɛː jiː   vjɛnujɛ]

Jestliže ji   miluje, srdce své jí   věnuje,
If   her   he loves, heart his to her gives up,

If he loves her, gives his heart to her,

[ʔa   pr̝ɛt ‿ svjɛtkɪ   bɛz ‿ nut͡sɛɲiː   vɪr̝knɛ]

a   před svědky   bez nucení   vyřkne,
and   before witnesses without pressure he declares

and declares freely before witnesses

[ʒɛ   sɛ   s ‿ ɲiː   ʔɔʒɛɲiː]

že   se   s   ní   ožení.
that   -   with her he'll marry.

that he'll marry her.

Kecal:

[vʃɛ   zapsaːnɔ fʃɛ   zapsaːnɔ jak   ʒaːdaːnɔ]

Vše   zapsáno, vše   zapsáno, jak   žádáno.
Everything written, everything written,   as   requested.

Everything's written, everything's written, as requested.

Sbor [Chorus]:

[jak   jɛn   mɔʒnaː   ʒɛ   ʔɔtstɔupɪl   mɪlɛŋku]

Jak   jen   možná,   že   odstoupil   milenku?
How   only   it's possbile that   he renounced sweetheart?

But how is it possible that he renounced his sweetheart?

Krušina:

(k Jeníkovi) (to Jeník)

[ɲɪgdɪ   bɪɣ bɪl   nɛʔuvjɛřɪl ʒɛ tag dɔbrɛː sr̩tsɛ   maːʃ]

Nikdy   bych byl   neuvěřil,   že tak dobré srdce   máš,
Never   would I have   believed   that so   good   heart   you have

Never would I have believed that you have such a good heart

[ʒɛ   bɪz   z ‿ nɛsnaːziː naːs vɪtr̩x   dɔbrɔvɔlɲɛ   sɛ pɔdːdaːʃ]

že   bys   z   nesnází nás vytrh',   dobrovolně   se poddáš.[18]
that you would from troubles us   pull out,   voluntarily   you will yield.

that you would pull us from our troubles, and of your own free will yield.

Kecal:

[jɛʃtʼɛ nɛⁱsmɛ   jɛʃtʼɛ nɛⁱsmɛ   jɛʃtʼɛ nɛⁱsmɛ   nɛⁱsmɛ   ʔu ‿ kɔnt͡sɛ]

Ještě   nejsme, ještě   nejsme, ještě   nejsme, nejsme   u konce.
Still   we're not, still   we're not, still   we're not, we're not at   end.

Still we're not, still we're not, still we're not, we're not finished.

[sluʃiː   dɔlɔʒɪtʼɪ]

Sluší   doložiti,
It is advisable   to add

It is advisable to add

[ʒɛ ⁱsmɛ sɛ zavaːzalɪ jɛɲiːkɔvɪ tŘɪ sta   zlatiːx   vɪplatʼɪtʼɪ]

že   jsme se zavázali Jeníkovi tři   sta   zlatých   vyplatiti.
that we have pledged   to Jeník three hundred gold ones to pay.

that we have pledged to pay Jeník three hundred gold coins.

[za ‿ tŘɪ   sta   ʔɔn sɛ naːm   pɔddal ʔa   svɔu mařɛŋku   prɔdal]

Za   tři sta   on   se nám   poddal[19] **a   svou Mařenku prodal.**
For three hundred he -   to us gave up and his   Mařenka   sold.

For three hundred he gave up and sold his Mařenka.

Sbor [Chorus]:

[ʔaⁱ tɔd' fianba   vjɛru fianba prɔdat'ɪ   mɪlɛŋku svɔu]

Aj,   tot' hanba,   věru   hanba, prodati   milenku svou!
Ah,   truly shame,   really shame, to sell   sweetheart his!

Ah, how shameful, truly shameful, to sell his sweetheart!

Krušina:

(k Jeníkovi) (to Jeník)

[bɛru   tɛt' svɔu   xvaːlu   spjɛt]

Beru[20] **ted' svou   chválu   zpět,**
I take now   my   praise   back,

Now I take back my praise—

[takɔvɛːfiɔ   fianɛbɲiːka   jakɔ   tɪs   nɛvɪd'ɛl   svjɛt]

takového   hanebníka,   jako   tys,   neviděl   svět.
such   shameful person, as   you are, didn't see world.

such a shameful person as you the world has never seen.

Kecal:

[puŋktum satɪs   puŋktum satɪs   puŋktum satɪs   piːsɛk na ‿ tɔ]

Punktum, satis,   punktum, satis,   punktum, satis,   <u>písek na to</u>![21]
Period, sufficient,   period, sufficient,   period, sufficient,   sand on   it!

Period, sufficient, period, sufficient, period, sufficient, some sand on it!

[pɔdɛpɪʃtɛ sɛ   neⁱpr̩f   tɪ   jɛɲiːku   pɔtɔm   svjɛtkɔvɛː]

Podepište se,   nejprv ty,   Jeníku, potom   svědkové!
Sign,   first   you,   Jeník,   then   witnesses!

Sign, first you, Jeník, then the witnesses!

Jeník:

(Chladně podepíše.) (Cooly he signs.)

[zdɛ   muːⁱ   pɔtpɪs   jɛɲiːk   fiɔraːk]

Zde můj   podpis—Jeník Horák.
Here my   signature—Jeník Horák.

Here's my signature—Jeník Horák.

Krušina:

(Podepíše.) (He signs.)

[vjɛru   ⁱsɛm tɛt'   tɔmu   raːt   naʔutʃɪl ⁱsɛm sɛ   t'ɛ   znaːt]

Věru   jsem   ted'   tomu   rád,   naučil jsem se   tě   znát.
Truly   I am   now   to that   glad,   I learned   you   to know.

Truly I am glad of this—I've learned to know you.

Sbor [Chorus]:

[prɔdal svɔːu mɪlɔːu   za ‿ tŘɪ sta   prɔdal svɔu mɪlɔːu]

Prodal svou milou   za tři sta;   prodal svou milou!
He sold his sweetheart for three hundred; he sold his   dear!

He sold his sweetheart for three hundred; he sold his dear one!

Sbor [Chorus], Krušina, Kecal:

[nɛɲiːt'   nɛɲiːt'   vjɛru draɦaː   nɛɲiːt'   nɛɲiːt'   vjɛru draɦaː]

Nenít',   nenít'   věru <u>drahá</u>,[22] nenít',   nenít'   věru drahá,
She's not, she's not really   dear,   she's not, she's not really   dear,

She's not, she's truly not dear, she's not, she's truly not dear,

[prɔdal svɔːu mɪlɔːu   za ‿ tŘɪ   sta]

prodal svou milou   za   tři sta,
he sold   his sweetheart for three hundred,

he sold his sweetheart for three hundred,

[svɔːu mɪlɔːu prɔdal za ‿ tŘɪ   sta   prɔdal]

svou milou prodal, za   tři sta   prodal,
his   dear   he sold, for three hundred he sold,

he sold his dear one, he sold her for three hundred,

[ʔɔː ɦanba ɦanba ɦanba ɦanba ɦanba ɦanba   ɦanba ɦanba]

ó,   hanba, hanba, hanba, hanba, hanba, hanba, hanba, hanba!
oh, shame, shame, shame, shame, shame, shame, shame, shame!

oh, shame, shame, shame, shame, shame, shame, shame, shame!

(Opona) (Curtain)   Konec II. jednání.   End of the second act.

Notes

1. The final note of *kuráže*, m. 31, can be a quarter. The same is true of *se váže*. The tempo also usually picks up at m. 31. The very last *Ejchuchu!* can end with an eighth.

2. In this great musical expression of stuttering, the effect should be that the singer is trying very hard to sing normally, on downbeats, but cannot. When he does get out a word, his stuttering soon cuts him off. There must be a struggle. Just singing what is written on the page will not capture the effect!

3. Loosen up the short-long rhythm on *celá* every time.

4. Remember the stress is on *za-*, not *-ji-*. Also hold the long vowel, *-sté*, slightly.

5. In the recitatives, Vašek's stuttering does not have to have the exact number of written repeated notes.

6. The word Vašek is trying to say is *nenechám*, so accent the first E. Otherwise, it just sounds like a lot of *ne*'s.

7. Bend the two eighth notes on this word, both times, for the short-long rhythm.

8. The phrase *pozdě bycha honiti* is a centuries-old expression used when someone regrets his/her own past action that in hindsight could have been prevented.

9. Czech singers bend the rhythm here, making *po-* shorter than an eighth so that *-čí-* can be lengthened slightly. This is done even though the orchestra doubles with straight eighths.

10. It is important to always pronounce two *t*'s on *od táty* so that the word *od* is clear.

11. The first edition had *věru málo* [truly little], but the autograph sources had *málo peněz*, which is set perfectly. See the notes in Bedřich Smetana and Karel Sabina, *Prodaná nevěsta*, piano/vocal score, 3d ed. (Prague: Editio Supraphon, 1982), 317. The rest is not necessary after *peněz*—just repeat the *z* going into *za*, or sing a long *z*.

12. Both [t] sounds must be pronounced in *odtud*. See Timothy Cheek, *Singing in Czech: A guide to Czech lyric diction and vocal repertoire* (Lanham, Md.: Scarecrow Press, 2001), 81–82, 88.

13. Change the rhythm on *penize* to sixteenth, eighth, sixteenth.

14. These words are preferred at the Prague National Theatre. Sing all three *anos*, as written; then sing two A's instead of one on *do smlou-*. Then continue as written with *-vy* and the remaining words.

15. The 1982 Supraphon piano/vocal score has the articulations missing on these two measures, 992–93. They are correct in: Bedřich Smetana and Karel Sabina, *Prodaná nevěsta*, orchestral score, 2d ed. (Prague: Státní nakladatelství literatury, hudby a umění v Praze; Museum Bedřicha Smetany v Praze, 1953), 375. Not quite the same as the next *Jak možná věřit, že bych*, there should be one slur over *Jak možná* and one over *věřit, že bych*, with staccatos over each note.

16. Czechs—both Kecal and the chorus—change the articulation of the quarter note at the end of *vykoná*. Because it is a long vowel, the *-ná* is sung as a half note, or as a half note with a *slight* separation after it.

17. The final note can be a quarter instead of a half.

18. The 1982 Supraphon piano/vocal score incorrectly has *podáš*, a different word. Pronounce an Italian double *d*, as in *freddo*. The orchestral score is correct: Smetana and Sabina, *Prodaná nevěsta*, orchestral score, 2d ed., 396.

19. Try to make the double *dd* clear in *poddal*, like an Italian double *dd*, as in *freddo*. *Podal*, with one *d*, means "he offered to help." See Cheek, *Singing in Czech*, 81.

20. Although the scores have *béřu*, this is so antiquated that Czechs always substi-

tute the common *beru* instead. (Because of the whole note, the first syllable still has to be long, but doing so serves to stress the word—lengthening normally short vowels is one common way Czechs stress a word.)

21. Sand was shaken on wet ink to help dry it.

22. Like the Italian *cara*, *drahá* can also mean "expensive." That's probably not a joke Sabina intended, though!

8

Act III

Jednání III

Dějiště jako v jednání prvním

Act III

Scene as in the first act

Výstup I Scene i

Vašek

[Opona] [Curtain] (Vašek vystoupí.) (Vašek appears.)

[tɔ tɔ mɪ v ⌣ ɦlavjɛ lɛ lɛʒiː ʔɔ ʔɔ ʒɪvɔt mɪ bjɛ bjɛʒiː]

To- to mi v hlavě le- leží, o- o život mi bě- běží;
That- that to me in head lie- lies, oh oh life to me ru- runs;

It's- it's stuck in my he- head, oh- oh, my life is fall- falling apart;

[jɛ jɛstlɪ mnɛ ʔɔtraː trraːviː]

je- jestli mne otrá- tráví,[1]
i- if me she will poi- poison,

i- if she'll poison me,

[fʃɛ fʃɛɦɔ mnɛ tu zba zba zbaviː]

vše- všeho mne tu zba- zba- zbaví,
of every- everything me then she will ri- ri- rid,

if she'll de- deprive me of every- everything,

195

[tɔ   tɔ   mɪ   v ‿ filavjɛ   lɛ   lɛʒiː   ʔɔ   ʔɔ   ʔɔ   ʒɪvɔt]

to-	to	mi	v	hlavě	le-	leží,	o-	o-	o	život,
that-	that	to me	in	head	lie-	lies,	oh	oh	oh	life,

it's- it's stuck in my he- head, oh- oh- oh, my life,

[ʔɔ   ʒɪvɔt   mɪ   bjɛ   bjɛʒiː]

o	život	mi	bě-	běží!
oh	life	to me	ru-	runs!

oh, my life is fall- falling apart!

[tɔ   tɔ   mɪ   v ‿ filavjɛ   lɛ   lɛʒiː   ʔɔ   ʔɔ   ʒɪvɔt   mɪ   bjɛ   bjɛʒiː]

To-	to	mi	v	hlavě	le-	leží,	o-	o	život	mi	bě-	běží;
That-	that	to me	in	head	lie-	lies,	oh	oh	life	to me	ru-	runs;

It's- it's stuck in my he- head, oh- oh, my life is fall- falling apart;

[va   vaʃɛk   ʔumr̝iːt   mu   mu   musiː   ʔɔx   ʔɔx]

Va-	Vašek	umřít	mu-	mu-	musí,	och,	och,
Va-	Vašek	to die	mu-	mu-	must,	oh,	oh,

Va- Vašek will have to die, oh, oh,

[t͡sɔ   pr̝ɪ ‿ tɔm   sku   sku   skussiː]

co	při	tom	zku-	zku-	zkusí,
what	with	that	he'll su-	su-	suffer,

and also su- su- suffer,

[tɔ   tɔ   mɪ   v ‿ filavjɛ   lɛ   lɛʒiː   ʔɔ   ʔɔ   ʔɔ   ʔɔ   ʔɔ   ʔɔ   ʒɪvɔt]

to-	to	mi	v	hlavě	le-	leží,	o-	o-	o-	o-	o-	o	život,
that-	that	to me	in	head	lie-	lies,	oh	oh	oh	oh	oh	oh	life,

it's- it's stuck in my he- head, oh- oh- oh- oh- oh- oh, my life,

[ʔɔ ʒɪvɔt mɪ bjɛ bjɛʒiː]

o život mi bě- běží!
oh life to me ru- runs!

oh, my life is fall- falling apart!

Výstup II Scene ii
Principál komediantů, Esmeralda, Indián, Vašek

Za jevištěm slyšeti jest tlučení na veliký buben.
Behind the stage is heard beating on a large drum.

Vstoupí principál, komediant s bubnem, Esmeralda.
The Principál, a comedian with the drum, and Esmeralda enter.

Pochod komediantů *March of the comedians*

Recitativ[2]
Principál komediantů [Head of the circus performers]:
(Tromba na jevišti) (Trumpet/bugle on the stage)

[ʔɔɦlaʃujɛmɛ slavnɛːmu publɪkum ʒɛ sɛ tu dnɛs]

Ohlašujeme slavnému publikum, že se tu dnes,
We announce to distinguished public that - here today,

We announce to the distinguished public that here today,

[jakɔʃtɔ pŘɪ ‿ slavnɛː pɔut'ɪ]

jakožto při slavné pouti
as on distinguished fair

on the occasion of your distinguished fair,

[prɔvɔzɔvat'ɪ budɛ znamɛɲɪtaː ɲɪɡdɪ pR̝ɛt ‿ t'iːm nɛviːdanaː kɔmɛdɪjɛ]

provozovati bude znamenitá, nikdy před tím nevídaná komedie
to operate   it will exceptional, never before that unprecedented comedy

an exceptional, never-before-seen, unprecedented show will be carried out

[na ‿ prɔvazɛ na ‿ kɔɲɪ ʔɪ na ‿ zɛmɪ]

na provaze, na koni i na zemi,
on rope,   on horse and even on earth,

on the tightrope, on the horse, and even on the ground,

[ɡdɛʃtɔ zvlaːʃt'ɛ slɛt͡ʃna ʔɛsmɛralda salamaŋka]

kdežto zvláště slečna Esmeralda Salamanka
whereas especially Miss Esmeralda Salamanka

whereas especially Miss Esmeralda Salamanka

[prɔvaːd'ɛt'ɪ budɛ znamɛɲɪtɛː ʔa nɛsliːxanɛː skɔkɪ]

prováděti bude znamenité a neslýchané skoky,
perform   she will exceptional and unheard-of leaps,

will perform exceptional and unheard-of leaps,

[pak ʔɔpravdɔviː jɛdɛn ʔɪndɪjaːn s ‿ ʔɔtafɪɪtaːnskiːx ʔɔstrɔvuː]

pak opravdový jeden Indián z Otahitánských ostrovů,
then genuine one Indian from Tahiti islands,

then a genuine Indian from the Tahitian islands,

[padɛsaːt t'ɪsiːt͡s mɪl ʔɔtsut vzdaːlɛniːx pɔlɪkat'ɪ budɛ ʒɪdl ɛː]

padesát tisíc mil odsud vzdálených, polykati bude židl (é)
fifty thousand miles from here distant, swallow he will chair— uh

fifty-thousand miles distant from here, will swallow storks[3]—uh,

(Opravuje se.) (He corrects himself.)

[vɪdlɪt͡ʃkɪ ʔa nɔʒɛ nat͡ʃɛʃ pak vɪstɔupiː nɛⁱznamɛɲɪt'ɛⁱʃiː kus]

vidličky a nože, načež pak vystoupí nejznamenitější kus,[4]
forks and knives, whereupon then enters most remarkable piece,

forks and knives, whereupon then the most remarkable item will enter,

[tɔt'ɪʃ | ʒɪviː ʔamɛrɪkaːnskiː mɛdvjɛt]

totiž živý amerikánský medvěd,
namely live American bear,

namely, a live American bear,

[budɛ sɛ prɔdut͡siːrɔvat'ɪ slavnɛːmu publɪkum]

bude se producírovati slavnému publikum
it will produce to distinguished public

which will perform for the distinguished public

[sɛ zvlaːʃt'ɛ drɛsiːrɔvaniːmɪ kumʃtɪ]

se zvláště dresírovanými kumšty,
with especially well-trained arts,

with remarkably well-trained skill,

[ʔa kɔnɛt͡ʃɲɛ sɛ ‿ slɛt͡ʃnou salamaŋkɔu]

a konečně se slečnou Salamankou
and finally with Miss Salamanka

at the very end, with Miss Salamanka,

[sɛm   zvlaːʃt'ɛ   s ‿ fraŋkraⁱxu   pR̝ɪvɛzɛniːm   kaŋkaːnɛm]

sem   zvláště   z Frankrajchu   přivezeným   kankánem.
to here   especially from France   with imported   can-can.

remarkably the dance imported here from France, the can-can.

(vážně) (seriously)
[ku ‿ ktɛrɛːmuʃtɔ   pR̝ɛtstavɛɲiː   slavnɛː   publɪkum]

Ku   kterémužto představení slavné   publikum,
To   which   performance distinguished public,

To which performance the distinguished public,

[sɛ ‿ vʃiː   ʔuːt͡stɔu   ʔa   vaːʒnɔst'iː sɛ   zvɛ]

se   vší   úctou   a   vážností se   zve!
with   all   respect and   dignity   itself invites!

with all due respect and dignity, is invited!

[fʃak   malɔu   skɔuʃku ʔufiliːdaː   slavnɛː   ʔɔbet͡sɛnstvɔ ʔɪfɪnɛt]

Však   malou   zkoušku uhlídá   slavné   obecenstvo⁵ ihned.
However small   rehearsal will perceive distinguished spectators   right away.

*However, a short rehearsal will be presented to our distinguished spectators
right away.*

[fiɔla   zat͡ʃɲɛtɛ]

Hola!   Začněte!⁶
Hey!   Begin!

Hey! Begin!

Skočná
Balet a produkce komediantů
Ballet and performance of the circus performers [Dance of the comedians]

Recitativ
Vašek:

[jɛ   jɛ   jɛ   jɛ   tɔ   budɛ   ɦɛsskɛː]

Je-   je-   je-   je!   To   bude   hezké!
Wow-   wow-   wow-   wow!   That   will be   pretty!

Wow- wow- wow- wow! That'll be nice!

[ʔa   ta   ta   ʔɪ   ʔɪ   ʔɪndɪjaːŋka   maː   ɦɛ   ɦɛ   ɦɛsskɛː   nɔʒɪt͡ʃkɪ]

A   ta-   ta   i-   i-   indiánka[7] **má   he-   he-   hezké   nožičky!**
And   that-   that   I-   I-   Indian girl   has   pre-   pre-   pretty   little legs!

And that- that I- I- Indian girl has pre- pre- pretty legs!

Esmeralda:

(Vaškovi se pokloníc) (To Vašek with a bow)

[panaːt͡ʃɛk   naːs   takɛː   naf ʃt'iːviː]

Panáček   nás   také   navštíví?
Dear sir   us   also   will visit?

The dear sir will visit us, too?

Vašek:

[ʔa   ʔa   ʔanɔ   raːd   bɪx   vɪ   vɪ   vɪd'ɛl   vaːs   na ‿ prɔvazɛ]

A-   a-   ano!   Rád   bych   vi-   vi-   viděl   vás   na   provaze!
Ye-   ye-   yes!   Glad   would I   se-   se-   see   you   on   rope!

Ye- ye- yes! I would like to se- se- see you on the tightrope!

(Esmeralda s ním mluví stranou.) (Esmeralda speaks with him aside.)

Indián:

(Přikvapí.) (He rushes in.)

[panɛ prɪnt͡sɪpaːl panɛ prɪnt͡sɪpaːl]

Pane principál, pane principál!
Mr. director, Mr. director!

Mr. director, Mr. director!

[stalɔ sɛ vɛlkɛː nɛʃt’ɛst’iː franta sɛ ʔɔpɪl v ‿ dɔlɛ^{i}ʃiː ɦɔspɔd’ɛ]

Stalo se velké neštěstí! Franta se opil v dolejší hospodě,
It happened big disaster! Franta got drunk in lower pub,

There's been a big diaster! Franta got drunk in the lower pub,

[tagʒɛ sɛ nɛmuːʒɛ ʔaɲɪ na ‿ nɔɦɪ pɔstavɪt’ɪ]

takže se nemůže ani na nohy postaviti
so that himself he can't even on legs stand up

so that he can't even stand up by himself,

[ʔa nɛxt͡sɛ dnɛs mɛrmɔmɔt͡siː d’ɛlat’ɪ mɛdvjɛda]

a nechce dnes mermomocí dělati medvěda.
and he doesn't want today be what may to do bear.

and he absolutely refuses to be the bear.

Principál:

[jagʒɛ jagʒɛ naːʃ nɛ^{i}pjɛkɲɛ^{i}ʃiː kus mɛdvjɛt bɪ nɛvɪstɔupɪl]

Jakže? Jakže? Náš nejpěknější kus? Medvěd by nevystoupil?
How's that? How's that? Our finest piece? Bear wouldn't appear?

What? What? Our finest act? The bear wouldn't appear?

[slavniː   kaŋkaːn   bɪ sɛ nɛprɔvɔzɔval]

Slavný   kankán   by se neprovozoval?
Celebrated   can-can   wouldn't run?

The celebrated can-can wouldn't happen?

[nɛ nɛ nɛ tɔ nɛmuːʒɛ tɔ   nɛsmiː   biːt]

Ne, ne, ne, to nemůže, to   nesmí   být!
No, no, no, that cannot, that   may not   be!

No, no, no, that cannot, that must not be!

[musiːmɛ filɛdatʼɪ jɪnɛːfiɔ snat   ɲɛgdɔ vɛ ‿ fsɪ   ɲɛktɛriː kluk]

Musíme   hledati jiného.   Snad někdo ve   vsi,   některý kluk?
We must   look for another. Maybe someone in   village, some   boy?

We have to look for someone else. Maybe someone in the village, some boy?

Indián:

[tɛn bɪ   tɔ   vɪbrɛptal ʔa   lɪdɛː   bɪ   sɛ   naːm   smaːlɪ]

Ten by   to   vybreptal a   lidé   by   se   nám   smáli.
That would   that blab   and   people would -   to us   laugh.

He would blab it all, and people would laugh at us.

[gdɛ   hɔ   takɛː finɛt   vziːtʼɪ]

Kde   ho   také   hned   vzíti?
Where him   also   right away take?

And where to find him right away?

[musiː   biːt'ɪ vɪrɔstliː   ʔabɪ   sɛ   mu   mɛdvjɛd'iː kuːʒɛ ɦɔd'ɪla]

Musí   býti vyrostlý, aby   se   mu   medvědí kůže hodila.
He must   be   grown,   so that it would -   to him bear   skin   fit.

He's got to be filled-out so the bearskin will fit him.

[lɪdɛː   sɛ   tam   ʔuʃ   sxaːzɛjiː]

Lidé   se   tam   už   scházejí,
People   -   there already meet,

People are already gathering over there,

[nɛzbiːvaː   ʔuʃ   ʔaɲɪ   t͡ʃasu   ɲɛkɔɦɔ   ɦlɛdat'ɪ]

nezbývá   už   ani   času   někoho hledati.
it doesn't remain already even   time   him   to look for.

there's not even enough time left to look for him.

Principál:

[ʔu ‿ ʃʃɛx   ʃʃudɪ   ʔɛsmɛraldɔ]

U   všech   všudy,   Esmeraldo!
At   everything everywhere, Esmeralda!

If that doesn't beat all, Esmeralda!

(Esmeralda přiskočí a mluví s ním stranou.)
(Esmeralda runs over and speaks with him aside.)

Vašek:

[ʔax   ta   ta   ʔu ʔumiː   mluvɪt]

Ach, ta-   ta   u- umí   mluvit.
Ah,   that- that kno- knows   how to speak.

Ah, that- that one kno- knows how to talk.

[tu   tu   bɪx   sɪ   fine   finet   vzal]

Tu-   tu   bych   si   hne- hned   vzal.
That- that   would I -   ri- right away   marry.

He- her I would marry ri- right away.

[tɔ   bɪ   bɪ   bɪ   bɪ   bɪ   bɪla   radɔst]

To   by-   by-   by-   by-   by-   byla   radost,
That   wou- wou- wou- wou- wou- would be   joy,

That wou- wou- wou- wou- wou- would be such joy,

[t͡sɛ   t͡sɛlaː   vɛz   bɪ   bɪ   sɛ   kɔ   kɔ   kɔukala]

ce-   celá   ves   by-   by   se   ko- ko- koukala.
who-   whole   village wou- would -   lo- lo- look.

the who- whole village wou- would ta- take notice.

Esmeralda:

[mɲɛ   sɛ liːbiːtɛ   jaː bɪx   vaːs   takɛː xtʼɛla]

Mně   se líbíte,   já bych   vás   také   chtěla.
To me   you are pleasing, I would you   also   want.

I like you, and I would like you for my own.

Vašek:

[xtʼɛla   bɪ   bɪ   bɪ   bɪ   bɪstɛ   mnɛ]

Chtěla   by-   by-   by-   by-   byste   mne?
Want you wou- wou- wou- wou- would   me?

You wa- wa- wa- wa- want me?

Indián:

(k principálovi) (to the Principál)

[tɔmu   bɪ   ta   mɛdvjɛdʼiː   kuːʒɛ   sluʃɛla]

Tomu   by   ta   medvědí   kůže   slušela,
To that one would   that   bear   skin   suit,

That one would fit the bearskin

[jakɔ bɪ   mu   bɪla   pŘɪrɔstla]

jako by   mu   byla   přirostla.
as if it   to him   were   grown into.

as if it were his second skin.

Principál:

(ke komediantům) (to the circus performers)

[ⁱdʼɛtɛ   ʔa   vɪfilaʃuⁱtɛ   daːlɛ   pɔ ‿ fsɪ]

Jděte   a   vyhlašujte   dále   po   vsi!
Go on   and   announce   further   all over village!

Go on announcing it all over the village!

[jaː tadɪ   prɔmluviːm   s ‿ panaːt͡ʃkɛm]

Já   tady   promluvím   s   panáčkem.
I   here   will speak   with   dear sir.

I'll speak here with the gentleman.

(Pochod na jevišti) (March on the stage), s. 212 (p. 212) [m. 94, opening of sc. ii]

(Indián a komedianti odcházejí, bubnujíce první pochod. Po skončeném
pochodu komediantů, vzdalujících se do kulis, pokračuje se v recitativech.)
(The Indian and circus performers go out, beating on the drum the opening
march. After the end of the march of the comedians, while they move to the
wings, he continues the recitative.)

(k Vaškovi) (to Vašek)

[nɔ panaːtʃku gdɪʃ sɛ vaːm ʔɛsmɛralda liːbiː   muːʒɛtɛ jɪ dɔstatʼɪ]

No, panáčku, když se vám Esmeralda líbí,   můžete ji   dostati.[8]
Well, dear sir, if   -   to you Esmeralda is pleasing, you can her receive.

Well, dear sir, if you like Esmeralda, you can have her.

[pɔiʼtʼtɛ   s ‿ naːmɪ firaite   kɔmɛdɪjɪ]

Pojďʼte   s   námi, hrajte   komedii
Come   with us,   play   comedy

Come with us, play the comedy,

[ʔa ʔɔstatɲiː sɛ   pak   pɔdːdaː   samɔ   sɛbɔu]

a ostatní   se   pak   poddá[9]   **samo   sebou.**
and   rest   -   then   will yield to nothing but itself.

and the rest, then, will take care of itself.

Vašek:

(udiven) (taken aback)

[kɔ kɔmɛdɪjɪ   jaː jaː   tɔ   nɛ nɛ nɛʔumiːm]

Ko- komedii? Já- já   to   ne- ne- neumím.
Co- comedy? I- I-   that do- do- don't know how.

Co- comedy? I- I- do- do- don't know how.

Esmeralda:

[maː laːska vaːs ffɛmu   naʔutʃiː]

Má láska vás všemu   naučí!
My love you everything will teach!

My love will teach you everything!

Vašek:

[laːska   tɔ   jɛ ɦɛsskɛː]

Láska? To je hezké.
Love? That is pretty.

Love? That's nice.

Principál:

[budɛtɛ   sɛ miːt'ɪ   ʔu ‿ naːz dɔbr̝ɛ]

Budete   se míti   u   nás dobře.
You will   have a time of it with us   well.

You'll have a great time with us.

[dluɦuː   ʔɛː pɛɲɛs   maːmɛ   vʒdɪt͡skɪ nazbɪt]

Dluhů   (éé) peněz   máme   vždycky   nazbyt,
Of debts   (uh) money   we have always   surplus,

Debts, uh, money we've got plenty of,

[jiːst   ʔa   piːt   t͡sɔ   fɪrdlɔ   raːtʃiː ʔa   pl̩nou   svɔbɔdu]

jíst   a   pít   co   hrdlo   ráčí,   a   plnou   svobodu.
to eat   and to drink what throat   pleases, and with full freedom.

we eat and drink our fill, and with complete freedom.

(tajemně) (secretively)

[ʔa   svɔbɔda   freⁱkumʃtiːr̝uː   znamɛnaː   mnɔɦɔ]

A   svoboda   frejkumštýřů   znamená   mnoho!
And freedom   of artists   means   much!

And freedom for artists means a lot!

[vuːbets   staf   kɔmɛdɪjantskiː   jɛ   vlastɲɛ   staf ː ʃʃɛx   stavuː]

Vůbec   stav   komediantský   je   vlastně   stav   všech   stavů!
Actually   state   comedian's   is   in fact   state   of all   of states!

As a matter of fact, the circus performer's condition is the condition of all conditions!,

[kumstus   kumstɔrum   jak   sɛ   pɔ ‿ latɪnsku   řiːkaː]   [praviː]

kumstus   kumstorum,[10] **jak   se   po   latinsku   říká.** [11] **[praví]**[11]
cumstus   cumstorum,   as   -   after   Latin   one says.

"cumstus cumstorum," as they say in Latin.

[skɔrɔ   ʃʃɪxɲɪ   lɪdeː   ⁱsɔːu   viːtsɛ   meːɲɛ   kɔmɛdɪjant'ɪ]

Skoro   všichni[12] **lidé   jsou   více   méně   komedianti,**
Almost   all   people   are   more   less   comedians,

Almost all people are more or less performers,

[jɛnʒɛ   nɛ   kaʒdiː   svou   kɔmɛdɪjɪ   tag   dɔbře   prɔvaːd'ɛt'ɪ   ʔumiː   jakɔ   mɪ]

jenže   ne   každý   svou   komedii   tak   dobře   prováděti   umí,   jako   my,
yet   not   each   his   comedy   to   well   to perform   knows how   like   we,

yet not everyone knows how to perform well like we do,

[jakɔ   mɪ]

jako   my!
like   we!

like we do!

Esmeralda:

[nuʒɛ muːⁱ drafiː pŘɪstuptɛ k ‿ naːm]

Nuže, můj drahý, přistupte k nám,
Well, my   dear, come up to us,

Well, my dear, join us,

[maː laːska vaːm budɛ slatkɔu ʔɔdmɲɛnɔu]

má   láska vám   bude sladkou odměnou.
my   love   to you will be sweet   reward.

my love will be your sweet reward.

Principál:

[nɛbudɛtɛ vaːzaːn ʔut͡ʃɪɲtɛ jɛn skɔuʃku jɛnɔm jɛdnu jɛnɔm dnɛs]

Nebudete   vázán,   učiňte jen zkoušku, jenom jednu, jenom dnes.
You won't be obligated, make   just test,   just   one,   just   today.

You won't be obligated, just give it a try, just once, just for today.

Esmeralda:

[ʔanɔ dnɛs jɛnɔm dnɛs ʔa pak muːⁱ zlatɔuʃku]

Ano dnes, jenom dnes, a pak, můj zlatoušku,
Yes today, just today, and then, my golden one,

Yes, today, just for today, and then, my darling,

[jɛnɔm dnɛs ʔa pak ʔa pag budu vaʃɛ]

jenom dnes, a pak, a pak budu   vaše!
just   today, and then, and then I will be yours!

just for today, and then, and then I'll be yours!

Vašek:

[ʔa t͡sɔ t͡sɔ maː maːm fɪraːt]

A   co-   co má-   mám hrát?
And what- what do I ha- have to play?

And what- what do I ha- have to do?

Esmeralda:

[kaŋkaːn]

Kankán!
Can-can!

The can-can!

Vašek:

[ka ka kaŋkaːn t͡sɔ tɔ jɛ]

Ka- ka- kankán! co   to je?
Ca- ca- can-can! what that is?

Ca- ca- can-can!, what's that?

Esmeralda:

[budɛtɛ tant͡ʃɪt jaː s ‿ vaːmɪ ʔa   vɪ   sɛ ‿ mnɔu]

Budete tančit, já s   vámi a   vy se   mnou.
You'll dance, I with you and you with me.

You'll dance, I with you and you with me.

Vašek:

[mɔ mɔ mɔjɛ maːma]

Mo- mo- moje máma!
M- m-   my   momma!

M- m- my momma!

Esmeralda:

[ta vaːs nɛpɔznaː]

Ta   vás   nepozná!
That you won't recognize!

She won't recognize you!

Duettino
Esmeralda:

[mɪlɔstnɛː   zvɪřaːtkɔ   ʔudʼɛlaːmɛ   z ‿ vaːs]

Milostné   zviřátko   uděláme   z   vás,
Graceful   little animal   we'll make   from   you,

We'll make a graceful little animal out of you,

[kɔlɛm   f̥r̩dla   daːmɛ   ʔɔzlat͡sɛniː   paːs]

kolem   hrdla   dáme   ozlacený   pás.
around   neck   we'll give   gilded   belt.

around your neck we'll put a golden collar.

Principál:

[zvɪřaːtkɔ   z ‿ vaːs   daːmɛ   paːs]

Zviřátko   z   vás,   dáme   pás.
Little animal   from   you,   we'll give   belt.

A little animal out of you, we'll give you a collar.

Esmeralda:

[přɛɦɛskaː   ʃkrabɔʃka   skrɪjɛ   tvaːřɪt͡ʃkɪ]

Přehezká   škraboška   skryje   tvářičky,
Very pretty   little mask   will hide   cute little cheeks/face,

A very pretty little mask will hide your cute little face,

[ʔa   v ‿ mɲɛkɔuŋkɛː   bɔtkɪ   daːtɛ   nɔʒɪt͡ʃkɪ]

a   v   měkounké   botky   dáte   nožičky.
and   in   nice and soft   little boots   you'll put   sweet little feet.

and you'll have nice and soft little boots for your sweet little feet.

Principál:

[pŘɛɦɛska: ʃkrabɔʃka   skrɪje   tvaːřɪt͡ʃkɪ]

Přehezká   škraboška   skryje   tvářičky,
Very pretty   little mask   will hide   cute little cheeks/face,

A very pretty little mask will hide your cute little face,

[ʔa   v ⌣ mɲɛkɔuŋkɛː   bɔtkɪ   daːtɛ   nɔʒɪt͡ʃkɪ]

a   v   měkounké   botky   dáte   nožičky.
and   in   nice and soft   little boots   you'll put   sweet little feet.

and you'll have nice and soft little boots for your sweet little feet.

Esmeralda:

[budɛtɛ   jak   miːlɛk   kraːsɲɛ   kraːsɲɛ   vɪpadat]

Budete   jak   Mílek   krásně,   krásně   vypadat.
You will   like   Cupid   beautiful,   beautiful   look.

You'll look beautiful, beautiful like Cupid.

Principál:

[budɛtɛ   jak   miːlɛk   kraːsɲɛ   vɪpadat]

Budete   jak   Mílek   krásně   vypadat.
You will   like   Cupid   beautiful   look.

You'll look beautiful like Cupid.

Esmeralda:

[svjet   zajaːsaː]

Svět   zajásá,
World   will rejoice,

The world will rejoice,

[svjet   zajaːsaː   gdɪʃ   vaːs   ʔuzřiː   tan͡tsɔvat   tan͡tsɔvat]

svět   zajásá,   když   vás   uzří   tancovat,   tancovat.
world   will rejoice   when   you   it will behold   dance,   dance.

the world will rejoice when it sees you dancing, dancing.

Principál:

[svjet   zajaːsaː   gdɪʃ   vaːs   ʔuzřiː   tan͡tsɔvat]

Svět   zajásá,   když   vás   uzří   tancovat,
World   will rejoice   when   you   will behold   dance,

The world will rejoice when it sees you dancing,

[tan͡tsɔvat   tan͡tsɔvat   tan͡tsɔvat   tan͡tsɔvat   tan͡tsɔvat]

tancovat, tancovat, tancovat, tancovat, tancovat,
dance,   dance,   dance,   dance,   dance,

dancing, dancing, dancing, dancing, dancing,

[zviřaːtkɔ   z ‿ vaːs   daːmɛ   paːs]

zviřátko   z   vás,   dáme   pás.
little animal   from   you,   we'll give   belt.

a little animal out of you, we'll give you a collar.

Esmeralda, Principál:

[mɪlɔstnɛː   zvɪřaːtkɔ   ʔud'ɛlaːmɛ   z ‿ vaːs]

Milostné   zviřátko   uděláme   z   vás,
Graceful   little animal   we'll make   from you,

We'll make a graceful little animal out of you,

[kɔlɛm fiṛdla   daːmɛ   ʔɔzlat͡sɛniː paːs]

kolem   hrdla   dáme   ozlacený   pás.
around   neck   we'll give   gilded   belt.

around your neck we'll put a golden collar.

[z ‿ vaːs   mɪlɔstnɛː   zvɪřaːtkɔ   z ‿ vaːs]

Z   vás   milostné   zviřátko,   z   vás,
From you   graceful   little animal, from you,

We'll make a graceful little animal out of you, out of you,

[ʔud'ɛlaːmɛ   z ‿ vaːs   ʔud'ɛlaːmɛ   z ‿ vaːs]

uděláme   z   vás, uděláme   z   vás!
we'll make   from you, we'll make   from you!

we'll make out of you, we'll make out of you!

(Odejdou.) (They leave.)

Výstup III   Scene iii
Háta, Vašek, Mícha, Kecal

Recitativ
Vašek:

[ʔɔx jaː nɛ   nɛ   nɛʃt'astniː]

Oh,   já ne- ne- nešt'astný!
Oh,   I   un- un- unhappy!

Oh, I'm un- un- unhappy!

[ffɛ ffɛ ffeʈ͡ skɪ   mnɛ xt'ɛjiː mɪ   mɪ mɪlɔvat ʔa ʔa zabiːt]

Vše- vše- všecky   mne chtějí mi- mi- milovat a-   a zabít!
Ev- ev- everybody me   wants to lo- lo- love   a- and to kill!

Ev- ev- everybody wants to lo- lo- love me a- and to kill me!

Háta:

[ʔaⁱ prɔʈ͡ʃ ⁱsɪ   tak smutɛn vaʃiːʈ͡ʃku but'   vɛsɛl   sɪnaːʈ͡ʃku]

Aj, proč jsi   tak smuten, Vašíčku? Bud' vesel,   synáčku.
Ah, why are you so   sad,   Vašíček? Be   happy,   dear little son.

Ah, why are you so sad, Vašíček? Be happy, dear little son.

[ʔɔʒɛɲ sɛ ʔa budɛ   t'ɪ   blazɛ ʔa budɛ   t'ɪ   blazɛ na ‿ zɛmɪ]

Ožeň se a bude   ti   blaze, a bude   ti   blaze na zemi.
Marry and it will be to you happy, and it will be to you happy on earth.

Marry, and you'll have happiness, and you'll have happiness on earth.

Vašek: Háta:

[jaː jaː jaː sɛ bɔjiːm]   [t͡ʃɛɦɔ   sɛ bɔjiːʃ   drafiɔuʃku]

Já- já- já se bojím.   **Čeho   se bojíš,   drahoušku?**
I- I- I   am afraid.   Of what   are you afraid, little dear?

I- I- I'm afraid.   *What are you afraid of, little dear?*

Háta:

[vʒdɪt'   sɛ   t'ɪ   ɲɪd͡z   zlɛːfiɔ nɛmuːʒɛ staːt'ɪ]

Vždyt'   se   ti   nic   zlého   nemůže státi.
To be sure -   to you nothing bad   can't   happen.

Surely nothing bad can happen to you.

[dɔstanɛʒ   ʒɛnu   ʔa   tɔ jɛ nɛⁱlɛpʃiː vjɛt͡s na ‿ svjɛt'ɛ]

Dostaneš   ženu   a   to je nejlepší   věc   na světě!
You'll get wife   and that is best   thing on world!

You'll get a wife, and that's the best thing in the world!

Kecal:

[ba   vjɛru vaʃiːt͡ʃɛk pɔdɛpiːʃɛ smlɔuvu ʔa budɛ   ʃʃɛt͡skɔ   f‿ pɔřaːtku]

Ba věru! Vašíček podepíše smlouvu a   bude   všecko   v pořádku!
To be sure! Vašíček will sign contract and it will be everything in order!

To be sure! Vašíček will sign the contract, and everything will be in order!

Vašek:

[na   na   nat͡ʃ sɛ   ma   ma maːm pɔdɛpsat]

Na-   na- nač se   ma-   ma- mám podepsat?
Why- why- why   -   do I ha- ha- have   to sign?

Why- why- why do I ha- ha- have to sign?

Mícha:

[ʒɛ   sɪ vɛzmɛʃ   mařɛŋku kruʃɪnɔvɔu   za ‿ ʒɛnu]

Že   si vezmeš   Mařenku Krušinovou   za   ženu!
That you'll take Mařenka Krušinová   as   wife!

So you'll take Mařenka Krušinová for your wife!

Vašek:

[jaː jaː jɪ   nɛ   nɛ nɛ   nɛxt͡sɪ]

Já- já ji   ne- ne- ne- nechci!
I-   I   her   do- do- do- don't want!

I- I do- do- do- don't want her!

Quartetto
Háta, Mícha, Kecal:

[ʔaⁱ   jagʒɛ   jagʒɛ   nɛxt͡sɛ   jɪ]

Aj!—Jakže?   jakže?—nechce   ji?
Ah!—How's that? how's that?—he doesn't want her?

Ah!—What? what?—he doesn't want her?

[jagʒɛ jagʒɛ nɛxt͡sɛ jɪ]

Jakže? jakže?—nechce ji?
How's that? how's that?—he doesn't want her?

What? what?—he doesn't want her?

[t͡sɔpak t͡sɔpak sɛ pR̝ɪfiɔd'ɪlɔ mluf mluf mluf vaʃku mluf]

Copak, copak se přihodilo? Mluv! mluv! mluv, Vašku, mluv,
What, what happened? Speak! speak! speak, Vašek, speak,

What, what happened? Speak! speak! speak, Vašek, speak,

[t͡sɔ tu mɪʃlɛŋku t'ɪ dɔ ˩ ɦlavɪ vlɔʒɪlɔ]

co tu myšlenku ti do hlavy vložilo?
what that notion to you to head inserted?

what put that notion into your head?

Vašek:
                                        (plačtivě) (tearfully)
[ʔɔ ʔɔna bɪ mnɛ ʔɔ ʔɔtraːvɪla ʒɪvɔta mnɛ zbavɪla mnɛ zbavɪla]

O- ona by mne o- otrávila, života mne zbavila, mne zbavila!
She- she would me po- poison, of life me rid, me rid!

She- she would po- poison me, take my life, take my life!

Háta, Mícha, Kecal:

[jakiː tɔ ɦlɔːupiː naːpat]

Jaký to hloupý nápad!
What kind of that stupid idea!

What a stupid idea!

[mluf   gde   ˡsɪ   tɔ   sɛbral   gdɛ   ˡsɪ   tɔ   sɛbral]

Mluv, kde jsi   to   sebral?   Kde   jsi   to   sebral?
Speak, where have you… that picked up? Where have you… that picked up?

Speak, where did you get it? Where did you get it?

Vašek:

(tajemně) (secretively)
[mɲɛ   tɔ   ɲɛ   ɲɛ   ɲɛgdɔ   dnɛs   pɔviːdal]

Mně   to   ně- ně- někdo   dnes   povídal.
To me   that   so- so- someone today   told.

So- so- someone today told me that.

Háta, Mícha, Kecal:	Vašek:
[gdɔ bɪl tɛn prɔstɔpaːʃɲiːk]	[jakaːs panɛŋka jakaːs panɛŋka]
Kdo byl ten prostopášník?	**Jakás panenka, jakás panenka.**
Who was that debauched one?	A certain maiden, a certain maiden.
Who was that scoundrel?	*A certain girl, a certain girl.*

Háta, Mícha, Kecal:

[ʔa   t͡sɔ   t'ɪ   pɔvjɛd'ɛla]

A   co   ti   pověděla?
And   what to you she said?

And what did she say to you?

Vašek:

[jɛ   ɦɛʒɔuŋkaː jɛ   ɦɛʒɔuŋkaː mnɛ rraːda maː   mnɛ rraːda maː]

Je   hezounká, je   hezounká, mne ráda   má,   mne ráda   má.
She's pretty,   she's pretty,   me   love she has, me   love she has.

She's pretty, she's pretty, she loves me, she loves me.

Háta:	Vašek:
	(Odběhne.) (He runs away.)
[ʔa znaːʃ lɪ jɪ]	[nɛ nɛznaːm]
A znáš-li ji?	**Ne- neznám.**
And do you know-if her?	I do- don't know.
And do you know her?	*I do- don't.*

Háta, Mícha, Kecal:

[f ‿ tɔm   vjɛziː   ɲaːkiː pɔdvɔt   f ‿ tɔm   vjɛziː   ɲaːkiː pɔdvɔt]

V   tom   vězí   ňáký   podvod. V   tom   vězí   ňáký   podvod,
In   that it sticks some deceit. In   that it sticks some deceit,

This reeks of deceit. This reeks of deceit,

[nɛɲiː   nɛɲiː   f ‿ tɔm   ɲɪgdɔ   jɪniː   nɛʃ   tɛn   paxɔlɛk   saːm]

není,   není   v   tom   nikdo   jiný, než   ten   pacholek sám,
it's not, it's not in   that no one other than that   groom   alone,

there's no one, there's no one else involved other than the groom himself,

[nɛɲiː   nɛɲiː   f ‿ tɔm   ɲɪgdɔ   jɪniː   nɛʃ   tɛn   paxɔlɛk   saːm]

není,   není   v   tom   nikdo   jiný, než   ten   pacholek sám.
it's not, it's not in   that no one other than that   groom   alone.

there's no one, there's no one else involved other than the groom himself.

Kecal:

[ja: fʃɛt͡skɔ   vɪskɔumaːm   ja: fʃɛt͡skɔ   vɪskɔumaːm]

Já všecko vyzkoumám, já všecko vyzkoumám.
I   everything will find out, I   everything   will find out.

I'll find out everything, I'll find out everything.

Kecal: Háta, Mícha, Kecal:

[f‿ tɔm vjɛziː   ɲaːkiː pɔdvɔt]   [f ‿ tɔm vjɛziː   ɲaːkiː pɔdvɔt]

V tom vězí   ňáký podvod.   **V   tom vězí   ňáký   podvod.**
In that it sticks some deceit.   In   that it sticks some deceit.

This reeks of deceit.   *This reeks of deceit.*

Kecal:

[nɛɲiː   nɛɲiː   f ‿ tɔm   ɲɪgdɔ   jɪniː   nɛʃ   tɛn   paxɔlɛk   saːm]

Není,   není   v   tom   nikdo   jiný,   než   ten   pacholek   sám.
It's not, it's not   in   that   no one   other than   that   groom   alone.

There's no one, there's no one else involved other than the groom himself.

Kecal:

[[ja: fʃɛt͡skɔ   vɪskɔumaːm   ja: fʃɛt͡skɔ   vɪskɔumaːm]

Já všecko vyzkoumám, já všecko vyzkoumám.
I   everything will find out, I   everything   will find out.

I'll find out everything, I'll find out everything.

Háta, Mícha:

[ʔɔn fʃɛ͡tskɔ   vɪskɔumaː ʔɔn   fʃɛ͡tskɔ   vɪskɔumaː]

On   všecko   vyzkoumá,   on   všecko   vyzkoumá,
He   everything   will find out, he   everything will find out,

He'll find out everything, he'll find out everything,

[ʔɔn fʃɛ͡tskɔ   vɪskɔumaː]

on   všecko   vyzkoumá.
he   everything   will find out.

he'll find out everything.

Výstup IV   Scene iv
Mařenka, Ludmila, Krušina
Předešlí bez Vaška   The previous, without Vašek

Mařenka:
(Rychle přikvapí. Za ní též otec Krušina a matka Ludmila.)
(She runs in quickly. Also behind her, her father Krušina and her mother, Ludmila.)

[nɛ nɛ nɛ nɛ nɛ nɛ nɛ nɛ tɔmu   nɛvjɛřiːm]

Ne! Ne! ne, ne, ne, ne, ne, ne, tomu   nevěřím,
No! No! no, no, no, no, no, no,   that   I don't believe,

No! No! no, no, no, no, no, no, that I don't believe,

[pɔufiɛː tɔ   ʃaːlɛɲiː   pɔufiɛː   tɔ   ʃaːlɛɲiː]

pouhé to   šálení,   pouhé   to   šálení,
sheer   that   deceiving, sheer   that   deceiving,

it's sheer deception, it's sheer deception,

[muːⁱ drafiː jɛɲiːt͡ʃɛk bɛzbɔʒniː tak bɛzbɔʒniː nɛɲiː]

můj drahý Jeníček bezbožný tak, bezbožný není.
my   dear Jeníček impious so, impious he's not.

my dear Jeníček isn't godless like that, he's not godless.

Krušina: # Kecal:

[ʔa prɛt͡ʃ tɔ prravda jɛ]   [ʔɔ ‿ t͡ʃɛm pɔxɪbujɛ]

A   preč to pravda je.   **O   čem   pochybuje?**
And yet that truth is.   About what does she doubt?

And yet that's the truth.   *What does she doubt?*

Krušina:

[ʒɛ   jɛɲiːk jɪ prɔdal]

Že Jeník ji prodal.
That Jeník her sold.

That Jeník sold her.

Kecal:

[vɪs   zdɛ   sɛ pɔdɛpsal vɪs   zdɛ   sɛ pɔdɛpsal]

Viz, zde   se podepsal, viz,   zde   se podepsal.
Look, here he signed,   look, here   he signed.

Look, here he signed, look, here he signed.

[tr̝ɪ   sta   mu   vɪplat'iːmɛ ʔa tak sɛ   ɦɔ   sprɔst'iːmɛ]

Tři   sta   mu   vyplatíme   a tak se   ho   sprostíme.
Three hundred to him we'll pay   and so -   him we'll get rid of.

We'll pay him three hundred, and so get rid of him.

Mařenka:

[ʔɔː ɦanɛbnɛː tɔ ʃaːlɛɲiː   ʔɔː muʃkɛː sr̂tsɛ klamnɛː]

Ó, hanebné to šálení!   Ó, mužské srdce klamné!
Oh, shameful that deceiving! Oh, male   heart false!

Oh, what shameful deception! Oh, a man's false heart!

[saːm   pR̂iːsaɦal ʒɛ t͡sɛliː svjɛt   bɪ ʔɔbjɛtɔval   za ‿mnɛ]

Sám   přísahal, že celý   svět   by obětoval,   za   mne,[13]
Himself he swore that whole world he would sacrifice for me,

He swore himself that he would give up the whole world for me,

[za ‿mnɛ   za‿ mnɛ]

za   mne, za   mne!
for   me   for   me!

for me, for me!

Krušina:

[nuʃ ʔut'ɪʃ sɛ   mařɛŋkɔ ʔaspɔɲz   ɦɔ   pɔznala]

Nuž, utiš se,   Mařenko, aspoň's   ho   poznala
Well, calm down, Mařenka, at least you… him found out

Well, calm down, Mařenka, at least you've found him out,

[ʔa   viːʃ   jak ⁱsɪ sɛ v ‿ mɪlɛːm svɛːm tr̂pt͡sɛ   sklamala]

a   víš,   jak jsi se v milém svém trpce   zklamala.
and you know how you - in dear your bitterly were disappointed.

and you know how bitterly disappointed you are in your sweetheart.

Kecal:

[nuʃ pɔdɛpɪʃ panɛŋkɔ   ʔɪ vaʃiːtʃɛk gdɛ   jɛ]

Nuž, podepiš, panenko, i Vašíček—kde je?
Well, sign, girl, and Vašíček—where is he?

Well, sign, girl, and Vašíček—where is he?

Ludmila:

[ʔaⁱ vɪstɛ tamɔ   zasɛ na ‿ fɪraːzɪ zɛvlujɛ]

Aj, vizte, tamo zase na hrázi zevluje!
Ah, see, over there again on dam he's hanging around!

Ah, look, he's over there again on the dam loafing around!

Mařenka:

[jaː ɲɪgdɪ nɛpɔtpiːʃu jaː nɛxt͡sɪ   vaʃka miːt   radʼɛjɪ samɔtʼɪŋkaː xt͡sɪ]

Já nikdy nepodpíšu, já nechci Vaška mít,   raději samotinká chci,
I never will sign, I don't want Vašek to have, rather all alone I want,

I'll never sign, I don't want Vašek, I'd rather be all alone,

[xt͡sɪ   vjet͡ʃɲe vjɛrɲɛ   ʒiːt   xt͡sɪ   vjet͡ʃɲe vjɛrɲɛ   ʒiːt]

chci věčně věrně žít, chci věčně věrně žít,
I want eternally faithfully to live, I want eternally faithfully to live,

I want to live eternally faithful, I want to live eternally faithful,

[xt͡sɪ   vjet͡ʃɲe vjɛrɲɛ   ʒiːt]

chci věčně věrně žít!
I want eternally faithfully to live!

I want to live eternally faithful!

Ludmila, Háta, Krušina, Mícha, Kecal:

[nɛdaː sɛ   jɪnag   d'ɛlat   tɔ   musiː musiː   tɔ   musiː biːt]

Nedá se   jinak   dělat,   to   musí, musí,   to   musí   být.
It's not possible   otherwise to do,   that must, must,   that must   be.

It can't be otherwise, it must, it must, it must be.

Kecal:
(Volá.) (He calls.)
[ɦɛⁱ vaʃku   ɦɛⁱ   vaʃiːtʃku ɦɛⁱ   vaʃku   ɦɛⁱ   vaʃiːtʃku]

Hej, Vašku! Hej, Vašíčku! Hej, Vašku! Hej, Vašíčku!
Hey, Vašek! Hey, Vašíček! Hey, Vašek! Hey, Vašíček!

Hey, Vašek! Hey, Vašíček! Hey, Vašek! Hey, Vašíček!

[pɔⁱt'   sɛm   pak   na ‿ xvɪlɪtʃku]

Pojď'   sem   pak   na   chviličku!
Come   here   then   for   little while!

Come here for a little while!

Výstup V   Scene v
Vašek, předešlí   Vašek, the previous

Vašek:

[t͡sɔ   t͡sɔ   t͡sɔ   t͡sɔ   pɔřaːdɛ   xt͡sɛtɛ]

Co- co- co- co   pořáde   chcete?
Wha- wha- wha- what   keep on   do you want?

Wha- wha- wha- what do you want now?

(Spatří Mařenku.) (He sees Mařenka.)

[ʔa   ta   ta   ta   ta   tɔ   bɪla]

A   ta- ta- ta- ta   to   byla!
And   that- that- that- that   that   she was!

And that- that- that- that one was her!

Ludmila, Háta, Krušina, Mícha, Kecal:

[mařɛŋka   ʒɛ   tɔ   bɪla]

Mařenka   že   to   byla?
Mařenka   that   that   she was?

It was really Mařenka?

Vašek:

[ʔa   ta   ta   ta   ta   ta   ta   tɔ   bɪla]

A   ta- ta- ta- ta- ta- ta   to   byla!
And   that- that- that- that- that- that   that   she was!

And that- that- that- that- that one was her!

Ludmila, Háta, Krušina, Mícha, Kecal:

[t͡sɔ   t'ɛ   tak   pɔstraʃɪla]

Co   tě   tak   postrašila?
What   you   so   frightened?

Why were you so scared?

Vašek:

[ta   ta   mɪ   pɔviːdala   ʒɛ   bɪ   mɲɛ   mɪlɔvala]

Ta-	**ta**	**mi**	**povídala,**	**že**	**by**	**mě**	**milovala,**
That-	that	to me	told	that	she would	me	love,

She's the one who told me that she would love me,

[ʒɛ   bɪ   mɲɛ   mɪ   mɪlɔvala]

že	**by**	**mě**	**mi-**	**milovala.**
that	she would	me	lo-	love.

that she would lo- love me.

Ludmila, Háta, Krušina, Mícha, Kecal:

[nuʃ   tɔ   jɛ   mařɛŋka   budɔut͡siː   ʒɛna   tvaː]

Nuž,   to je Mařenka, budoucí žena   tvá,[14]
Well,   that is Mařenka,   future   woman   your,

Well, that's Mařenka, your future wife,

[nuʃ   tɔ   jɛ   mařɛŋka   budɔut͡siː   ʒɛna   tvaː]

nuž,   to   je Mařenka, budoucí žena   tvá![15]
well,   that   is Mařenka,   future   woman   your!

well, that's Mařenka, your future wife!

Vašek:

[ta   ta   sɛ   mɪ   liːbiː   ta   ta   sɛ   mɪ   liːbiː]

Ta-	**ta**	**se**	**mi**	**líbí,**	**ta-**	**ta**	**se**	**mi**	**líbí,**
That-	that	-	to me	is pleasing,	that-	that	-	to me	is pleasing,

It's he- her that I like, it's he- her that I like,

[ta   ta sɛ mɪ   liːbiː]

ta-   ta se mi   líbí.
that- that - to me is pleasing.

it's he- her that I like.

(Odejde.) (He leaves.)

Kecal:

[tak tɛdɪ   bɛs ‿ prɔt͡sɛsuː ʔa   bɛzɛ   fʃɛx   ʔɛkst͡sɛsuː]

Tak tedy bez   procesů   a   beze   všech   excesů[16]
So   then without legalities and   without   all   of excesses

So, then, without redress and without excess,

[pɔtpɪʃtɛ smlɔuvu   finɛt]

podpište smlouvu   hned!
sign   contract   right away!

sign the contract right away!

Mařenka:

(Pláče.) (She cries.)

[tak mnɛ nɛxtɛ   xviːlɪ   jaː sɪ rɔzmɪsliːm]

Tak mne nechte   chvíli,   já   si rozmyslím![17]
So   me   leave   little while, I   will think it over!

So, leave me alone for a little while, I'll think it over!

Sextetto
Ludmila, Krušina, Kecal:

[rɔzmɪslɪ sɪ mařɛŋkɔ rɔzmɪslɪ   rɔzmɪslɪ sɪ mařɛŋkɔ rɔzmɪslɪ]

Rozmysli si, Mařenko, rozmysli,   rozmysli si, Mařenko, rozmysli,
Think it over, Mařenka, think it over, think it over, Mařenka, think it over,

Think it over, Mařenka, think it over, think it over, Mařenka, think it over,

Háta:

[rɔzmɪslɪ sɪ   rɔzmɪslɪ sɪ]

Rozmysli si!,   rozmysli si.
Think it over!,   think it over.

Think it over!, think it over.

Ludmila, Krušina, Kecal:

[na ‿ svɛː   ʃt'ɛst'iː   dɔbřɛ pɔmɪslɪ   na ‿ svɛː   ʃt'ɛst'iː]

na   své   štěstí   dobře pomysli, na   své   štěstí,
on   your   happiness   well   think,   on   your   happiness,

reflect well on your happiness, on your happiness,

[na ‿ svɛː   ʃt'ɛst'iː   dɔbřɛ   pɔmɪslɪ]

na   své   štěstí   dobře   pomysli!
on   your   happiness   well   think!

on your happiness reflect well!

Ludmila, Háta, Krušina, Mícha, Kecal:

[rɔzmɪslɪ sɪ   mařeŋkɔ   rɔzmɪslɪ   na ‿ svɛː   ʃtʼɛstʼiː   dɔbře   pɔmɪslɪ]

Rozmysli si,   Mařenko, rozmysli,   na   své   štěstí   dobře   pomysli!
Think it over,   Mařenka,   think it over,   on   your   happiness   well   think!

Think it over, Mařenka, think it over, on your happiness reflect well!

[maːʃ   t͡sɛstu   pŘɛt ‿ sɛbɔu   pŘevaːbivɔu]

Máš   cestu   před   sebou   převábivou,
You have   path   before   you   attractive,

You have a path before you that's very appealing,

[maːʃ   t͡sɛstu   pŘɛt ‿ sɛbɔu   pŘevaːbivɔu]

máš   cestu   před   sebou   převábivou,
you have   path   before   you   attractive,

you have a path before you that's very appealing,

[nɛdɛⁱ sɛ   nɛdɛⁱ sɛ   svɛːstʼɪ   svɛːɦlavɔstʼiː   svɔu]

nedej se,   nedej se   svésti   svéhlavostí   svou,
keep your ground,   keep your ground   to manage   stubborness   your,

don't let, don't let your stubborness get the better of you,

[rɔzmɪslɪ sɪ   panɛŋkɔ   rɔzmɪslɪ]

rozmysli si,   panenko,   rozmysli,
think it over,   girl,   think it over,

think it over, girl, think it over,

[na ‿ svɛː ʃtʼɛstʼiː dɔbřɛ pɔmɪslɪ pɔmɪslɪ]

na své štěstí dobře pomysli, pomysli!
on your happiness well think, think!

on your happiness reflect well, reflect!

Mařenka:

[ʔanɔ dɔbřɛ rɔzmɪsliːm dɔbřɛ rɔzmɪsliːm]

Ano, dobře rozmyslím, dobře rozmyslím,
Yes, well I'll think it over, well I'll think it over,

Yes, I'll consider it well, I'll consider it well,

[dɔbřɛ dɔbřɛ rɔzmɪsliːm rɔzmɪsliːm]

dobře, dobře rozmyslím, rozmyslím!
well, well I'll think it over, I'll think it over!

well, I'll consider it well, I'll consider it!

(Rodiče a Kecal odejdou.) (The family and Kecal leave.)

Výstup VI   Scene vi
Mařenka:
(sama) (alone)

[ʔɔx jakiː ʒal jakiː tɔ ʒal]

Och, jaký žal! jaký to žal,
Oh, what kind of grief! what kind of it grief,

Oh, what grief! what grief

[gdıʃ   sr̩t͡sɛ   ʔɔklamaːnɔ]

když   srdce   oklamáno!
when   heart   deceived!

when a heart is deceived!

[fʃak   pR̂et͡sɛ   jɛst'ɛ   nɛvjɛřiːm]

Však   přece   ještě   nevěřím,
Though   yet   still   I don't believe,

Yet, I still don't believe it,

[ʔat͡ʃ   stɔjiː   tam   napsaːnɔ]

ač   stojí   tam   napsáno.
although   it stands   there   written.

although it stands there in writing.

[nɛvjɛřiːm   ʔaʃ   s ‿ ɲiːm   prɔmluviːm]

Nevěřím,   až   s   ním   promluvím.
I don't believe,   until   with   him   I will speak.

I won't believe it until I speak with him.

[snat   ʔaɲı   ʔɔ ‿ tɔm   nɛviː]

Snad   ani   o   tom   neví!
Maybe   not even   about   it   he doesn't know!

Maybe he doesn't even know about it!

[ʔɔː   kiːʃ   sɛ   mɪ   v ‿ nɛsnaːzɪ   tɛː   skutɛt͡ʃnaː]

Ó   kýž   se   mi   v   nesnázi   té   skutečná,
Oh,   let   -   to me   in   distress   this   real,

Oh, in my distress let the real,

[skutɛt͡ʃnaː   pravda   zjɛviː]

skutečná   pravda   zjeví!
real   truth   reveals!

the real truth be revealed to me!

[tɛn   laːskɪ   sɛn   jak | kraːsniː   bɪl   tɛn   laːskɪ   sɛn]

Ten   lásky   sen,   jak   krásný   byl,   ten   lásky   sen,
This   of love   dream,   how   beautiful   it was,   this   of love   dream,

This dream of love, how beautiful it was, this dream of love,

[jak   kraːsniː   bɪl   jak   nad'ɛ¹ɲɛ   rɔskviːtal]

jak   krásný   byl,   jak   nadějně   rozkvítal!
how   beautiful   it was,   how   hopefully   it blossomed!

how beautiful it was, how hopefully it blossomed!

[ʔa   nat‿ʔubɔɦiːm   sr̩t͡sɛm :   miːm   t͡sɔ   t'ɪxaː   ɦvjɛzda   sviːtal]

A   nad   ubohým   srdcem   mým   co   tichá   hvězda   svítal,
And   over   wretched   heart   my   what   silent   star   shone,

And over my wretched heart it was shining like a silent star,

[ʔa nat‿ʔubɔɦiːm   sr̩t͡sɛm ꞉ miːm t͡sɔ tʼɪxaː fivjɛzda sviːtal]

a	nad	ubohým	srdcem	mým	co	tichá	hvězda	svítal.
and	over	wretched	heart	my	what	silent	star	shone.

and over my wretched heart it was shining like a silent star.

[jag blaɦiː   ʒɪvɔt   s ‿ mɪlɛnt͡sɛm]

Jak	blahý	život	s	milencem
How	blissful	life	with	beloved

How in this dream a blissful life

[f ‿ snu   tɔmtɔ   ⁱsɛm   sɪ   pR̝adla]

v	snu	tomto	jsem	si	přadla!
in	dream	this		I was spinning!

with my beloved I imagined!

[tu ʔɔsut pR̝ɪvaːl vɪxŘ̝ɪt͡sɪ ʔa   ruːʒɛ   laːskɪ   svadla]

Tu	osud	přivál	vichřici	a	růže	lásky	svadla.
Now	fate	blew	tempest	and	rose	of love	withered.

Now fate blew in a tempest, and love's rose has withered.

[nɛ nɛɲiː   mɔʒniː takiː klam   nɛ nɛ nɛ nɛ nɛ   nɛɲiː]

Ne,	není	možný	taký	klam,	ne, ne, ne, ne, ne,	není,
No,	it is not	possible	such	deception,	no, no, no, no, no,	it is not,

No, such deception is not possible, no, no, no, no, no, it's not,

[nɛɲiː   mɔʒniː   takiː   klam]

není   možný   taký   klam!
it is not   possible   such   deception!

such deception is not possible!

[tɛnt'   smutnɔu   bɪ bɪl   ranɔu]

Teňť   smutnou   by byl   ranou,
It   sad   would be   wound,

It would be a sad wound,

[ʔa   rɔsplakala bɪ sɛ   zɛm   nad ‿laːskɔu pɔxɔvanɔu]

a   rozplakala by se   zem   nad   láskou   pochovanou,
and   would burst into tears   earth   over   love   buried,

and the earth would burst into tears over the buried love,

[nad ‿ laːskɔu   laːskɔu   pɔxɔvanɔu]

nad   láskou,   láskou   pochovanou!
over   love,   love   buried!

over the buried love, love!

(zádumčivě) (sadly, gloomily, pensively)

[tɛn   laːskɪ   sɛn   jak | kraːsniː   bɪl]

Ten   lásky   sen,   jak   krásný   byl!
This   of love   dream,   how   beautiful   it was!

This dream of love, how beautiful it was!

[ʔa   nat‿ʔubɔɦiːm   sr̩t͡sɛm ː miːm   t͡sɔ   t'ɪxaː   fivjɛzda   sviːtal]

A   nad   ubohým   srdcem   mým   co   tichá   hvězda   svítal,
And   over   wretched   heart   my   what   silent   star   shone,

And over my wretched heart it was shining like a silent star,

[t͡sɔ   t'ɪxaː   fivjɛzda   sviːtal]

co   tichá   hvězda   svítal!
what   silent   star   shone!

shining like a silent star!

[tɛn   laːskɪ   sɛn   jak | kraːsniː   bɪl]

Ten   lásky   sen,   jak   krásný   byl!
This   of love   dream,   how   beautiful   it was!

This dream of love, how beautiful it was!

Výstup VII   **Scene vii**
Mařenka, Jeník

Jeník:

(Přikvapí.) (He runs in.)

[mařɛŋkɔ maː mařɛŋkɔ maː tɪ   fivjɛzdɔ mɛːɦɔ   ʒɪt'iː]

Mařenko má, Mařenko má, ty hvězdo mého žití!
Mařenka my, Mařenka my, you star of my living!

My Mařenka, my Mařenka, you star of my life!

Recitativ

[ʔɔː mluf jak stɔjiː naʃɛ vjet͡s ʔa t͡ʃɛɦɔ sɛ nadʔiːtʔɪ]

Ó, mluv, jak stojí naše věc a čeho se nadíti?
Oh, speak, how stands our matter and of what to expect?

Oh, speak, how does our matter stand, and what can we expect?

Mařenka:

[ˈdɪʃ pak tɪ ˈsɪ mnɛ ʔɔklamal tɪz ɦanɛbɲɛ sɛ xɔval]

Jdiž pak! Ty jsi mne oklamal, tys hanebně se choval!
Go then! You have... me deceived, you have shamefully behaved!

Go away! You've deceived me, you've behaved disgracefully!

Recitativ

[ktɛrak ˈsɪ sɲiːʒɪl sɛbɛ saːm ʒɛ ˈsɪ mɛː sr̩t͡sɛ prɔdal]

Kterak jsi snížil sebe sám, že jsi mé srdce prodal!
How you lowered yourself alone, that you have... my heart sold!

How you degraded yourself when you sold my heart!

[mluf jɛ tɔ pravda t͡ʃɪlɪ ɲɪt͡s ʔanɔ nɛp nɛ ɲɪ slɔva viːt͡s]

Mluv! Je to pravda, čili nic?—Ano, neb ne—ni slova víc!
Speak! Is that right, or not?—Yes, or no—not word more!

Speak! Is that right, or not?—Yes, or no—not a word more!

Jeník:

[jɛn dɔvɔl bɪx   t'ɪ   vɪlɔʒɪl]

Jen dovol, bych   ti   vyložil!
Just   allow   I would to you explain!

Just let me explain to you!

Mařenka:

[jaː nɛxt͡sɪ   ʒaːdniːx viːkladuː rt͡sɪ pravd'ɪvjɛlɪ psaːnɔ]

Já   nechci   žádných výkladů. Rci, pravdivě-li psáno?
I   don't want of no   comments. Say, truly-if   written?

I don't want any comments. Tell me, did you really write it?

Jeník:

[nuʃ tɛdɪ ʔanɔ ʔanɔ ʔanɔ]

Nuž, tedy—ano! ano! ano!
Well, then—yes! yes! yes!

Well, then—yes! yes! yes!

Mařenka:

                                    (Pláče.) (She cries.)
[nuʃ tɛdɪ ⁱd'ɪ ʔa nɛʔɔbjɛf sɛ mɪ   pʀɛt ‿ | tvaːʀiː viːt͡sɛ]

Nuž, tedy jdi a   neobjev se   mi   před   tváří   více!
Well, then go   and don't appear to me before face   more!

Well, then go, and don't show up in front of me ever again!

Jeník:

[jɛn dɔvɔl mɪ   bɪɣ   zuliːbal tvɛː krːaːsnɛː drafiɛː liːt͡sɛ]

Jen dovol mi,   bych zulíbal tvé   krásné, drahé   líce!
Just allow to me, I would kiss your beautiful, dear visage!

Just let me kiss your beautiful, dear face!

Mařenka:

[naʃiː ʔuʃ   laːskɪ kɔnet͡s jɛ ʔa jaː jaː sɪ vɛzmu   vaʃka]

Naší   už   lásky konec je, a já—já si vezmu   Vaška!
Of our already of love end is, and I—I   I will marry Vašek!

Our love is now over, and I—I will marry Vašek!

Jeník:

(Směje se.) (He laughs.)

[fia fia fia fia fia fia fia fia   ʔaⁱ tɔdʼ   bɪ bɪla]

Ha ha ha ha, ha ha ha ha, aj,   totʼ   by byla,
Ha ha ha ha, ha ha ha ha, ah,   of course   it would,

Ha, ha, ha, ha; ha, ha, ha, ha; ah, that would certainly—

[fia fia fia fia tɔdʼ   bɪ bɪla   fia fia fia fia]

ha ha ha ha, totʼ   by byla, ha ha ha ha,
ha ha ha ha, of course   it would, ha ha ha ha,

ha, ha, ha, ha, that would certainly—ha, ha, ha, ha,

[rɔskɔʃna: vɛssɛla: vjɛru vɛssɛla: fraʃka]

rozkošná, veselá věru, veselá fraška!
delightful, lively truly, lively farce!

be a delightful, truly lively, lively farce!

Mařenka:

[tak   tɪ   sɛ   jɛʃt'ɛ   vɪsmɲɛjɛʃ]

Tak? ty se ještě vysměješ?
So?   you -   still mock?

What? you can still mock me?

Jeník:

[ma:mt' vjɛru   prɔtʃ sɛ sma:t'ɪ jɛn   dɔvɔl bɪx   t'ɪ   vɪlɔʒɪl]

Mámt' věru proč se smáti—Jen dovol, bych   ti   vyložil!
I have   truly reason to laugh—just allow, I would to you explain!

I have every reason to laugh—just let me explain!

Mařenka:

[ja: nɛxt͡sɪ   pɔslɔuxat'ɪ]

Já nechci   poslouchati!
I   don't want   to listen!

I don't want to listen!

Jeník:

[tak tvr̩dɔʃiː'naː d'iːfkɔ 'sɪ   ʒɛ nɛxt͡sɛʃ   pravdu zvjɛd'ɛt]

Tak tvrdošíjná, dívko, jsi,   že nechceš   pravdu zvědět,
So   stubborn,   girl, are you, that you don't want truth   to come to learn,

Are you so stubborn, girl, that you don't want to hear the truth,

[ʒɛ nɛxt͡sɛʃ   pravdu zvjɛd'ɛt]

že nechceš   pravdu zvědět?
that you don't want truth   to come to learn?

that you don't want to hear the truth?

[t͡sɔʃ   mɔfil̩ bɪɣ dɔ ‿ tvaːr̝iː tviːx tak   smɲɛlɛ pr̝iːmɔ fil̩ɛd'ɛt]

Což   mohl bych do tváří tvých tak směle, přímo hledět?
No doubt   could I   to cheeks your   so boldly, directly gaze?

Could I really look directly into your face so boldly?

[tak tvr̩dɔʃiː'naː d'iːfkɔ 'sɪ   ʒɛ nɛxt͡sɛʃ   pravdu zvjɛd'ɛt]

Tak tvrdošíjná, dívko, jsi,   že nechceš   pravdu zvědět.
So   stubborn,   girl, you are, that you don't want truth   to come to learn.

You are so stubborn, girl, that you don't want to hear the truth.

Mařenka:

[tak ʔɔʃɛmɛtniː muʃ 'sɪ   tɪ   nɛxt͡sɪ   ʔɔ ‿ tɔbjɛ   vjɛd'ɛt]

Tak ošemetný muž jsi ty,   nechci   o   tobě   vědět,
So   deceitful man are you, I don't want about you   to know

You are such a deceitful man, I don't want to know about you,

[nɛxt͡sɪ   ʔɔ ‿ tɔbjɛ   vjɛd'ɛt]

nechci   o   tobě   vědět,
I don't want   about you   to know,

I don't want to know about you,

[ɲɪ dɔ‿falɛʃniːx   tvaːr̝iː tviːx t͡sɔ ʒɪva viːt͡sɛ ɦlɛd'ɛt]

ni   do falešných tváří tvých co   živa více   hledět!
not to false   cheeks your what alive more gaze!

nor to ever see your false face while I'm alive!

[tak ʔɔʃɛmɛtniː muʃ ⁱsɪ tɪ   nɛxt͡sɪ   ʔɔ ‿ tɔbjɛ   vjɛd'ɛt]

Tak ošemetný muž jsi ty, nechci   o   tobě   vědět!
So   deceitful man are you, I don't want about you   to know!

You are such a deceitful man, I don't want to know about you!

Jeník:

[tak tvr̩dɔʃiːⁱnaː d'iːfkɔ ⁱsɪ   ʒɛ   nɛxt͡sɛʃ   pravdu zvjɛd'ɛt]

Tak tvrdošíjná, dívko, jsi,   že   nechceš   pravdu zvědět?
So   stubborn,   girl, are you, that you don't want truth   to come to learn?

Are you so stubborn, girl, that you don't want to hear the truth?

Mařenka:

[tak ʔɔʃɛmɛtniː muʃ ⁱsɪ tɪ   nɛxt͡sɪ   ʔɔ ‿ tɔbjɛ   vjɛd'ɛt]

Tak ošemetný muž jsi ty, nechci   o   tobě   vědět,
So   deceitful man are you, I don't want about you   to know

You are such a deceitful man, I don't want to know about you,

[nɛxt͡sɪ   ʔɔ ‿ tɔbjɛ   vjɛdˈɛt]

nechci   **o   tobě   vědět,**
I don't want   about you   to know,

I don't want to know about you,

[ɲɪ   dɔ‿falɛʃniːx tvaːr̝iː tviːx   t͡sɔ   ʒɪva   viːt͡sɛ fɪlɛdˈɛt]

ni   do falešných tváří tvých co   živa   více   hledět!
not to false   cheeks your what alive more gaze!

nor to ever see your false face while I'm alive!

Jeník:

[t͡sɔʃ   mɔfi̩l bɪɣ   dɔ ‿ tvaːr̝iː tviːx   tak smɲɛlɛ pR̝iːmɔ fɪlɛdˈɛt]

Což   mohl bych do   tváří tvých tak směle, přímo hledět?
No doubt   could I   to   cheeks your so   boldly, directly gaze?

Could I really look directly into your face so boldly?

[tak tvr̩dɔʃiːiˈnaː dˈiːfkɔ ˈsɪ   ʒɛ nɛxt͡sɛʃ   pravdu zvjɛdˈɛt]

Tak tvrdošíjná, dívko, jsi,   že nechceš   pravdu zvědět!
So   stubborn,   girl, you are, that you don't want truth   to come to learn!

You are so stubborn, girl, that you don't want to hear the truth!

Výstup VIII   Scene viii
Mařenka, Jeník, Kecal

Recitativ

Kecal:

(Přikvapí.) (He runs in.)

[ɦlɛ ɦlɛ xasɲiːku   t͡ʃekaːʃ   ʔuʃ   na ‿ pɛɲiːzɛ]

Hle, hle! Chasníku,   čekáš   už   na   peníze?
Hey, hey! Farm boy, are you waiting already for   money?

Hey, hey! Farm boy, are you already waiting for your money?

[nɔ   mɲɛⁱ jɛn malɛː str̩pɛɲiː]

No,   měj jen malé strpení.
Well, have just small patience.

Well, just have a little patience.

[jag   budɛ   smlɔuva pɔdɛpsaːna budɛʃ   vɪplat͡sɛn ː na ‿ krɛⁱt͡sar]

Jak   bude   smlouva podepsána, budeš   vyplacen   na   krejcar.
How   will be contract   signed,   you will be paid   in   coin.

As soon as the contract is signed, you'll be paid your money.

Mařenka:

[ɦa   tɛː   ɦanɛbnɔstʼɪ]

Ha! té   hanebnosti!
Ha! of that villainy!

Ha! such villainy!

Kecal:

[nɔ ʔa tɪ mařɛŋkɔ vɛzmɛʃ sɪ sɪna miːxɔva]

No, a ty, Mařenko? Vezmeš si syna Míchova?
Well, and you, Mařenka? Will you marry son of Mícha?

Well, and you, Mařenka? Will you marry the son of Mícha?

Jeník:

[tɔ't sɛ rɔzumiː ʒɛ sɪ ɦɔ vɛzmɛ]

Tot' se rozumí, že si ho vezme
Of course she understands that - him she'll marry,

She certainly understands that she'll marry him,

[ʔa ɲɪgdɔ jɪniː jɪ dɔstat'ɪ nɛsmiː na ‿ tɔ přiːsafiaːm]

a nikdo jiný ji dostati nesmí, na to přísahám!
and no one other her to get may not, on that I swear!

and no one else may have her, that I swear!

Kecal:

[tɪz fiɔdniː fiɔx ʔa maːʃ s ‿ tɔfiɔ rɔzum]

Tys hodný hoch a máš z toho rozum!
You are nice boy and you have from that reason!

You're a nice boy, and you have intelligence!

Mařenka:

[tɪz   ɦanɛbɲiːk   ʔa   lɦaːŘ]

Tys   hanebník   a   lhář!
You are   villain   and   liar!

You're a villain and a liar!

[nɛ nɛ tɛd' zrɔvna nɛ nɛvɛzmu sɪ   ɦɔ ʔa   gdɪbɪx   mɲɛla ʔumři:t'ɪ]

Ne, ne, ted' zrovna ne, nevezmu si   ho,   a   kdybych měla   umříti!
No, no, now   at all   not, I'll not marry   him, and   if I had   to die!

No, no, I would never marry him, even if I had to die!

Jeník:

(k dohazovači) (to the broker)

[t͡sɔ   mɪ   daːtɛ]

Co   mi   dáte,
What   to me   will you give,

What will you give me

[gdɪʃ jɪ   pŘemluviːm   ʔabɪ   sɪ vzala sɪna miːxova]

když ji   přemluvím,   aby   si vzala syna Míchova?
if her I'll persuade   that she would   marry   son of Mícha?

if I talk her into marrying the son of Mícha?

Mařenka:

[jag3ɛ   tɪ mnɛ   jɛʃt'ɛ x͡tsɛʃ k ‿ tɔmu pR̃ɛmlɔuvat'ɪ]

Jakže?   ty mne ještě chceš k   tomu přemlouvati?
How's that? you me   even   want to that persuade?

What? you even want to talk me into it?

[nɛ takɔvɛːɦɔ ɲɛ͡tsɔ   svjɛt jɛʃt'ɛ nɛvɪd'ɛl ʔa   nɛslɪʃɛl]

Ne, takového něco   svět   ještě neviděl   a   neslyšel!
No, of such   something world even didn't see and didn't hear!

No, something like this the world has not seen nor heard!

(Dá se do pláče.) (She gives in to tears.)

Terzetto
Jeník:

[ʔut'ɪʃ sɛ   ʔut'ɪʃ sɛ   d'iːfkɔ]

Utiš se, utiš se,   dívko,
Calm down, calm down, girl,

Calm down, calm down, girl,

[ʔut'ɪʃ sɛ ʔut'ɪʃ sɛ   ʔa   duːvjɛřuⁱ f ‿ slɔva   maː]

utiš se, utiš se,   a   důvěřuj v   slova má!
calm down, calm down and trust   in words my!

calm down, calm down and trust in my words!

[v3dɪt'   nɛviːʃ   jakɛː   za ‿ t'iːm fʃiːm]

Vždyt'   nevíš,   jaké   za   tím   vším
Certainly you don't know what kind of after that everything

You don't know what happiness, after all this,

[sɛ ʃt'ɛst'iː   prɔ‿ t'ɛ xɔvaː]

se   štěstí   pro   tě   chová!
– happiness   for   you   keeps!

is waiting for you!

[sɪn miːxuːf   sɪn miːxuːf   tɛbɛ mɪlujɛ jak ɲɪgdɔ na‿ tɔm svjɛt'ɛ]

Syn Míchův, syn Míchův tebe miluje, jak nikdo na   tom světě.
Son Mícha's, son Mícha's you loves, how no one on this world.

The son of Mícha, the son of Mícha loves you like no one else in this world.

[ʔɪ   vjɛř   ʒɛ   zɛ ‿ tɔɦɔ sɲatku   t'ɪ   pl̩nɔ blaɦa vɪkvɛtɛ]

I   věř,   že   ze   toho sňatku   ti   plno blaha vykvete,
And believe that from this marriage to you fully bliss will bloom,

And believe that from this marriage bliss will fully blossom,

[t'ɪ   pl̩nɔ blaɦa vɪkvɛtɛ]

ti   plno blaha vykvete.
to you fully bliss will bloom.

will fully blossom.

[ʔut'ɪʃ sɛ   d'iːfkɔ ʔut'ɪʃ sɛ   ʔut'ɪʃ sɛ   ʔa duːvjɛřuⁱ f ‿ slɔva maː]

Utiš se, dívko, utiš se,   utiš se   a důvěřuj v   slova má,
Calm down, girl, calm down, calm down and trust   in words my,

Calm down, girl, calm down, calm down and trust in my words,

[ʔa   duːvjɛřuⁱ f ‿ slɔva   maː]

a   důvěřuj   v   slova   má!
and   trust   in   words   my!

and trust in my words!

Mařenka:

[ʔɔː bɔʒɛ ʔɔː bɔʒɛ slɔva   tvaː mnɛ   vjɛru ʔusmr̥t͡sujiː]

Ó   bože, ó   bože, slova   tvá mne věru   usmrcují.
Oh   God, oh   God, words your me   truly   destroy.

Oh, God, oh, God, your words truly destroy me.

Kecal:

[jaː nɛslɪʃɛl ⁱsɛm ː mɔudřeⁱʃiːx   jaː   nɛslɪʃɛl ⁱsɛm ː mɔudřeⁱʃiːx]

Já   neslyšel jsem   moudřejších, já   neslyšel jsem   moudřejších
I   didn't hear   of more wise, I   didn't hear   of more wise,

I've never heard anything more wise, I've never heard anything more wise,

[ʔa   fʃɛmu   fʃɛmu   pŘɪsvjɛtt͡ʃujɪ]

a   všemu,   všemu   přisvědčuji.
and to everything, to everything   I agree.

and with everything, everything I agree.

[tɛt'   tɛt'   tɛt'   tɛt'   pŘɪvɛdu   sɛm   rɔd'ɪt͡ʃɛ]

Ted', ted', ted', ted' přivedu   sem   rodiče,
Now, now,   now, now   I'll fetch to here parents,

Now, now, now, now I'll bring your parents here,

[ʔa   svjɛtkɪ   zavɔlaːmɛ]

a   svědky   zavoláme
and   witnesses   we'll call

and we'll call the witnesses,

[ʔa   fʃɛmu   tɔmu zdraːfiaːɲiː   ʔuʃ   kɔnɛt͡s   ʔudˀɛlaːmɛ]

a   všemu   tomu zdráhání   už   konec   uděláme.
and   to everything   that   hestitating   already   end   we'll make.

and right away we'll put an end to all this hesitating.

Mařenka:

[jaː   pR̝ɪvɔlaːm   sɛm   rɔdˀɪt͡ʃɛ ʔa   fʃɛt͡skɪ   svɔjɛ   znaːmɛː]

Já   přivolám   sem   rodiče   a   všecky[18]   svoje   známé
I   will call in   here   parents   and   all   my   familiar

I'll call for my parents and all my friends,

[ʔa   ʔɔkamʒɛɲiː   trapnɛːmu   ʔuʃ   kɔnɛt͡s   ʔudˀɛlaːmɛ]

a   okamžení   trapnému   už   konec   uděláme.
and   to moments   awkward   already   end   we'll make.

and we'll put an end to this awkward moment.

Jeník:

[tɛtˀ   pR̝ɪvɛtˀtɛ   sɛm   rɔdˀɪt͡ʃɛ ʔa   svjɛtkɪ   zavɔlaːmɛ]

Teď   přiveď'te sem   rodiče   a   svědky   zavoláme,
Now   fetch   to here   parents   and   witnesses   we'll call,

Now bring her parents here, and let's call the witnesses,

[ʔa t͡sɛlɛː kɔmɛdɪjɪ tɛː ʔuʃ kɔnɛt͡s ʔudʼɛlaːmɛ]

a   celé komedii té   už   konec uděláme.
and whole comedy this already end   we'll make.

and we'll put an end to this whole comedy.

[tɛtʼ   tɛtʼ pR̬ɪvɛːtʼtɛ sɛm   rɔdʼɪt͡ʃɛ]

Ted', ted' přived'te sem   rodiče!
Now, now fetch   to here parents!

Now, now bring in her parents!

Mařenka:

[tɛtʼ   tɛtʼ pR̬ɪvɔlaːm sɛm   rɔdʼɪt͡ʃɛ]

Ted', ted' přivolám sem   rodiče!
Now, now I'll call to here parents!

Now, now I'll call for my parents!

Kecal:

[tɛtʼ tɛtʼ tɛtʼ tɛtʼ pR̬ɪvɛdu sɛm   rɔdʼɪt͡ʃɛ]

Ted', ted', ted', ted' přivedu sem   rodiče,
Now, now, now, now I'll fetch to here parents,

Now, now, now, now I'll bring your parents here,

[ʔa   svjɛtkɪ zavɔlaːmɛ]

a   svědky   zavoláme
and witnesses we'll call

and we'll call the witnesses,

[ʔa   fʃɛmu   tɔmu   zdraːɦaːɲiː   ʔuʃ   kɔnɛt͡s   ʔud'ɛlaːmɛ]

a   všemu   tomu   zdráhání   už   konec   uděláme.
and   to everything   that   hestitating   already   end   we'll make.

and right away we'll put an end to all this hesitating.

(Odejde.) (He leaves.)

Recit.
Jeník:

[t͡sɔʃ   jɛʃt'ɛ   nɛpɔxɔpujɛʃ]

Což   ještě   nepochopuješ?
No doubt   still   you don't understand?

So you still don't understand?

Recit.
Mařenka:

[ⁱd'ɪ   t͡sɔ   tu   jɛʃt'ɛ   xt͡sɛʃ]

Jdi!   Co   tu   ještě   chceš?
Go!   What   then   still   do you want?

Go! What else do you want?

(Poodstoupí stranou.) (He steps back.)

Výstup IX   Scene ix
Mařenka, Ludmila, Háta, Jeník, Krušina, Mícha, Kecal
Sbor lidu [Chorus of people]

Finale

Sbor [Chorus]:

[jak ⁱsɪ sɛ   mařɛŋkɔ   rɔzmɪslɪla   mluf   mluf   rɔzmɪslɪla]

Jak   jsi se,   Mařenko, rozmyslila? Mluv! mluv! rozmyslila,
How have you... Mařenka, reconsidered? Speak! speak! reconsidered,

What have you decided, Mařenka? Speak! speak! how have you decided,

[bɪ sɛ   vjɛd͡z dɔbřɛ ʔukɔnt͡ʃɪla ʔukɔnt͡ʃɪla]

by se   věc   dobře ukončila, ukončila,
it would matter well   finish,   finish,

so everything will come out well in the end, in the end,

[jak ⁱsɪ sɛ   mařɛŋkɔ   rɔzmɪslɪla   mluf   mluf   rɔzmɪslɪla]

jak   jsi se,   Mařenko, rozmyslila? Mluv! mluv! rozmyslila!
how have you... Mařenka, reconsidered? Speak! speak! reconsidered!

what have you decided, Mařenka? Speak! speak! what have you decided!

Mařenka:

(stranou pro sebe) (aside to herself)

[ja: pɔmst'i:m sɛ   ʔa ʔut͡ʃɪɲi:m f ⌣ t͡sɔ ʔon snat   sa:m   nɛvjɛřɪl]

Já   pomstím se   a   učiním, v co on snad sám   nevěřil.
I   will take revenge and I'll do in what he maybe alone didn't believe.

I'll take revenge and do what he himself didn't believe.

[ʔo: kˇʀɪvjɛ   kˇʀɪvjɛ jɛɲi:ku ⁱsɪ   stˇʀɛlɪ svɛ: zamɲɛřɪl]

Ó,   křivě,   křivě,   Jeníku, jsi   střely své   zaměřil.
Oh, wrongly, wrongly, Jeník,   have you... bullets your aimed.

Oh, badly, badly, Jeník, have you aimed your bullets.

(k ostatním) (to the others)

[ja: ʔutʃɪɲiːm jag   ʒaːdaːtɛ]

Já   učiním, jak   žádáte!
I   will do how   you request!

I'll do what you want!

Sbor [Chorus]:

[buď zdraːva mařɛŋkɔ]

Buď zdráva, Mařenko!
Be   well,   Mařenka!

Long live Mařenka!

[tak : kɔnɛt͡s fʃemu rɔzbrɔjɪ ʔa svadba   finɛt   sɛ vɪstrɔjiː]

Tak konec všemu rozbroji a   svatba hned   se vystrojí,
So   end   of all   dissent and wedding right away will be in preparation,

This puts an end to all dissent, and the wedding will take place right away,

[ʔa svadba   finɛt   sɛ vɪstrɔjiː]

a   svatba hned   se vystrojí!
and wedding right away will be in preparation!

and the wedding will take place right away!

Jeník:

(Předstoupí.) (He steps forward.)

[ba svadba   vɪstrɔji: sɛ   finɛt]

Ba, svatba   vystrojí se[19]   hned
Yes, wedding will be in preparation right away,

Yes, the wedding will take place right away,

[ʔa   vɛssɛlɪt   ʔa   vɛssɛlɪt sɛ   budɛ   svjɛt]

a   veselit,   a   veselit se   bude   svět!
and   to make merry   and   to make merry   will   world!

and will be celebrated, celebrated by the world!

Háta, Mícha:

(v úžasu) (in amazement)

[ɦlɛ   jɛɲiːk   gdɛ   sɛ   tadɪ   vzal]

Hle,   Jeník!   Kde   se   tady   vzal?
Hey,   Jeník!   Where   -   here   he came to be?

Look, Jeník! Where did he come from?

Jeník:

[nuʃ   ʔɔttʃɛ   dɔstˈɪ   dlɔːuɦɔ]

Nuž,   otče,   dosti   dlouho
Well,   father,   rather   long time

Well, father, for a pretty long time

[ⁱsɛm sɛ   f ‿ tsɪzɪɲɛ   ʔuʃ   pɔtlɔukal]

jsem se   v   cizině   už   potloukal.
I have…   in   foreign country   already   wandered.

I roamed in a foreign country.

[jɛtˈ   tuʃiːm   svr̩xɔvaniː   tʃas bɪɣ   dɔmuː   pɔdˈiːval sɛ   zas]

Jeť,   tuším,   svrchovaný   čas,   bych   domů   podíval se[20]   zas.
It is,   I guess,   absolute   time   I would   home   see   again.

It is, I guess, the perfect time that I should see home again.

Kecal:

[ʔaⁱ pravda lɪ t͡ʃɪ pɔufiː sɛn]

Aj, pravda-li, či pouhý sen,
Ah, truth-if,   or sheer dream,

Ah, is it the truth, or merely a dream,

[ʒɛ sprrɔstiː xudiː xasɲiːk tɛn jɛst jɛɲiːk starʃiː miːxuːf sɪn]

že sprostý, chudý chasník ten jest Jeník, starší Míchův syn?
that vulgar, poor   farm boy that is   Jeník, older Mícha's son?

that that vulgar, poor farm boy is Jeník, Mícha's older son?

[vʒdɪt'   pravɛnɔ ʒɛ jɛst vɔjiːn]

Vždyť'   praveno, že jest vojín!
To be sure it is said that he is private (soldier)!

It is said that he's a soldier!

Jeník:

[fskutku ⁱsɛm ʔɔt͡sɛ miːxɪ sɪn jak vɪd'iːtɛ]

Vskutku jsem otce Míchy syn, jak vidíte.
Really   I am father Mícha's son, as   you see.

Really I am Mícha's son, as you see.

[ʔat͡ʃ   nɛ vɔjiːn]

Ač   ne vojín,
Although not private,

Although not a soldier,

[pр̌ɛt͡s mnɔɦɔ bɔjuː   s ‿ ʔɔsudɛm]

pр̌ec   mnoho bojů   s   osudem
yet   many   of battles with   fate

I still waged many battles with fate

[na ‿ t͡sɛstaːx sviːx   pɔtstɔupɪl ⁱsɛm]

na   cestách svých   podstoupil jsem.
on   paths   my   I waged.

on the paths I took.

Háta:

[ʔaⁱ mɲɛl ⁱsɪ jɛʃtʼɛ t͡ʃasu   dɔst   k ‿ svɛːmu   pɔtulɔvaːɲiː]

Aj,   měl jsi ještě času   dost   k   svému   potulování!
Ah,   you had still of time enough to   your   wandering!

Ah, you still had enough time in your wanderings!

Jeník:

[ʔaⁱ viːmtʼ   jaː   bɛz ‿ ɦaːdaːɲiː   ʒɛ   viːtaniː   vaːm   nɛⁱsɛm   ɦɔst]

Aj, vímt' já   bez hádání,   že   vítaný   vám   nejsem host.
Ah, I know I   without quarreling that welcome to you I'm not guest.

Ah, without arguing about it, I know that I'm not a welcome guest to you.

[fʃak   nɛʃkɔdʼiː   tɔtʼ   malɪt͡ʃkɔst]

Však   neškodí!   tot'   maličkost!
However   does no harm! certainly trifle!

But no harm's been done!, it matters little!

[jɛn   gdɪʃ   k ‿ svɛː   mɪlɛː   praːvɔ   maːm]

Jen   když   k   své   milé   právo   mám,
Only   when   to   my   dear   right   I have,

Only what matters is I have the right to my sweetheart,

[ˈsa   sɪnɛm   ʔɔt͡sɛ   miːxɪ   saːm]

jsa   synem   otce   Míchy   sám!
I am   son   of father   Mícha   alone!

I alone am the son of Mícha!

Háta:

[tɔ   nɛplatʼiː   tɔ   pɔdvɔt   jɛst]

To   neplatí,   to   podvod   jest!
That   is not valid,   that   deceit   is!

That's not valid, that's deceit!

Jeník:

[nɛ   pɔdvɔt   pɔuɦaː   jɛnɔm   lɛst   t͡sɔ   psaːnɔ   jɛ   tɔ   psaːnɔ]

Ne   podvod, pouhá   jenom   lest.   Co   psáno   je,   to   psáno!
Not   deceit,   mere   just   trick.   What   written   is,   that   written!

Not deceit, just a mere trick. What is written, is written!

[ɦlɛ   ˈsmɛ   tu   dva]

Hle,   jsme   tu   dva,
Hey,   we are   here   two,

Look, there are two of us here,

[ktɛrɛːmu   z ‿ naːz daː   sama   mařɛŋka svuːⁱ ɸilas]

kterému   z nás dá   sama   Mařenka svůj hlas,
to whom from us   gives she herself Mařenka her voice,

to whichever of us Mařenka herself chooses,

[tɔmu   but'   ʃt'ɛst'iː   pŘaːnɔ]

tomu   bud' štěstí   přáno!
to that   be   happiness wished!

may he be wished happiness!

Mařenka:

(radostně) (joyfully)

[ʔax   tɛt' ⁱsɛm   t'ɛ   pɔxɔpɪla   jɛɲiːtʃku   muːⁱ]

Ach, ted' jsem   tě   pochopila, Jeníčku   můj!
Ah,   now I have... you   understood, Jeníček   my!

Ah, now I understand, my Jeníček!

[ⁱsɛm   tvaː   ⁱsɛm   tvaː]

Jsem tvá! jsem   tvá!
I am   yours! I am   yours!

I'm yours! I'm yours!

Kecal:

[ʔaⁱ   prɔɸinaniː   tɔ   t͡ʃlɔvjɛk jɛst]

Aj, prohnaný to   člověk jest.
Ah,   astute   that man   is.

Ah, that man is clever.

[jɪʃ   pɔraʒɛn   ⁱsɛm fʃadɪ   ʔaⁱ prɔfinaniː tɔ t͡ʃlɔvjɛk jɛst]

Již   poražen jsem všady,   aj, prohnaný to   člověk   jest,
already defeated   I am completely, ah, astute   that   man   is,

I'm already completely defeated, ah, that man is clever,

[jɪʃ   pɔraʒɛn   ⁱsɛm   fʃadɪ]

již   poražen jsem   všady!
already defeated   I am   completely!

I'm already completely defeated!

[ʔɔ ⌣ rɛputa͡tsɪ mɔu ʔa   t͡ʃɛst mnɛ pR̝ɪpravɪla jɛɦɔ lɛst]

O   reputaci mou a   čest mne připravila jeho lest,
Of   reputation my and honor me   it deprived   his   trick,

His trick deprived me of my reputation and honor,

[ʔɔ ⌣ rɛputa͡tsɪ mɔu ʔa   t͡ʃɛst mnɛ pR̝ɪpravɪla jɛɦɔ lɛst]

o   reputaci mou a   čest mne připravila jeho lest!
of   reputation my and honor me   it deprived   his   trick!

his trick deprived me of my reputation and honor!

[nɛviːm   nɛviːm   sɪ   vjɛru radɪ]

Nevím,   nevím   si   věru rady!
I don't know, I don't know   -   truly of advice!

I don't know, I truly don't know what to do!

Mícha:

(k dohazovači) (to the broker)

[ta   vaʃɛ mɔudrɔst vaːs na ‿ xviːlɪ ʔɔpustˈɪla]

Ta   vaše   moudrost   vás   na   chvíli   opustila!
That your   wisdom   you for   awhile abandoned!

That wisdom of yours abandoned you for awhile!

Háta:

[ba   r͡tsɛmɛ pŘ̩iːmɔ ɦlɔupaː vjɛt͡s ɦlɔupaː vjɛt͡s sɛ vaːm tu pŘ̩iɦɔdˈɪla]

Ba,   rceme   přímo: hloupá   věc,   hloupá   věc   se   vám   tu   přihodila.
Yes, let's say directly: stupid thing, stupid thing - to you now happened.

Yes, let's put it bluntly: a stupid thing, a stupid thing happened to you now.

Sbor [Chorus]:

[ɦa ɦa ɦa ɦa ba ɦlɔupaː vjɛt͡s ba ɦlɔupaː vjɛt͡s sɛ vaːm   tu pŘ̩iɦɔdˈɪla]

Ha ha ha ha, ba hloupá věc, ba hloupá věc se vám   tu přihodila.
Ha ha ha ha, yes stupid thing, yes stupid thing - to you now happened.

Ha, ha, ha, ha, yes, a stupid thing, yes, a stupid thing happened to you now.

Mařenka, Jeník:

[ta   vaʃɛ mɔudrɔst ta   vaʃɛ mɔudrɔst vaːs na ‿ xviːlɪ ʔɔpustˈɪla]

Ta   vaše moudrost, ta   vaše moudrost vás   na   chvíli   opustila!
That your wisdom, that your wisdom you for   awhile abandoned!

That wisdom of yours abandoned you for awhile!

Háta:

[ba   r͡tsɛmɛ pR̝iːmɔ fɪlɔupaː vjet͡s fɪlɔupaː vjet͡s sɛ   vaːm   tu   pR̝ɪfiɔd'ɪla]

Ba, rceme přímo: hloupá věc, hloupá věc se vám tu přihodila.
Yes, let's say directly: stupid thing, stupid thing - to you now happened.

Yes, let's put it bluntly: a stupid thing, a stupid thing happened to you now.

Ludmila, Krušina:

[ta   vaʃɛ mɔudrɔst   vaːs na ‿ xviːlɪ   ʔɔpust'ɪla]

Ta vaše moudrost vás na chvíli opustila!
That your wisdom you for awhile abandoned!

That wisdom of yours abandoned you for awhile!

Mařenka, Jeník:

[ta   vaʃɛ mɔudrɔst kmɔtR̝ɛ vaːs na ‿ xviːlɪ   ʔɔpust'ɪla]

Ta vaše moudrost, kmotře, vás na chvíli opustila!
That your wisdom, neighbor, you for awhile abandoned!

That wisdom of yours, neighbor, abandoned you for awhile!

Kecal:

[ʔaⁱ prɔfinaniː   tɔ t͡ʃlɔvjɛk jɛst ʔaⁱ prɔfinaniː   tɔ   t͡ʃlɔvjɛk jɛst]

Aj, prohnaný to člověk jest, aj, prohnaný to člověk jest,
Ah, astute that man is, ah, astute that man is,

Ah, that man is clever, ah, that man is clever,

[jɪʃ   pɔraʒɛn   ˡsɛm   fʃadɪ]

již   poražen   jsem   všady,
already defeated   I am   completely,

I'm already completely defeated,

[ʔɔ ‿ rɛputa͡tsɪ   mɔu   ʔa   ͡tʃɛst   mnɛ   pR̝ɪpravɪla   jɛɦɔ   lɛst]

o   reputaci mou   a   čest   mne   připravila   jeho   lest,
of   reputation my   and   honor   me   it deprived his   trick,

his trick deprived me of my reputation and honor!

[nɛviːm   sɪ   radɪ   prɔfinaniː tɔ ͡tʃlɔvjɛk jɛst]

nevím   si   rady,   prohnaný to člověk jest.
I don't know -   of advice, astute   that man   is.

I don't know what to do, that man is clever.

Sbor [Chorus]:

[ɦa ɦa ɦa ɦa   ɦlɔupaː vjɛ͡ts sɛ   vaːm   tu   pR̝ɪɦɔdˈɪla]

Ha ha ha ha, hloupá věc   se   vám   tu   přihodila.
Ha ha ha ha,   stupid thing -   to you now   happened.

Ha, ha, ha, ha, a stupid thing happened to you now.

[ɦa ɦa ɦa ɦa ɦlɔupaː vjɛ͡ts sɛ   vaːm   tu   pR̝ɪɦɔdˈɪla]

Ha ha ha ha, hloupá věc   se   vám   tu   přihodila,
Ha ha ha ha, stupid thing -   to you now   happened,

Ha, ha, ha, ha, a stupid thing happened to you now,

[sɛ vaːm sɛ vaːm pR̝ɪfiɔd'ɪla]

se vám, se vám přihodila.
- to you, - to you happened.

to you, happened to you.

Háta, Ludmila, Mícha, Krušina:

[ba r̂t͡sɛmɛ pR̝iːmɔ]

Ba, rceme přímo:[21]
Yes, let's say directly:

Yes, let's put it bluntly:

[filɔupaː vjɛt͡s sɛ vaːm tu pR̝ɪfiɔd'ɪla sɛ vaːm sɛ vaːm pR̝ɪfiɔd'ɪla]

hloupá věc se vám tu přihodila, se vám, se vám přihodila.[21]
stupid thing - to you now happened, - to you, - to you happened.

a stupid thing happened to you now, to you, happened to you.

Výstup X   **Scene x**
Předešlí, Vašek, Kluci   The previous, Vašek, boys

(Za jevištěm hluk a pokřik. Kluci vyběhnou a přes jeviště ubíhají.)
(Off-stage noise and cries. The boys run out across the stage.)

Jeden kluk [One boy]:

[spasstɛ duʃɛ mɛdvjɛt sɛ ʔutr̝x]

Spaste duše! Medvěd se utrh'!
Save souls! Bear is loose!

Save yourselves! The bear is loose!

Druhý kluk [Second boy]:

[mɛdvjɛt sɛ splaʃɪl bjɛʒiː zrɔvna sɛm]

Medvěd se splašil, běží zrovna sem!
Bear was startled, he's running right to here!

The bear got spooked, he's running straight here!

(Uteče.) (He runs away.)

Recitativ
Vašek, Háta, Krušina

Vašek:

(Vyběhne jako medvěd oblečený, strhne medvědí kůži s hlavy a křičí.)
(He runs out dressed as a bear; he takes off the bearskin from his head, and cries out.)

[nɛ nɛbɔɪtɛ sɛ jaː nɛɪsɛm mɛdvjɛt jaː jaː jaː ɪsɛm vaʃɛk]

Ne- nebojte se, já nejsem medvěd, já- já- já jsem Vašek![22]
Do- don't be afraid, I am not bear, I- I- I am Vašek!

Do- don't be afraid, I'm not a bear, I- I- I'm Vašek!

(Všichni se dají do hlasitého smíchu.) (Everyone bursts with loud laughter.)

Háta:

[tɪ blɔudɛ t͡sɔs tɔ ʔutʃɪɲɪl jakaː tɔ ɦanba]

Ty bloude, cos to učinil? Jaká to hanba!
You fool, what have you... that done? What kind of that shame!

You fool, what have you done? How shameful!

[klɪt' sɛ   ʔɔtsut   darɛbɔ   ʔa   svlɛt͡ʃ sɛ   s ‿ tɛː   maʃkarɪ]

Klid' se   odsud,   darebo,   a   svleč se   z   té   maškary!
Go away   from here,   brat,   and   take off   from those   masks!

Get out of here, brat, and take off that costume!

(Odejde s Vaškem.) (She leaves with Vašek.)

Krušina:

(k Míchovi) (to Mícha)

[nuʒɛ   kmɔtR̝ɛ   miːxɔ]

Nuže, kmotře   Mícho!
Well, neighbor   Mícha!

Well, neighbor Mícha!

[tɛt' snat   pR̝e͡t͡sɛ   ʔuznaːtɛ   ʒɛ   s ‿ vaʃkɛm   ɲɪt͡ʃɛɦɔ   nɛɲiː]

Ted' snad   přece   uznáte,   že s   Vaškem   ničeho   není.
Now perhaps   to be sure   you will admit   that with   Vašek   of nothing   he's not.

Now perhaps you'll admit that Vašek's good for nothing.

[vʒdɪt'   nɛmaː   jɛʃt'ɛ   rɔzum]

Vždyt'   nemá   ještě   rozum!
To be sure   he doesn't have   still   reason!

He still has no sense!

Závěr   *Conclusion*

[pɔmɲɛtɛ kmɔtŘɛ jɛɲiːk ʒɛ vaːʃ sɪn vaːʃ sɪn jɛ krɛvniː]

Pomněte, kmotře, Jeník že váš syn, váš syn je krevný!
Remember, neighbor, Jeník that your son, your son is blood!

Remember, neighbor, that Jeník is your son, your son by blood!

Ludmila:

[raːd but'tɛ ʒɛ ⁱstɛ pɔ ‿ dlɔufieːm zas sɪna nabɪl t͡ʃasɛ]

Rád bud'te, že jste po dlouhém zas syna nabyl čase.
Glad be, that you have... after long again son got time.

Be glad that after such a long time you've got your son again.

[pɔdeⁱtɛ ruku Ɂɔt͡tsɔfskɔːu Ɂa smɪŘtɛ sɛ s ‿ ɲiːm zasɛ]

Podejte ruku otcovskou a smiřte se s ním zase,
Offer hand fatherly and reconcile with him again,

Offer a father's handshake, and reconcile with him again,

[Ɂa smɪŘtɛ sɛ s ‿ ɲiːm zasɛ]

a smiřte se s ním zase!
and reconcile with him again!

and reconcile with him again!

Mícha:

[staɲɪʃ sɛ tɛdɪ staɲɪʃ sɛ daːm vaːm svɛː pɔʒɛfinaːɲiː]

Staniž se tedy, staniž se! Dám vám své požehnání![23]
Let it happen then, let it happen! I give to you (plural) my blessing!

So be it, then, so be it! I give you both my blessing!

Mařenka, Ludmila, Jeník, Mícha, Krušina, Sbor [Chorus]:

[dɔbraː vjɛt͡s   sɛ pɔdařɪla   dɔbraː vjɛt͡s   sɛ pɔdařɪla]

Dobrá věc   se podařila,   dobrá věc   se podařila,
Good   thing   turned out well, good   thing   turned out well,

A good cause has turned out well, a good cause has turned out well,

[vjɛrnaː laːska   zviːt'ɛzɪla   vjɛrnaː laːska   zviːt'ɛzɪla]

věrná   láska   zvítězila,   věrná   láska   zvítězila.
true   love   has prevailed, true   love   has prevailed.

true love has won out, true love has won out.

[ʃt'astɲɛ ʔukɔnt͡ʃɛn jɛ   bɔⁱ   ʃt'astɲɛ ʔukɔnt͡ʃɛn jɛ   bɔⁱ]

Šťastně ukončen je²⁴ boj,   šťastně ukončen je²⁴ boj,
Happily finished is dispute, happily finished is dispute,

The dispute has ended happily, the dispute has ended happily,

[vɛssɛlaː sɛ   svadba   strɔⁱ   sɛ   svadba   strɔⁱ]

veselá   se   svatba   stroj,   se   svatba   stroj!²⁵
merry   -   wedding   prepare, -   wedding   prepare!

may a merry wedding be prepared, a wedding be prepared!

(Opona dolů) (Curtain down)

Notes

1. Czechs roll *r*'s for expression. Feel free to roll *r*'s for expressive words.
2. Remember to bend rhythms to bring out short and long vowels. Sometimes this will result in dotted rhythms even if the notes are written equally. Also, remember to place stress on first syllables, or on prepositions (see chapter 5). Finally, feel free to roll *r*'s for days—this would be typical for someone like the Principál making his pitch.
3. The Principál almost said *židličky* [little chairs] instead of *vidličky* [forks]. The word-slip doesn't work in English if translated literally. Thus, *storks/forks*.

4. The fanfare here doesn't have to be played just once. Bohumil Gregor liked to do it three times.

5. Disregard the rest (but not the glottal!) after *obecenstvo*.

6. Make sure the stress is on *Zač-*, not on *-ně-* or *-te*.

7. The American Indian girl is either Esmeralda (dressed exotically enough that Vašek takes her for an Indian) or some other Komediant.

8. Loosen up the rhythm here: make *mů-* an eighth note, and then *-žete ji* a triplet.

9. Try to sing a double *dd* on *poddá*, as in the Italian *freddo*. *Podá* is a different word.

10. This Latin is completely made up!

11. One source has *říká*, while all others have *praví*. They mean the same thing, but *říká* is far more common, and is preferred in the Prague National Theatre. If you sing *říká*, then use two eighth notes instead of what is written. In the orchestral score, *říká* is given first: Bedřich Smetana and Karel Sabina, *Prodaná nevěsta*, orchestral score, 2d ed. (Prague: Státní nakladatelství literatury, hudby a umění v Praze; Museum Bedřicha Smetany v Praze, 1953), 472, 661.

12. The word *všichni* is spelled wrong in the 1982 piano/vocal score.

13. If necessary, sing the *m* of *mne* on the lower note with *za*—an exception because of the high note! Then, when *za mne* is repeated, sing the *m* clearly on the second note with *-ne*, both times.

14. Observe all the musical accent marks.

15. Hold the last *tvá* for two measures.

16. Loosen up the repeated Cs and hold the long vowels.

17. The *-my-* of *rozmyslím* begins on the grace note.

18. The 1982 piano/vocal score incorrectly has *svědky* here. It is correct in: Smetana and Sabina, *Prodaná nevěsta*, orchestral score, 2d ed., 565, 664.

19. Although Smetana wrote *se vystrojí*, like the chorus, some Czechs sing *vystrojí se* here instead because the inflection is better. The chorus should remain as written, though.

20. Similar to *se vystrojí*—although Smetana wrote *se podíval*, some Czechs sing *podíval se* for better inflection.

21. Háta does sing above Ludmila here. See the note for these measures in Bedřich Smetana and Karel Sabina, *Prodaná nevěsta*, piano/vocal score, 3d ed. (Prague: Editio Supraphon, 1982), 319; and: Smetana and Sabina, *Prodaná nevěsta*, orchestral score, 2d ed., 665.

22. The word *Vašek* is often spoken.

23. In the 1982 piano/vocal score, m. 1477, piano part, left hand, don't play the third beat D. The left hand should only have an octave D in whole notes on the first beat.

24. Smetana and Sabina have *jest*, but Czech choruses usually sing *je* instead. Both words mean the same, but *jest* is antiquated and *je* is easier.

25. Put the final off-glide [ⁱ] of *stroj* on the last eighth of the measure—think of it as coming just before the downbeat of the next measure.

Appendix A

Editions and English Translations

Czech Editions

Except for some nonprofessional productions, the author advocates singing *Prodaná nevěsta* in the original Czech. This has been done with non-Czechs at as high a level as with any other language, in both professional and student productions. The argument that *Prodaná nevěsta* is a comedy does not hold, since other comic operas, such as *Le nozze di Figaro, L'elisir d'amore*, etc. are performed successfully in their original languages. Audiences get the jokes because of supertitles. The trick is to make supertitles that don't give away lines before they are delivered! The opera is not just about jokes, though. There are plenty of serious moments, and when performed well, it is the humanity of the characters that shines through. Where the argument for performing in English is strong is when there is extensive dialogue, as in *Die Zauberflöte. Prodaná nevěsta* has recitatives instead, and they are not extensive.

Orchestral Score

In 1953, Czechs published their second, critical edition of the orchestral score to *Prodaná nevěsta*:

Smetana, Bedřich, and Karel Sabina. *Prodaná nevěsta*. Orchestral score. 2d ed. Prague: Státní nakladatelství literatury, hudby a umění v Praze; Museum Bedřicha Smetany v Praze, 1953. H 1100

The publisher is currently Editio Bärenreiter Praha. The score only has Czech words. It is out of print, but editions can be found in music libraries, or rented from:

DILIA
Theatrical, Literary, and Audiovisual Agency
Music Department
Krátkého 1
190 03 Praha 9 Czech Republic
Tel/Fax: 420/ 283 893 709   http://www.dilia.eu/

Instrumental parts can be rented from DILIA, as well, or parts can be found from German or English editions.

Another orchestral score, published by Edition Kunzelmann in Switzerland, contains Czech, German, and English (the translation by Eric Crozier; see below). It is octavo-sized. Kunzelmann's distributor is C.F. Peters:

> Smetana, Bedřich, and Karel Sabina. *Prodaná nevěsta*. Orchestral score. Zürich: Albert J. Kunzelmann, 1980. OCT 10016

http://www.edition-peters.com

Piano/Vocal Score

In 1982, the third, critical edition of the piano/vocal score was published:

> Smetana, Bedřich, and Karel Sabina. *Prodaná nevěsta*. Piano/vocal score. 3d ed. Prague: Editio Supraphon, 1982. H 531

The publisher is currently Editio Bärenreiter Praha. The score only has the original Czech words. It is out of print, but editions can be found in music libraries, or rented from DILIA (see above). Another possibility is to purchase authorized copies directly from the publisher in the Czech Republic:

Customer Service
Editio Bärenreiter Praha
Běchovická 26
100 00 Praha 10 Czech Republic

Tel: 420/274 001 932, 420/274 001 933
Fax:420/274 001 920   zcentrum@epb.cz
http://www.editio-baerenreiter.cz or http://www.sheetmusic.cz

Still another source for reprints of this edition is:

Classical Vocal Reprints
2701 South Van Hoose Drive
Fayetteville, AR 72701 USA
Tel: 800-298-7474   sales@classicalvocalrep.com
http://www.classicalvocalrep.com

The 1982 Czech critical edition is excellent, and there is plenty of room to write notes, fingerings, translations, and IPA. Reprints actually mean more durable paper, too, than the original. The piano reduction was made by Smetana, including a four-hands version of the overture. Also included is a two-hands reduction of the overture made by Jindřich Kàan von Albest (1852–1926).

Another published piano/vocal score that contains the original Czech words is:

Smetana, Bedřich, and Karel Sabina. *Prodaná nevěsta*. Piano/vocal score. English translation by Mark Herman and Ronnie Apter. Shepherd, Mich.: M. Herman and R. Apter, 2003.

This edition can be ordered through Classical Vocal Reprints, as well. However, although it is a beautiful edition and provides an excellent English singing translation, there are misprints in the Czech, and there is little room to write in any IPA or translations unless you white-out the English. Pianists may also find it difficult to write in fingerings and notes in places.

Finally, an old Czech edition of the piano/vocal score is:

Smetana, Bedřich, and Karel Sabina. *Prodaná nevěsta*. Piano/vocal score. Prague: Umělecká beseda, no date (1909). U. 3 B.

This edition can be downloaded in seconds, for no cost, at:

IMSLP/Petrucci Music Library
http://imslp.org/wiki/Main_Page
IMSLP no. 26611

Any discrepancies can be checked against a copy of the Czech critical edition. Also, Kecal in this score is usually indicated by "Dohaz." This stands for "Dohazovač," "marriage broker," which is how Smetana originally marked Kecal's part in his pencil sketch of the opera.[1]

English Translations

Whereas today an opera in English-speaking lands will either be performed in the original language with English supertitles or in an English translation, this practice was not always the case. In the early twentieth century, operas were sung in whatever language was most convenient. *Faust* and *Lohengrin* were frequently sung in Italian in the United States if that language was easiest for the singers and conductors involved. Similarly, it was not uncommon to hear *Don Giovanni* sung in German. Scottish soprano Mary Garden (1874–1967) sang *Tosca* and *Salome* in French. At this time, no American company felt equipped to produce an opera in a Slavic language. *Eugene Onegin* and *Boris Godunov* were heard in Italian, unless the Russian bass Feodor Chaliapin (1873–1938) was singing Boris, in which case he sang in Russian while everyone else sang in Italian. Later, the Slavic operas were sung in English. As late as 1974, New York critic Harold C. Schonberg was writing:

"Nobody expects a Czech opera at the Metropolitan to be sung in the original language."[2]

Very soon after this, both Russian and Czech operas in the original language became standard fare at the Met.

For *Prodaná nevěsta*, all this meant that many early productions, especially in larger houses in the United States and the United Kingdom, were performed in German, almost until 1940. After the Prague National Theatre's famous performance in Vienna in 1892, in Czech, Vienna mounted its own production of the opera in 1893. It was called *Die verkaufte Braut*, and was sung to a German translation by Max Kalbeck (1850–1921). Mahler conducted this version at the Vienna State Opera in 1896. The German version soon spread throughout every German opera house, and it was again used by Mahler when he conducted the work at the New York Metropolitan Opera in 1909. Not only did Mahler know the German well, but overall it was the most convenient language for the cast members. It was used in Chicago in 1930, and conductor Alfred Hertz took it with him to San Francisco in 1934. The opera was sung in German at Covent Garden in 1939 because this language was easiest for the cast. Before looking at English translations, we must first look at the German one.[3]

Max Kalbeck was a prominent German critic, a writer on music, and a translator. Two of his poems were set to music by Brahms ("Nachtwandler" and "Letztes Glück"). After *Die verkaufte Braut* premiered at the Prague Neues Deutsches Theater (now the Státní opera) on October 18, 1925, under Alexander Zemlinsky (1871–1942), critic Ernst Rychnowsky (1879–1934) wrote two days later in the *Prager Tagblatt*:

> "The sore point of the performance is the insufficient German translation of Kalbeck. Certainly it is written with such perfection like all that the word-virtuoso Kalbeck has taken into his hands. But it is—since Kalbeck had no idea of the original Czech—prepared by the eye."[4]

So, for example, instead of the opening chorus singing (a literal translation of the Czech):

> "Why shouldn't we have a great time, when the Lord God grants us health? Who of us knows if the next fair will be so cheerful?"

Kalbeck has the chorus sing:

> "Seht am Strauch die Knospen springen, hört die munter'n Vögel singen! Glanz und Jubel weit und breit! O, du schöne Frühlingszeit!"[5]

This translates as:

> "See on the bush the buds bursting, hear the cheerful birds singing! Splendor and rejoicing far and wide! Oh, you beautiful springtime!"

Kalbeck does not always stray so far from the Czech, but there are still many liberties, so that the characters do not come across in their true guises. Those English translators who based their English on Kalbeck's version strayed even further.[6]

Piano/Vocal Score

The main English versions are listed below. All but two contain only English words. The Czech critical orchestral score, second edition, lists the major errors in the English editions.[7]

While some English editions give the option of performing the recitatives as spoken dialogue, it should not be an option. Smetana was clearly satisfied with the recitatives, Czechs have never replaced them with dialogue, and they are not extensive.

Several English translations were adapted from Kalbeck's free German translation, and cannot be recommended:

Kalmus

> Smetana, Bedřich, and Karel Sabina. *Die verkaufte Braut/The Bartered Bride.* Piano/vocal score. German by Max Kalbeck. English by Paul Csonka and Ariane Theslöf. Huntington Station, N.Y.: Kalmus, 1968.

This is a reprint of the Peters 1936 edition, with an added English singing translation that is clearly a translation of Kalbeck's German. At times the English strays even further from the original Czech than Kalbeck did. For example, Jeník (Hans) sings of "my noble birth" in the Act I duet with Mařenka (Marie). Jeník's father owned a farm and had some money, but he was no nobleman!

Schirmer

> Smetana, Bedřich, and Karel Sabina. *The Bartered Bride.* Piano/vocal score. English by Marion Farquhar. New York: G. Schirmer, 1956.

This may not be a direct translation from the German, but Kalbeck seems to have served as a springboard for some fanciful English writing. For example, in this version, Mařenka's first aria, in Act I, begins:

> "Ah, my darling, we could grow together like a single vine, if I am yours and you are mine. All the flower of my hope will wither if this cannot be."

instead of, in the original Czech:

> "If I learned anything like that about you, with cruel, spiteful anger I would come to hate you."

To be sure, the music is warm and loving, but we must know what Mařenka is really singing!

"Graham Jones"

> Smetana, Bedřich, and Karel Sabina. *The Bartered Bride*. Libretto. English by
> Graham Jones, a free version based on the German. (New York: Fred
> Rullman, 1936).

This version was originally for the 1936 production at the Met, and was used at least as late as 1973 for a production at Juilliard.[8] It was not by someone named Graham Jones, nor even by the diction coach Madeleine Marshall (1900–93), although Marshall contributed, helped shape it, and later modified it. It was actually a collective enterprise instigated by Muriel Dickson (1903–90), the Mařenka in that 1936 Met production (see chapter 2), who was appalled by the translation by Libushka Bartusek (see below) that she was supposed to sing. Dickson, other cast members, and Marshall then came up with their own version, which Dickson said they based on the German, since they knew no Czech. The group of translators decided on a collective pseudonym while munching on graham crackers, and they all received royalties for years from the enterprise.[9]

The "Graham Jones" translation was a hit with audiences, for two reasons. English was not the norm for performances at that time—the diction was excellent in the 1936 production, and Met audiences were thrilled to be able to understand what was being sung. Also, people loved the funny lines, such as Kecal's in the Act II Kecal/Jeník duet:

> "I know a honey with lots of money, I have a tootsie, sweet tootsie wootsie."[10]

Intoxicated by the ready laughter, the performers strayed further and further from the spirit of the original until the work became more like Gilbert and Sullivan or American musical theater than a Czech comic folk opera (see chapter 2). The following English translations were based on the original Czech:

Rosa Newmarch

> Smetana, Bedřich, and Karel Sabina. *The Bartered Bride*. Piano/vocal score.
> English by Rosa Newmarch. London: Hawkes & Son, 1934.

Newmarch (1857–1940) was an English writer on music, and an early English champion of Slavic music, especially Russian. Some of her books were *Tschaikovsky* (1940) and *The Music of Czechoslovakia* (1942). She dedicated her English version of *Prodaná nevěsta* to the first president of Czechoslovakia, Tomáš Garrigue Masaryk. Her English singing version of *Prodaná nevěsta* is based firmly on the original Czech, and is really very good. The problem lies with out-of-date phrases that make the English hard to understand, or quaint. One of many examples is in the Kecal/Jeník duet, where the alliteration also cloys:

> "Pretty girls with pauper lads their promise will not plight."

Libushka Bartusek

> Smetana, Bedřich, and Karel Sabina. *The Bartered Bride*. Piano/vocal score.
> English by Libushka Bartusek. Chicago: Gamble Hinged Music Co., 1934.

Bartusek (1896–1999) was a Czech-American dancer and writer who during her long life saw the landmark 1892 Prague production of *Prodaná nevěsta* (around 1905), heard and met Emy Destinnová and Otakar Bartík, and danced in the Chicago Civic Opera's German performances of *Prodaná nevěsta* in 1930 (see chapters 2 and 3). In 1930, her young son Harry John Brown (1924–2000), who would grow up to be a prominent conductor, attended both her mother's performance and the Ravinia Opera's German performance, and complained that he could not understand the words. This led Bartusek to make her translation, which was first used in the 1933 Chicago production by the American Operetta corporation.[11] It was published the following year and used by English-speaking countries throughout the world. Based firmly on the Czech, it is very good and lovingly done. The problem again lies with certain phrases that call attention to themselves as being old-fashioned and stilted. After coming to the following line, Muriel Dickson wrote that she could go no further and had to write her own translation for her 1936 debut at the Met:

> ". . . water, cold, would be her grave, coal gas she'd coolly brave; forever . . ."[12]

Eric Crozier/Joan Cross

> Smetana, Bedřich, and Karel Sabina. *The Bartered Bride*. Piano/vocal score.
> English by Joan Cross and Eric Crozier. London: Boosey & Hawkes, 1945, revised in 1978.

This edition can be ordered from Boosey & Hawkes, at:

http://www.boosey.com

Eric Crozier (1914–94) and Joan Cross (1900–93) originally made this translation for a production in 1943 at Sadler's Wells, where Cross was head and Crozier was producer. They based their version on Rosa Newmarch's translation. Crozier wrote the English for the recitatives, which in 1943 were done as spoken dialogue; and Cross wrote words for the musical numbers. They were also graced with the advice and help of Czech choreographer Saša Machov (1903–51), who convinced them to perform the dialogue as recitatives in later productions. (Their translation is dedicated to Machov; see chapters 2 and 3.)[13] The English was revised and updated through 1978. It is an excellent singing translation, and has been used around the world. (The Kunzelmann orchestral score has this version.) However, the translation weaves in and out between staying true to the original and veering off to add a joke or seemingly to make the English flow naturally. So, for example, Kecal does not threaten to have Jeník run out of town if he doesn't accept the final offer of three hundred gold coins. Nor does Kecal mention that he has a wife. There are some gag lines here and there that were not in the original. These, along with a caricatured performance, prompted critic Olin Downes to write about New York City Opera's first performance of *Prodaná nevěsta* in 1945:

> "The text is bowdlerized, and filled with cheap gags not in the original. It may be funny in a cheap way; it is very far from the simplicity, the shrewdness, the naiveté of the original."[14]

Tony Harrison

> Smetana, Bedřich, and Karel Sabina. *The Bartered Bride*. Libretto. English by Tony Harrison. New York: G. Schirmer, 1978.

The English poet and playwright Tony Harrison (b. 1937) wrote this translation expressly for the Met's 1978 production of *Prodaná nevěsta*. It was touted as capturing the essence of the original while being true to the Czech rhythms.[15] However, even in 1978 New York critic John Rockwell called it a "stilted translation." For the 1996 revival, New York critic Allan Kozinn referred to it as:

> ". . . Tony Harrison's dated and sometimes goofy English translation."

When used for Opera Boston's 2009 production, it was referred to as a "clunky translation," "more *Iolanthe* than Iowa," where the opera was set.[16]

In fact, all of the above translations have been criticized at some time as "outdated," which is an interesting aspect of opera translations, since the original libretto itself becomes "dated" at some point. No one would think of "updating" an original English opera libretto, such as Purcell's *Dido and Aeneas*!

Kit Hesketh-Harvey

Hesketh-Harvey (b. 1957) is a British writer and comedian, with a background in choral singing. He has translated quite a few operas into English, including one for Sir Charles Mackerras's performances of *Prodaná nevěsta* with the Royal Opera House in 2001. For a revival in 2006, London critic Rupert Christiansen noted:

> "Kit Hesketh-Harvey's translation is neatly rhymed and perfectly serviceable without recourse to unjustified vulgarity. But one day I'd like to hear Tony Harrison's more poetically ambitious version, commissioned for New York's Metropolitan Opera but never to my knowledge used in Britain."[17]

Although very well done, the translation does have reminiscences of W.S. Gilbert, of Gilbert and Sullivan, that pulls us away from the Czech atmosphere at times. Also, Hesketh-Harvey found Jeník to be too cruel in the original—even though it is Mařenka who doesn't give him a chance to explain his actions—and so found it necessary to have Jeník explain that Háta had cheated him of his inheritance. He then manages to "sell" Mařenka for a much higher sum than in the original, a sum equal to what his inheritance would have been. Reviewing the CD recorded in 2005, critic Stephen Francis Vasta faults the English version:

". . . Kit Hesketh-Harvey's translation keeps to most of the written rhythms, which is no small feat in a Czech-to-English adaptation; but if it avoids a stilted, impersonal quality, it doesn't quite achieve naturalness. Aside from the occasional overt Britishism—the adults tell Vasek, 'You're talking total rot' in the Act III quartet—the English won't always scan comfortably in rhythms fashioned for Czech sentences. The fast patter is pretty much unintelligible here; some of Jenik's Act I recitative is a bit frenetic. And while a construction such as Jenik's 'the birthright out of which I was cheated by that woman there' in the final scene may be grammatically permissible, it sounds as clumsy as it reads."[18]

Mark Herman and Ronnie Apter

Smetana, Bedřich, and Karel Sabina. *Prodaná nevěsta/The Bartered Bride.* Piano/vocal score. English by Mark Herman and Ronnie Apter. Shepherd, Mich.: M. Herman and R. Apter, 2003.

This version was commissioned by the Bronx Opera Company in New York for their 2003 production. Both Herman and Apter are writers, and have collaborated on many English singing translations of operas. Some are published by Ricordi, while others are self-published.

This is probably the best current English translation of *Prodaná nevěsta*. It is clearly based on the original Czech, and maintains well the difficult balance between being true to the rhythms, spirit, and meaning of the original while having natural, singable English.

This version can be ordered through Classical Vocal Reprints (see above), or through the translators, at:

hermanapter@earthlink.net

Notes

1. See throughout: Bedřich Smetana and Karel Sabina, *Prodaná nevěsta; první náčrtek*, facsimile of holograph sketches, preface and notes by Mirko Očadlík (Prague: Společnost Bedřicha Smetany, Melantrich, 1944).

2. Harold C. Schonberg, "Opera: *Jenůfa* is revived by Met after 50 years," *New York Times*, 16 November 1974, 20.

3. Max Kalbeck's translation can be heard on a 1982 DVD, recorded live at the Vienna State Opera, Deutsche Grammophon 073 4360, with Slovak soprano Lucia Popp (Lucia Poppová) (1939–1993) and German heldentenor Siegfried Jerusalem (b. 1940).

With Kalbeck, some of the characters have different names:

> Mařenka = Marie
> Jeník = Hans
> Ludmila = Kathinka
> Vašek = Wenzel
> Háta = Agnes
> Principál = Springer
> Indián = Muff

4. Translation from the German by the author. Rychnowsky was a German-speaking Czech columnist and musicologist who wrote the first German biography of Smetana. Pamela Tancsik, *Die Prager Oper heißt Zemlinsky: Theatergeschichte des Neuen Deutschen Theaters Prag in der Ära Zemlinsky von 1911 bis 1927* (Vienna: Böhlau, 2000), 582.

5. Bedřich Smetana and Karel Sabina, *Die verkaufte Braut* [Bartered bride], libretto, German version by Max Kalbeck (New York: Fred Rullman, 1908), 4.

6. A similar problem can be seen in Janáček's opera *The Cunning Little Vixen*. The score prints the original Czech, with German by Max Brod (1884–1968), who significantly changed parts of the opera in his translation. Those who perform the opera in Czech but base their ideas on the German can have a rude awakening!

7. Bedřich Smetana and Karel Sabina, *Prodaná nevěsta*, piano/vocal score, 3d ed. (Prague: Editio Supraphon, 1982), xxxiii. Errors in various editions are also listed throughout the endnotes, 645–66.

8. Harold C. Schonberg, "Opera: *Bartered Bride* at Juilliard," *New York Times*, 16 December 1973, 75.

9. Muriel Dickson, *There and back: A light-hearted, sentimental autobiography* (Billingham, U.K.: The Gaiety, 2004), 18–19.

10. "*Bartered Bride* repeated," *New York Times*, 24 May 1936, 35.

11. Libushka Bartusek Brown, *Everything but circus and burlesque* (Oak Park, Ill.: Libushka Bartusek Brown, 1994), 93; and Edward Moore, "Opera you can understand gets enthusiastic welcome," *Chicago Daily Tribune*, 4 December 1933, 21.

12. From the Mařenka/Vašek duet in Act II. Dickson, *There and back*, 18–19.

13. Přemysl Pražák, *Smetanova Prodaná nevěsta* (Prague: Lidová demokracie, 1962), 281–82.

14. Olin Downes, "*Bartered Bride* heard in English," *New York Times*, 4 October, 1945, 26.

15. Gary D. Lipton, "Czech mates," *Opera News* 43, no. 6 (2 December 1978): 41.

16. John Rockwell, "Patricia Craig sings title role in *Bartered Bride* at the Met," *New York Times*, 27 November 1978, C16; Allan Kozinn, "Finding complexity in a seemingly simple *Bride*," *New York Times*, 7 October 1996, C12; and Lloyd Schwartz, "Here comes the bride," *Boston Phoenix*, 12 May 2009, http://thephoenix.com (18 May 2009).

17. Rupert Christiansen, "Long road to the fun and games," *Telegraph*, 11 January 2006, http//:www.telegraph.co.uk (13 February 2009).

18. Stephen Francis Vasta, "Smetana: *The Bartered Bride* (in English)," *Opera News* 70, no. 9 (1 March 2006): 80.

Appendix B

Recordings

Recordings are presented in chronological order. Although there are quite a few recordings in German, only Czech and English are presented here, along with singers who performed the main roles. Recordings on major labels, such as Supraphon, EMI, Naxos, and Chandos are readily available. Others may be difficult to find. For those, check:

Berkshire Record Outlet, at http://www.berkshirerecordoutlet.com
Premiere Opera, at http://premiereopera.com
House of Opera, at http://store.operapassion.com

CDs and LPs

In Czech

1.
This was the first complete recording of the opera, originally made on fifteen 78s. The tempi are very fast, probably because of the time limits on each record.

Ada Nordenová, Mařenka	Otakar Ostrčil, conductor
Vladimír Tomš, Jeník	Prague National Theatre Orchestra
Jaroslav Gleich, Vašek	Recorded 1933
Emil Pollert, Kecal	Supraphon 1016 3201-03 (LPs)
	Naxos (not available in USA) 8.110098-99 (CDs)

2.
Toward the end of December 1940, conductor Václav Talich recorded the complete opera on wax disks in the studio of Český rozhlas [Czech radio], Prague. As of 2009, the disks have still not been found.[1]

3.

Miluše Dvořáková (and Ota Ho-ráková, and Marie Budíková), Mařenka	Rudolf Vašata, conductor
	Prague National Theatre Orchestra
Jindřich Blažíček, Jeník	Recorded 194?, composite recording
Oldřich Kovář, Vašek	Ultraphone G 22397-22403 (78s)
Eduard Haken (and Luděk Mandaus), Kecal	

4.

Ludmila Červinková, Mařenka	Karel Ančerl, conductor
Beno Blachut, Jeník	Prague Radio Symphony Orchestra
Rudolf Vonásek, Vašek	Recorded 1947, radio performance
Karel Kalaš, Kecal	Multisonic 310 185-2 (CDs)

5.

Milada Musilová, Mařenka	Jaroslav Vogel, conductor
Ivo Žídek, Jeník	Prague National Theatre Orchestra
Oldřich Kovář, Vašek	Recorded 1952
Karel Kalaš, Kecal	Supraphon SU 39802 (CDs)

6.

Vilma Bukovetz, Mařenka	Dimitri Gebré, conductor
Miro Branjnik, Jeník	Slovenian National Opera
Janec Lipusek, Vašek	Recorded 1956
Latko Koroshetz, Kecal	Epic SC 6020 (LPs)

7.

Drahomíra Tikalová, Mařenka	Zdeněk Chalabala, conductor
Ivo Žídek, Jeník	Prague National Theatre Orchestra
Oldřich Kovář, Vašek	Recorded 1959
Eduard Haken, Kecal	Supraphon SU 0040-2 612 (CDs)

8.

Gabriela Beňačková, Mařenka	Zdeněk Košler, conductor
Peter Dvorský, Jeník	Czech Philharmonic Orchestra
Miroslav Kopp, Vašek	Recorded 1981
Richard Novák, Kecal	Supraphon SU 3707-2 632 (CDs)

9.

Oksana Krovytska, Mařenka	Zdeněk Mácal, conductor
Miroslav Dvorský, Jeník	Opéra de Nancy
John Cogram, Vašek	Recorded 1999, live performance
Jiří Sulženko, Kecal	Celestial Audio CA 003 (CDs)

10.

Christiane Oelze, Mařenka	Jiří Bělohlávek, conductor
Aleš Briscein, Jeník	L'Opéra National de Paris
Christoph Homberger, Vašek	Recorded 2008, live performance
Franz Hawlata, Kecal	Premiere Opera 3162-2 (CDs)

In English

1.

Hilda Burke, Mařenka	Wilfrid Pelletier, conductor
Mario Chamlee, Jeník	Metropolitan Opera
George Rasely, Vašek	Recorded 1937, live performance
Louis D'Angelo, Kecal	Bensar Records OL 5837 (CDs)

2.

Ava June, Mařenka	James Lockhart, conductor
Donald Smith, Jeník	Sadler's Wells Opera
Kevin Miller, Vašek	Recorded 1962, excerpts
John Homes, Kecal	EMI 585 010-2 (CDs)

3.

Teresa Stratas, Mařenka	James Levine, conductor
Nicolai Gedda, Jeník	Metropolitan Opera
Jon Vickers, Vašek	Recorded 1978, live performance
Martti Talvela, Kecal	Bensar OL 12278 (CDs)

4.

Susan Gritton, Mařenka	Sir Charles Mackerras, conductor
Paul Charles Clarke, Jeník	Philharmonia Orchestra
Timothy Robinson, Vašek	Recorded 2004
Peter Rose, Kecal	Chandos CHAN 3128 (CDs)

DVDs

In Czech

1.

Gabriela Beňačková, Mařenka	Zdeněk Košler, conductor
Peter Dvorský, Jeník	Czech Philharmonic Orchestra
Miroslav Kopp, Vašek	Recorded 1981, Czech TV
Richard Novák, Kecal	Supraphon SU 7011-9

2.

Soile Isokoski, Mařenka	Bernard Haitink, conductor
Jorma Silvasti, Jeník	Covent Garden
Ian Bostridge, Vašek	Recorded 1998, live performance
Franz Hawlata, Kecal	Encore 2222

In English

1.

Elsie Morison, Mařenka	Clive Douglas, conductor
Victor Franklin, Jeník	Victoria Symphony Orchestra
Raymond MacDonald, Vašek	Recorded 1957, Australian TV
Keith Nelson, Kecal	House of Opera 438

2.

Teresa Stratas, Mařenka	James Levine, conductor
Nicolai Gedda, Jeník	Metropolitan Opera
Jon Vickers, Vašek	Recorded 1978, live performance
Martti Talvela, Kecal	House of Opera DVDM 1060

Films

1.

The first film of the opera was a silent one, but featured singers famous for these roles. Adolf Krössing was admired by Smetana himself for his protrayal of Vašek.

Prodaná nevěsta

Marie Šlechtová, Mařenka   Max Urban (1882–1959), director
Tadeusz Dura, Jeník   Filmed 1913, silent, 45 minutes
Adolf Krössing, Vašek
Emil Pollert, Kecal

2.

The following was a silent Czech documentary that featured actors instead of singers. It caused somewhat of a scandal, as purists objected to a prologue in which Mařenka and Kecal traveled by train to a contemporary Prague to meet Jeník.[2]

Prodaná nevěsta

Laura Želenská, Mařenka   Oldřich Kmínek (1892–1946), director
František Smolík, Jeník   Filmed 1922, silent
František Beranský, Vašek
Karel Noll, Kecal

3.

Even though the following film is in German, it is included here because it was the first real opera film—utilizing some of the possibilities of cinematography, rather than merely filming a regular stage performance. The opening credits make it clear that this film is freely based on Smetana's opera. In this version, Jeník drives a coach, and Mařenka is the mayor's daughter. They sing their Act I duet in a boat floating downstream. The Principál's name is Brummer. He is married, and Esmeralda is the Brummers' daughter. In the end, not only are Jeník and Mařenka free to be together, but Vašek and Esmeralda are, too.

Die verkaufte Braut

Jarmila Novotná, Mařenka (Marie)   Max Ophüls (1902–57), director
Willy Domgraf-Fassbaender,   Theo Mackeben (1897–1953), conductor
    Jeník (Hans)   Filmed 1932, 77 minutes
Paul Kemp, Vašek (Wenzel)   Available for viewing at Internet Archive:
Otto Wernicke, Kecal   http://www.archive.org

4.

The following film was the first sound film of the complete opera in its original form, in Czech. Whereas Max Ophüls took many liberties with the story and music, but managed to explore some possibilities of the film medium, Innemann basically presented a stage version of the opera. Assisting Innemann as directors were Jaroslav Kvapil (1868–1950), the librettist for Dvořák's *Rusalka*; and Emil Pollert (1877–1935), a noted Kecal.

Prodaná nevěsta

Ota Horáková, Mařenka	Svatopluk Innemann (1896–1945), director
Vladimír Tomš, Jeník	Jožka (Josef) Charvát, conductor
Jaroslav Gleich, Vašek	Prague National Theatre Orchestra
Emil Pollert, Kecal	Filmed 1933, 131 minutes

5.

The next film is more complicated. Two versions were made, one in Czech and one in German. In the German film, Teresa Stratas and René Kollo both sang and acted the lead roles. The Czech version was filmed in the beautiful historic Czech village of Holašovice, west of České Budějovice. Vanda Švarcová (b. 1948) was the actress portraying Mařenka, Petr Skarke (b. 1943) played Jeník, Václav Sloup (b. 1936) played Vašek, and Čestmír Řanda (1923–86) was Kecal, but the singing voices were different:[3]

Prodaná nevěsta

Gabriela Beňačková, Mařenka	Václav Kašlík (1917–89), director
Ivo Žídek, Jeník	Jaroslav Krombholc, conductor
Alfréd Hampel, Vašek	Prague National Theatre Orchestra
Karel Berman, Kecal	Filmed 1975, 114 minutes

Notes

1. Jan Panenka and Taťána Součková, *Prodaná nevěsta na jevištích Prozatímního a Národního divadla 1866–2004* (Prague: Gallery and Národní divadlo, 2004), 117.

2. Panenka and Součková, *Prodaná nevěsta na jevištích Prozatímního a Národního divadla 1866–2004*, 102–103.

3. Panenka and Součková, *Prodaná nevěsta na jevištích Prozatímního a Národního divadla 1866–2004*, 167; and "Český film," *Volný*, http://www.volny.cz/czfilm (14 June 2009).

Bibliography

Abraham, Gerald. "The genesis of *The Bartered bride*." Pp. 28–39 in *Slavonic and Romantic music: Essays and studies*. New York: St. Martin's Press, 1968.

"Adolf Bolm." *MetOpera Database*. http://archives.metoperafamily.org/archives/frame. htm (16 May 2009).

"Alan Crofoot." *MetOpera Database*. http://archives.metoperafamily.org/archives/frame. htm (7 April 2009).

"Antonín Landa." *Národní divadlo*. http://archiv.narodni-divadlo.cz (18 May 2009).

Asche, Gerhart. "Retrospektive: Die Macht des Schicksals." *Opernwelt* 46, no. 8 (August 2005): 68–71.

"Bartered Bride," *MetOpera Database*. http://archives.metoperafamily.org/archives/ frame.htm (16 May 2009).

"Bartered Bride," *Royal Opera House: Collections online*. http://www.rohcollections. org.uk/performances.aspx (13 February 2009).

"Bartered Bride." *San Francisco Opera performance archive*. http://archive.sfopera.com/ qry1operalist.asp (22 May 2009).

"*The Bartered Bride* mosaic." In English-language program booklet for the Prague National Theatre *Prodaná nevěsta*. Helena Havlíková, ed. Prague: National Theatre, 1992.

Bartoš, František. *Bedřich Smetana: Letters and reminiscences*. Translated from the Czech by Daphne Rusbridge. Prague: Artia, 1955.

Bartoš, Josef. *Prozatímní divadlo a jeho opera* [The Provisional Theater and its opera]. Prague: Sbor pro zřízení druhého národního divadla v Praze, 1938.

Billman, Larry. *Film choreographers and dance directors: An illustrated biographical encyclopedia, with a history and filmographies, 1893 through 1995*. Jefferson, N.C.: McFarland & Co., 1997.

Bloomfield, Arthur. *The San Francisco Opera: 1922–1978*. Sausalito, Calif.: Comstock Editions, 1978.

Bonuš, František. *Tance, písně a hudba Plzeňského kraje* [Dance, songs, and music of the Plzeň region]. Prague: Státní nakladatelství Krásné literatury, hudby a umění, 1955.

Brodenová, Lída. *Notes on Smetana's opera Prodaná nevěsta*. Edited by Judith Fiehler. Washington: K. Maier, 1990.

Brodská, Božena. *Dějiny českého baletu do roku 1918* [History of Czech ballet up to the year 1918]. Prague: Akademie múzických umění, 1983.

Brown, Libushka Bartusek. *Everything but circus and burlesque*. Oak Park, Ill.: Libushka Bartusek Brown, 1994.

Carey, Hugh. *Duet for two voices: An informal biography of Edward Dent compiled from his letters to Clive Carey*. Cambridge: Cambridge University Press, 1980.

"Český film" [Czech film]. *Volný*. http://www.volny.cz/czfilm (14 June 2009).

Cheek, Timothy. CD notes for recording *Vítězslava Kaprálová: Songs*. Prague: Supraphon, 2003.

————. "Inflection and word setting in Czech vocal music." *Journal of Singing* 62, no. 3 (January/February 2006): 299–313.

————. *Singing in Czech: A guide to Czech lyric diction and vocal repertoire*, with a foreword by Sir Charles Mackerras. Lanham, Md.: Scarecrow Press, 2001.

Chekhov, Anton. "A happy ending." Pp. 141–47 in *The horse-stealers and other stories*, vol. 10 of *The tales of Chekhov*. Translated by Constance Garnett. New York: The Macmillan Company, 1921.

Čornej, Petr. *Dějiny českých zemí* [A history of the Czech lands]. 3d ed. Havlíčkův Brod: Fragment, 2003.

Daňek, Petr, and Jana Vyšohlídová. "Dokumenty k operní soutěži o cenu hraběte Harracha" [Documents on the operatic prize competition of Count Harrach]. *Miscellanea musicologia*, XXX (1983): 154.

De Mille, Agnes. *Speak to me, dance with me*. Boston: Little, Brown and Co., 1973.

Dickson, Muriel. *There and back: A light-hearted, sentimental autobiography*. Billingham, U.K.: The Gaiety, 2004.

Ducloux, Walter. "From the heart of Bohemia." *Opera News* 43, no. 6 (2 December 1978): 12–19.

Dvořák, Antonín. *Rusalka*. Piano/vocal score. Kasel: Bärenreiter, 2006.

Dyer, Richard. "Daniel Pelzig profile." *Opera Boston*. http://www.operaboston.org/operas_bride_specialfeatures.php (18 May 2009).

————. "Patricia Craig profile." *Opera Boston*. http://www.operaboston.org/operas_bride_specialfeatures.php (21 May 2009).

Ebert, Peter. *In this theatre of man's life: The biography of Carl Ebert*. Sussex: The Book Guild, 1999.

"Emerich Gabzdyl." *Národní divadlo*. http://archiv.narodni-divadlo.cz (18 May 2009).

Erben, Karel Jaromír. *Nápěvy písní národních v Čechách* [National song melodies in Bohemia]. Vol. 2. Prague: J. Hoffmann, no date.

Fanger, Iris M. "Daniel Pelzig: New kid in town." *Dance Magazine* 70, no. 10 (October 1996): 54–57.

Foreman, Carolyn Thomas. *Indians abroad 1493–1938*. Norman, Okla.: University of Oklahoma Press, 1943.

"František Vajnar." *Národní divadlo*. http://archiv.narodni-divadlo.cz (25 May 2009).

Freeman, John W. "The theater of Josef Svoboda." *Opera News* 43, no. 6 (2 December 1978): 43–46.

————. "In review." *Opera News* 61, no. 7 (28 December 1996): 41.

Freestone, Peter. "Czech Republic." *Opera* 60, no. 2 (February 2009): 172–73.

"George Rasely." *MetOpera Database*. http://archives.metoperafamily.org/archives/frame.htm (10 April 2009).

"Gateway to the Australian performing Arts." *AusState*. http://www.ausstage.edu.au/ (25 May 2009).

Gogol, Nikolai. *Marriage*. Trans. by Bella Costello. Manchester: Manchester University Press, 1969.

Hájek, Ladislav. *Paměti Augustina Bergra: Choreografa a baletního mistra národního divadla v Praze a několika světových scén* [Memoirs of Augustín Berger: Choreography and ballet master of the National Theatre in Prague, and some world scenes]. Prague: Orbis, 1942.

Heinsheimer, Hans. "An enemy of the people." *Opera News* 43, no. 6 (2 December 1978): 27–30.

Heřman, Jiří, ed. *Prodaná nevěsta* [Bartered bride]. Introductory material, libretto, and appendices. Prague: Petrklíč, 2001.

Horne, Marilyn, with Jane Scovell. *Marilyn Horne: My life*. New York: Atheneum, 1983.

Hostinský, Otakar. "O české deklamaci hudební" [On Czech musical declamation]. Pp. 259–97 in *O hudbě* [On music]. Miloslav Nedbal, ed. Prague: Státní hudební vydavatelství, 1961, reprinted from 1886.

"In memoriam: Walter Ducloux." *The University of Texas at Austin*. http://www.utexas. edu/faculty/council/1999-2000/memorials/Ducloux/ (27 May 2009).

"James Levine." *The Metropolitan Opera*. http://www.metoperafamily.org/metopera/ about/whoweare/levine.aspx (10 April 2009).

Janota, Dalibor, and Jan P. Kučera. *Malá encyklopedie České opery* [Small encyclopedia of Czech opera]. Prague: Paseka, 1999.

"Jiří Němeček." *Národní divadlo*. http://archiv.narodni-divadlo.cz (18 May 2009).

Kezys, Algimantas, and Ada Sutkus. "Posters by Ada Sutkus." *Lituanus* 42, no. 2 (Summer 1996), from http://www.lituanus.org/1996/96_2_04.htm (22 May 2009).

Kolodin, Irving. *The Metropolitan Opera 1883–1966: A candid history*. New York Alfred A. Knopf, 1966.

Krist, Jan Miroslav, and Jitka Matuszková. "Zpívání na pivo" [Singing to beer]. *Národní ústav lidové kultury* [National foundation of folk culture]. http://www.nulk.cz/ Informace.aspx?sid=133 (24 October 2008).

Kutsch, K.J., and Leo Riemens. *Großes Sängerlexikon* [Large singers' lexikon]. 3d ed. Bern: K.G. Saur, 1997.

"Ladislava Košíková," *Národní divadlo*, http://archiv.narodni-divadlo.cz (18 May 2009).

Large, Brian. *Smetana*. New York: Praeger Publishers, 1970.

"Libor Vaculík," *Národní divadlo*, http://archiv.narodni-divadlo.cz (18 May 2009).

Link, Karel. *Beseda, český salonní tanec* [Beseda, the Czech ballroom dance]. 2nd ed. Prague: A. Storch Syn, 1882.

Lipton, Gary D. "Czech mates." *Opera News* 43, no. 6 (2 December 1978): 41.

Locke, Brian S. *Opera and ideology in Prague: Polemics and practice at the National Theater 1900–1938*. Rochester: University of Rochester Press, 2006.

Löwenbach, Jan. *Hudba v Americe* [Music in America]. Prague: Hudební matice, 1948.

Loewenberg, Alfred. *Annals of opera 1597–1940*. 3d ed. Totowa, N.J.: Rowman and Littlefield, 1978.

"Lucielle Browning." *MetOpera Database*. http://archives.metoperafamily.org/archives/ frame.htm (21 March 2009).

Ludwig, Christa. *In my own voice*. Translated by Regina Domeraski. New York: Limelight, 1999.

Macy, Laura, ed. *The Grove book of opera singers*. Oxford: Oxford University Press, 2008.

Mahler, Alma. *Gustav Mahler: Memories and letters*. 3d ed. Translated by Basil Creighton. Edited by Donald Mitchell. Seattle: University of Washington Press, 1975.

Marsh, Robert C. *150 years of opera in Chicago*. Completed and edited by Norman Pellegrini. Dekalb, Ill.: Northern Illinois University Press, 2006.

Martínková, Alena. *Bohumil Gregor: Chtěl jsem sloužit divadlu* [I wanted to serve the theater]. Prague: Jalna, 2006.

"Miroslav Kůra." *Národní divadlo*. http://archiv.narodni-divadlo.cz (18 May 2009).

Mladina: Plzeňský lidový soubor [Plzeň folk group]. http://www.mladina.cz (5 June 2009).

Moses, L.G. *Wild West shows and the images of American Indians 1883–1933.* Albu-
    querque: University of New Mexico Press, 1996.
"Muriel Dickson." *MetOpera Database.* http://archives.metoperafamily.org/archives/
    frame.htm (10 April 2009).
"Nicholas Goldschmidt, Tavikovice, Moravia, December 6, 1908—Toronto, February 8,
    2004." *Opera News* 69, no. 1 (1 July 2004): 69.
Novák, Ladislav. *O těch, kteří odešli* [About those who have departed]. Prague: Máj,
    1940.
"Octave Dua." *The digital opera archives of La Monnaie.* http://carmen.demunt.be (2
    April 2009).
"Opera in English," *Time* 36, no. 23 (2 December 1940). http://www.time.com/time/
    magazine/article/0,9171,772496,00.html.
"Ottokar Bartik." *MetOpera Database.* http://archives.metoperafamily.org/archives/
    frame.htm (11 May 2009).
"Our uppish and defiant fellows." *Národní divadlo* [National Theatre]. http://www.
    narodni-divadlo.cz (29 May 2009).
Paller, Rebecca. "Sound Bites: Simon O'Neill." *Opera News* 70, no. 3 (September 2005):
    14.
Panenka, Jan, and Taťána Součková. *Prodaná nevěsta na jevištích Prozatimního a Ná-
    rodního divadla 1866–2004* [The Bartered bride on the stages of the Provisional and
    National Theatres 1866–2004]. Prague: Gallery and Národní divadlo, 2004.
Pennino, John. *Risë Stevens: A life in music.* Fort Worth: Baskerville Publishers, 1999.
"Petr Zuska." *Národní divadlo.* http://archiv.narodni-divadlo.cz (18 May 2009).
Poster listing premieres of *Prodaná nevěsta* throughout the world. Hanging in Smetana
    Museum, Prague, 2008.
Pražák, Přemysl. *Bedřich Smetana.* Prague: Státní nakladatelství dětské knihy, 1955.
———. *Smetanova Prodaná nevěsta* [Smetana's Bartered bride]. Prague: Lidová demo-
    kracie, 1962.
"Přemysl Kočí." *Národní divadlo.* http://archiv.narodni-divadlo.cz (25 May 2009).
Procházka, Vladimír, ed. *Národní divadlo a jeho předchůdci: Slovník umělců divadel
    Vlastenského, Stavovského, Prozatimního a Národního* [The National Theatre and
    its predecessors: Dictionary of the Patriotic, Estates, Provisional and National
    artistic theaters]. Prague: Academia Praha, 1988.
"Prodaná nevěsta." *Národní divadlo.* http://archiv.narodni-divadlo.cz (8 May 2009).
"Productions." *Glyndebourne.* http://www.glyndebourne.com/archive/productions/ (25
    May 2009).
Rosenthal, Harold. *Two centuries of opera at Covent Garden.* London: Putnam, 1958.
"Rudolf Innemann." *Národní divadlo.* http://archiv.narodni-divadlo.cz (20 May 2009).
"Šárka Hejnová." *Národní divadlo.* http://archiv.narodni-divadlo.cz (25 May 2009).
Schönzeler, Hans-Hubert. *Dvořák.* London: Marion Boyars Publishers, 1984.
Slavoj. No. 11 (December 1, 1863): 203.
Smetana, Bedřich. *Wedding scenes.* Miami Lakes, Fla.: Masters Music Publications,
    1989.
Smetana, Bedřich, and Karel Sabina. *The Bartered Bride.* Piano/vocal score. English by
    Marion Farquhar. New York: G. Schirmer, 1956.
———. *Prodaná nevěsta* [Bartered bride]. Orchestral score. 2d ed. Czech only. Prague:
    Státní nakladatelství literatury, hudby a umění v Praze; Museum Bedřicha Smetany
    v Praze, 1953.
———. *Prodaná nevěsta* [Bartered bride]. Orchestral score, with Czech, German, and
    English. Zürich: Albert J. Kunzelmann, 1980.

———. *Prodaná nevěsta* [Bartered bride]. Piano/vocal score. 3d ed. Czech only. Prague: Editio Supraphon, 1982.

———. *Prodaná nevěsta; první náčrtek* [Bartered bride; first draft]. Facsimile of holograph sketches. Preface and notes by Mirko Očadlík. Prague: Společnost Bedřicha Smetany, Melantrich, 1944.

———. *Prodaná nevěsta.* Piano/vocal score. Czech only. Prague: Umělecká beseda, no date (1909).

———. *Prodaná nevěsta* [Bartered bride]. Piano/vocal score. English translation by Libushka Bartusek. Chicago: Gamble Hinged Music, 1934.

———. *Prodaná nevěsta* [Bartered bride]. Piano/vocal score. English translation by Joan Cross and Eric Crozier. London: Boosey & Hawkes, 1945, rev. 1978.

———. *The Bartered Bride.* Libretto. English by Tony Harrison. New York: G. Schirmer, 1978.

———. *Prodaná nevěsta* [Bartered bride]. Piano/vocal score. English translation by Mark Herman and Ronnie Apter. Shepherd, Mich.: M. Herman and R. Apter, 2003.

———. *Die verkaufte Braut/The Bartered Bride.* Piano/vocal score. German by Max Kalbeck. English by Paul Csonka and Ariane Theslöf. Huntington Station, N.Y.: Kalmus, 1968.

———. *Die verkaufte Braut* [Bartered bride]. Libretto. German translation by Max Kalbeck. New York: Fred Rullman, 1908.

Šmok, Pavel. "My meetings with *The Bartered Bride.*" In English-language program booklet for the Prague National Theatre *Prodaná nevěsta.* Ed. Helena Havlíková. Prague: National Theatre, 1992.

Smolka, Jaroslav. *Smetanova vokální tvorba: Písně, sbory, kantáta* [Smetana's vocal works: Songs, choruses, cantata]. Vol. 2 of *Dílo a život Bedřicha Smetany* [Work and life of Bedřich Smetana]. Prague: Editio Supraphon, 1980.

Sokol, Martin L. *The New York City Opera: An American adventure.* New York: Macmillan Publishing Co., 1981.

Štefánek, Josef, ed. *O lidovém tanečním umění* [On the art of folk dance]. Prague: Orbis, 1954.

Svoboda, Josef, with Milena Honzíková. *Tajemství divadelního prostoru* [Secrets of theater space]. Prague: Odeon, 1990.

"Swatches and splashes," *Time* 85, no. 10 (5 March 1965), at http://www.time.com/time/magazine/article/0,9171,839323,00.html (15 May 2009).

Tancsik, Pamela. *Die Prager Oper heißt Zemlinsky: Theatergeschichte des Neuen Deutschen Theaters Prag in der Ära Zemlinsky von 1911 bis 1927* [The Prague Opera is called Zemlinsky: Theater history of the New German Theater, Prague, in the era of Zemlinsky from 1911 to 1927]. Vienna: Böhlau, 2000.

Taper, Bernard. *Balanchine.* New York: Harper & Row, 1960.

Telegraph. 11 January 2006.

Thomas, Theodore. *Theodore Thomas: A musical autobiography.* Vol. 2. Edited by George P. Upton. Chicago: A.C. McClurg & Co., 1905.

Thomson, J.M. "Crozier, Eric." In *Grove music online. Oxford music online.* http://www.oxfordmusiconline.com/subscriber/article/grove/music/45792 (11 April 2009).

"2008–2009 season: *The Bartered Bride.*" *Opéra national de Paris.* http://www.operadeparis.fr (26 May 2009).

Tyrrell, John. *Czech opera.* Cambridge: Cambridge University Press, 1988.

University of Michigan School of Music, *School of Music programs* (Ann Arbor: University of Michigan School of Music, 1967–68), March 21–24.

"Václav Talich." *Národní divadlo* [National Theatre]. http://archiv.narodni-divadlo.cz (5 May 2009).

Vasta, Stephen Francis. "Smetana: *The Bartered Bride* (in English)." *Opera News* 70, no. 9 (1 March 2006): 80–82.

Vašut, Vladimír. *Saša Machov.* Prague: Panorama, 1986.

Věžník, Václav. "Divadelní jubilea—vzpomínky" [Theatrical jubilees—memories] *Zpravodaj* (Klub přátel opery a baletu Národního divadla v Brně), February 2009: 1.

"Vlastimil Jílek." *Národní divadlo* [National Theatre]. http://archiv.narodni-divadlo.cz (14 May 2009).

Wellwood, Joan. "*The Bartered Bride.*" *The Point*, University of British Columbia's weekly activities and events guide (26 February 2003): 3.

Index

About the Author

Pianist and vocal coach Timothy Cheek is a leading expert on Czech vocal music. His books—*Singing in Czech: A Guide to Czech Lyric Diction and Vocal Repertoire* with a foreword by Sir Charles Mackerras, and a series on Janáček's opera libretti—are recognized internationally as authoritative resources for singing in Czech. He has been especially instrumental in championing the works of Czech female composer Vítězslava Kaprálová (1915–40). In order to promote this extraordinary composer, Dr. Cheek has presented lectures and recitals throughout North America and Europe; performed in several world premieres of her songs; recorded the complete songs of Kaprálová with soprano Dana Burešová on a Supraphon CD, nominated for the best recording of 2003 by the Czech journal *Harmonie*; and edited a critical edition of the songs for the Czech publisher Amos Editio in 2006. He is on the International Advisory Board of the Kapralova Society, based in Toronto.

After completing an opera internship at the National Theatre in Prague under the great Janáček conductor Bohumil Gregor in 1995 (with *The Cunning Little Vixen*, in Czech), Cheek went on to receive several prestigious grants from the International Research and Exchanges Board in Washington, D.C., for hands-on research in the Czech Republic. He has coached, performed, and taught masterclasses on Czech repertoire at opera companies, summer festivals, and music schools in the United States, Canada, Israel, Italy, Slovakia, and South Africa. Since 1994 he has been on the faculty of the University of Michigan, where he instituted a new course in "Slavic Vocal Repertoire" with his colleague Martin Katz, covering Russian and Czech art song. His duties at the university include teaching diction classes, serving as music director of Opera Workshop, and coaching opera productions. He is also an Associate Faculty member of the university's Center for Russian and East European Studies. His education includes a doctorate in collaborative piano from the University of Michigan, degrees in piano performance from the University of Texas at Austin and the Oberlin Conservatory, and a Fulbright award to study as an opera coach in Florence, Italy. Dr. Cheek's performances as a collaborative pianist have brought him to fifteen countries on four continents and have been broadcast worldwide.

Lightning Source UK Ltd.
Milton Keynes UK
UKHW021815270219
338134UK00005B/102/P